Imagining Archives

Essays and Reflections by Hugh A. Taylor

Edited by Terry Cook and Gordon Dodds

D1591064

Society of American Archivists and
Association of Canadian Archivists
in association with
The Scarecrow Press, Inc.
Lanham, Maryland, and Oxford
2003

SCARECROW PRESS, INC.

Published in the United States of America
by Scarecrow Press, Inc.
A wholly owned subsidiary of
The Rowman & Littlefield Publishing Group, Inc.
4501 Forbes Boulevard, Suite 200
Lanham, Maryland 20706
www.scarecrowpress.com

PO Box 317
Oxford
OX2 9RU, UK

British Cataloging in Publication Information Available

Library of Congress Cataloging-in-Publication Data

Taylor, Hugh A.
  Imagining archives : essays and reflections by Hugh A. Taylor / edited by
  Terry Cook and Gordon Dodds.
      p. cm.
  Includes bibilographical references.
  ISBN 0-8108-4771-X (pbk. : alk. paper)
1. Archives—Administration. 2. Archival materials.
I. Cook, Terry, 1947–. II. Dodds, Gordon. III. Title.
CD950.T395 2003
027—dc21

                                                    2003008837

Printed in the United States of America

♾™ The paper used in this publication meets the minimum requirements
of American National Standard for Information Sciences—Permanence of
Paper for Printed Library Materials, ANSI/NISO Z39.48-1992.
Manufactured in the United States of America.

In loving memory of my daughter, Mary Margery Taylor, 1961–2001

This book is dedicated with affection to my wife, Daphne, whose support in so many different ways has made possible my archival career and these writings.

I want also to acknowledge Terry Cook and Gordon Dodds for suggesting this book and then undertaking the work to produce it, as without their vision it would not have happened. The support they received in turn from Candace Loewen, Jean-Stéphen Piché, and Tom Nesmith pleases me. And I am grateful to Jane Turner and Daphne Taylor, who between them have typed all my papers.

—*Hugh A. Taylor*

Hugh and Daphne Taylor in their garden, Victoria, British Columbia, June 2002, with Hugh's "boxes" of compost in the background, "still preserving and still recycling," using the old to create the new, in life and ecology as in the archival ideas in the essays in this book.

Contents

Introduction

Hugh A. Taylor is one of the most important thinkers in the English-speaking world of archives. His provocative essays have pushed the borders of professional thinking. From his sensitive reading in diverse fields, Hugh has ever been excited by new ideas and the prospect of teasing out their significance for archivists. His best essays link archives to social life and contemporary ideas. Long before postmodern scholars' recent fascination with "the archive," Hugh was intent on constructing archives anew, imagining them as places where archivists connect their records with social issues, with new media and technologies, with the historical traditions of archives, with the earth's ecological systems, and with broader spiritual meaning.

The leading thinkers writing in English about archives, such as Hilary Jenkinson, Theodore Schellenberg, Margaret Cross Norton, Helen Samuels, Richard Cox, and David Bearman, have focused their writings primarily on administering archives as institutions and meeting the challenges of complex modern records. Their books variously offer strategies, methodologies, and guidelines for appraisal, arrangement and description, records management, electronic records, preservation, and general archival administration, with shorter passages sometimes on the history of archives and their core working principles. Hugh's collective work easily ranks with that of these sterling pioneers. Yet his writing is different—in tone, in style, and in approach.

Hugh once remarked that archives administration left him cold. He cares more for the meaning of archives as social and cultural institutions and as documentary and media artifacts. What do archives signify? In the great memory systems of humankind, are archives a critical support or academic indulgence? Is collective memory itself as fragile as our global ecosystem, and as holistically interconnected? Is the very act of collective remembering not filled with deep spiritual meaning, a kind of transcendent evidence of faith in humankind and its continued shared existence? Indeed, following Marshall McLuhan, Hugh would ask whether archives are not as important as a medium of accountability, memory, and culture as they are for any message of historical content found in their holdings. By existing, archives signify. And sometimes Hugh's own medium carried his message—a lively, literary prose, filled with pastiches, metaphors, and nonlineal thinking, so different from the turgid writing of the average archival manual or textbook, so evidently sending a signal that a different way of thinking about archives is both necessary *and* going on in his work. Given the serious challenges facing the archival profession with electronic records and information overload, with widespread illegal records destruction and a "dumbing-down" commodification of culture, Hugh's stimulating ideas and his engaging style provide a bright beacon of hope in times of professional change, technological anxiety, and occasional hubris.

Hugh Taylor has many accomplishments, not least being named to the prestigious Order of Canada, his nation's highest civilian award. A senior manager at the National Archives of Canada; provincial archivist of Alberta, New Brunswick, and Nova Scotia; a rare non-American President of the Society of American Archivists; archival educator *par excellence* in theory and practice; winner of numerous awards and prizes; and much-admired mentor for an entire generation of archivists, Hugh was accordingly honoured for his long career with a festschrift published in his honour in 1992. Written mainly by members of the generation he inspired, and edited by Barbara Craig, the festschrift was entitled *The Archival Imagination: Essays in Honour of Hugh A. Taylor*. The present volume, *Imagining Archives: Essays and Reflections by Hugh A. Taylor*, deliberately resonates with that earlier title as a kind of companion piece. While the first volume was about Hugh Taylor, the present volume is by Hugh Taylor. While that earlier volume carried the scholarly apparatus of a full bibliography of Hugh's work, a time-line of his career, and detailed references to his ideas and work, the present volume is more personal and impressionistic in its editorial interventions and intentionally does not duplicate what can be found in the earlier book. Yet the idea of imagination runs through both books. This is hardly surprising, for more than any other single archival writer, Hugh has tried to imagine what archives could be within society. "Imagining archives" on a sustained basis has been Hugh's major contribution to world archivy and the principal reason for his many honours. We believe the present book shows why.

* * * * *

Unlike the other leading English-speaking archival thinkers mentioned above, however, Hugh's work has never been gathered together in one place. The impact of his ideas has been based on a widely scattered series of remarkable essays written over the last third of the twentieth century. This volume brings the most important of these together for the first time. But this book intentionally is more than a compendium of past work, no matter how distinguished that work may be. Hugh has written at our request a short reflection on each essay to explain (where useful) the context in which he wrote the original piece and, especially, his thoughts on it today, as well as a longer afterword to the book. It is rare in the world of letters that a writer in a field revisits his own work, reflecting on its origins and continued meaning—thus addressing the questions many thoughtful readers will have had when reading his provocative work: "I wonder what he was thinking when he wrote that?" or "I wonder what he would say about that today?" Hugh provides here some of those answers, and of course, as always, generates more questions.

As editors, we have contributed two original essays to the book to explore the person, the archivist, and the colleague; and his ideas and their significance within the framework of international archival theory and the Canadian archival tradition. Both essays intentionally lack the scholarly tone and footnoting apparatus of our past articles in favour of personal reflection and more whimsical tone. We have together known Hugh for a long time; we have both been influenced by his ideas and his person; and we both without apology approach this task with fealty, though not uncritically, to our mentor and friend. These are our personal readings of Hugh and his impact, not a detailed explication of his ideas. We hope our reflections on what Hugh's ideas have meant to us will invite readers to appreciate anew Hugh's essays from their personal perspectives.

Overall, the whole of this work, with its original and reprinted components, is more than the sum of its parts that, until now, were scattered in journals in three countries or unpublished. The book is not intended as a "convenience" collection that brings old work together, but as a renewed and powerful statement about the archival ethos at the start of the new millennium by the profession's grand visionary, placed for the first time together, in sequence, in context, and in sharpened focus. The essays remain a touchstone for the ongoing debate about archival identity in the face of social, technological, and philosophical change.

* * * * *

Our first debt is of course to Hugh Taylor for writing the new reflections and afterword, and for granting permission to reprint his previously published and unpublished work. When we approached him with this project, Hugh was nearing 80 years of age and had very resolutely "retired from retirement," as he put it, deciding to say no more in published form about archives. We thank him for acceding so graciously and skilfully—and imaginatively—to our request to say more, and for his patience as the text gradually moved to publication. Hugh also helped us choose which essays should be published, given our space limitations. We also solicited advice on which pieces were the "best" from two long-time admirers of Hugh, Tom Nesmith, and Candace Loewen. Our final decision has been to include those essays that are, to us, the most stimulating, that reduce duplication in themes across essays between those chosen and not chosen, and that give a sample of the several phases and breadth of Hugh's career. The essays are presented in chronological order, so that readers may appreciate the broadening evolution and rich interconnections in Hugh's thought as these occurred over more than three decades.

As a member of the Association of Canadian Archivists' Publication Committee, Candace Loewen again was a pillar of strength on several points, including helping to hone our publication proposal and obtaining reliable electronic versions of some of the essays. More came very kindly from Jane Turner who, with Daphne Taylor, had earlier typed much of Hugh's work; Jane's input was helpfully converted by Dan Moore from incompatible software for our ease of editorial formatting. For well over one-half of the chosen essays, however, there was no existing electronic version, and Jean-Stéphen Piché kindly converted these essays page-by-page into digital text using a sophisticated scanner. We as editors have proofread the scanned versions to ensure their conformity with the original texts: the essays all appear here as they were originally published or written, save for the correction of incidental typographical errors and limited standardizing of formats. Original footnoting conventions have largely been retained from the original sources.

Throughout these essays, some inconsistencies of spelling, capitalization, and general style arise from variations in British, Canadian, and American English. Over time, Hugh's native British English took on a hint of Canadian style. To complicate matters further, his British and Canadian usage may have been edited out altogether in some American publications. And what of his Australian editors? In any case, rather than wrangling these linguistic differences into artificial conformity, we have chosen to retain Hugh's original language where possible. In a way, the adaptation and evolution of his prose is a subtle record of his voice and story.

Teresa Brinati, Director of Publishing, and Richard Cox, Publications Editor, both for the Society of American Archivists; and Elizabeth Diamond and Cheryl Avery, Chairs, Association of Canadian Archivists' Publication Committee, all extended welcome encouragement for this joint ACA-SAA publication. We thank as well the publishers of the journals and books where Hugh's work first appeared for generously granting permission for republication without any fees or royalties being charged; they are acknowledged in the source citation on the first page of each essay.

Terry Cook, Ottawa/Winnipeg
Gordon Dodds, Winnipeg

Part 1

ABOUT HUGH A. TAYLOR

Chapter 1

Hugh Taylor:
The Far-Away Archivist

Gordon Dodds

I could easily believe that, when Hugh Taylor was a boy, his schoolteacher constantly had to bring him back to the presence of the class. In my mind's eye, I can see a lad who heard just enough to get his imagination rolling and his thought processes into another realm. I don't know if this was the case, but it wouldn't surprise me if it were so because that seemed to be the man I met when my path ran into his a little more than forty years ago.

It might explain his trademark ever-dusty reading glasses, his preoccupation with pacifist issues following wartime experiences in the Royal Air Force, the inviting dance with Marshall McLuhan in the 1970s, the staff gift of a bicycle when Hugh left the (then) Public Archives of Canada (he doesn't drive), his ecological commitments in Nova Scotia and British Columbia, maybe even his lifelong Anglicanism and latter-day interest in spirituality. I have no way of knowing whether any of this is symptomatic of Hugh's outlook on life, but it has always been my impression that his mind was ever freewheeling and searching. Once he worked some flight of thought out to his satisfaction, he would come swooping in with galvanizing energy and glinting eyes to tell us all.

I first met Hugh when he was the County Archivist of Northumberland. The summer of my first year as a history undergraduate at the University of Durham took me to see him on the recommendation of the chair of History at the (then) King's College. I guess I had shown some interest in local history and who better to talk to than an archivist—at least in those days. I made contact with him in a dingy and disheveled room in County Hall, a Greek revival building crammed with offices, sturdily and crudely planted on the site of the new castle overlooking the historic, but industrial, River

Tyne at Newcastle, where an explosion of nineteenth-century railway trackage curved sinuously around the castle keep still standing sturdily to the west of the county offices. There he was—tall almost lofty, head slightly tilted upwards from broad shoulders, glasses firmly set and forgotten on a broad face, and a utility smock wrapped around his frame signifying I suppose that he was someone who worked with his hands. "Come along," he said to me within moments of my arrival, "let me show you what I am doing." I followed him along the corridor to what Hugh would often refer to in later years as "the heap on the floor."

What he was doing, of course, was making sense of the county records, both those deriving from Northumbrian public administration and those "deposited" by the owners or estates of businesses, organizations, and individuals. County archives in England were, in their way, just as much about "total archives" as Canadian public archives. No doubt Hugh Taylor would have been deeply engaged in what I would come to know as records appraisal, arrangement, description, and access, if not conservation as we value that function today. I have to say that he piqued my curiosity. I was impressed by his purposefulness and recognition of the inherent organic character of the records in front of us, but Hugh appeared to me a little austere and remote. Hugh's tasks, Sisyphean—as David Bearman has dubbed such work—appeared to me that day as lonely, dirty, arcane, and not immediately attractive.

We left the clutter of County Hall, walking across a parking lot, which in more military times would have been the castle courtyard, to the second floor of a northerly gatehouse known as the Black Gate Museum. Not much passed between us, possibly because I was a hesitant student and he at a loss to know what to say to this callow youth. Perhaps it had something to do with being born and raised in English culture. Or was it because Hugh was lost in thought? I couldn't tell then but I am persuaded now it was the latter. Hugh set me down in the library of the Society of Antiquaries of Newcastle upon Tyne where I began my first more or less archival and volunteer job. I was instructed briefly on how to list and describe the correspondence of a local family, which had fallen into the care of the Society.

From time to time, Hugh, who was the Society's honorary librarian, looked in from his "heap" at County Hall on my scribblings and contemplation amid the quiescent half light of the Black Gate's bindings and document miscellany. Before the end of the summer, and for no obvious reason that I can recall, Hugh talked one day with me about the University of Liverpool's graduate diploma programme in archival administration. He suggested that I seriously consider it as a career when I got my degree in history and generously offered to sponsor my application if I were so inclined.

Having been archivist at the Liverpool City Library for a time and a graduate of the Liverpool programme, no doubt Hugh's word might well have been useful. I have to admit, so many years on, that the prospect was not altogether exciting to me as a young student. Perhaps the peace and obscurity of the Black Gate, where heavy stone walls dulled the roar of the city's traffic and the regular shuttling of trains negotiating the complex switches east of Newcastle upon Tyne's central station, had sunk too deeply into my psyche. If what I saw Hugh doing, however briefly, and what I had spent the summer doing, was a career, its attraction seemed singularly remote. Archival activity looked dull, despite the excitement of reading other people's correspondence. At that moment, doing research and telling others what I had found seemed infinitely more dynamic. I let the matter settle for a few days and reported to Hugh that teaching history was what really interested me.

On various evenings during the next year or two, I saw Hugh in public performance as it were. As the Society of Antiquaries librarian, he was called upon to give his report to its members of which I had become one in pursuit of my burgeoning interest in local history and Romano-British archaeology. The librarian didn't have a leading role in Society business and no doubt his duties could have been dispatched perfunctorily, but Hugh was distinctive. I glimpsed in those few minutes something of the arresting figure he was to assume not long after in North American archivy. There was the physical presence, chin forward, arms and hands in delivery, eyes glinting and darting behind the characteristically crooked spectacles, and the melodious, clear, authoritative voice giving the Society's mostly venerable members one treat of a report. There was little sign of the "thinking" Hugh Taylor whom Canadian archivists came to cherish but, it seemed to me, perched on the darkened upper tiers of the Mining Institute lecture hall, that this was clearly someone worth listening to.

I also saw a little more of archives in action—initially, under the guidance of Michael Cook at the Newcastle City Archives as I gathered together some detail about the city's dealings with an early nineteenth-century architect/engineer and, again, with Hugh Taylor at the Northumberland County Archives as I explored the toll-road administration of turnpike trusts. Most of this research was done in the evenings, following a day's teaching for me and a day's archival work for Hugh. He had offered to let me work at the archives after closing on days when he continued to work on the county records. The first county archival facility was tucked away in the woods on the edge of a horse racecourse. This bunker of a building had been used as a military communications centre and probably caused Hugh all kinds of logistical problems. To my untutored eye, and I think to Hugh's affectionate recollection, the bunker served its new purpose admirably well. One feature was especially useful—a raised gallery around a central "ops" floor (you could imagine it from those British post–Second World War movies with a natty, shrewd-eyed John Mills and neatly suited Sylvia Sims) which lent itself quite effectively to archival exhibits. I remember with real admiration Hugh's documentary displays on a host of local historical themes such as coal mining, railway development, coastal shipping, estate farming, and the like. I took a busload of schoolchildren on more than one occasion to see these rich expressions of life in the county and drew from them ideas for a class or two at my Workers Education Association evenings. I probably did not appreciate the depth of planning that went into these exhibits or that Hugh was not only the instigator but, more often than not, the designer and the operator. Hugh's exhibitions were imaginative within the constraints of mid-1960s technology and his gallery talks to classes quite evocative. He would simply light up when he did his "show and tell." Somehow he did what most archivists would give their eyeteeth to achieve—he made the documents, as he would say later, "move and speak."

I saw little of the mundane office duties of the County Archivist nor his struggles for funding. It must have been tough, but Hugh gave little outward sign of this to me. He has referred to this period in Northumberland, where his father hailed from and where he spent his adolescence, as "an archivist's dream." In more than one English county archives (Devon, Essex, Kent, and Northamptonshire come readily to mind), a burst of archival energy, some of it understandably idiosyncratic, was released in the post-war decades as centuries of public and private records were identified, gathered-in, and given rudimentary protection. Hugh was one of a band of archivists who readily seized the opportunity to reveal with a flourish how their "nearby" records, as one American historian aptly labeled them, made sense to citizens. Today, with sophisticated digital instruments that seem to make possible any document transmission to any ear or eye, it is easy to overlook the early efforts to open the door into memory and understanding.

Sometimes we talked along the pathways back to our respective bus routes at the end of an evening. Perhaps because I had turned away from being an archivist or maybe it was Hugh Taylor's excellent impression of being on a different plane, we did not touch much on archival work. I got no sense in those days of the "paper archaeology" that fired Hugh's archival commitment—the stripping away of layers of activity and interaction to establish context and meaning. Certainly, the northeast borders with Scotland were brimming with settlement from prehistoric times, and it was comfortable for historians, archivists, librarians, museum curators, genealogists, geographers, antiquarians, and many others to delve in and out of what we would now call the natural, the built, and the archival heritage. I suspect Hugh himself had not then given this much thought and realized intuitively, as he looked back much later in life during a visit to Australia, that "there was no time." Doing was the order of the day.

Our paths were soon to divide, though in a curiously coincidental way. Hugh's direction was to become the first Provincial Archivist of Alberta in Edmonton, mine to take up historical research in Vancouver. We would both leave Northumberland before the summer of 1965 had passed. In our own fashion, we looked forward with enormous excitement to these ventures in Western Canada and shared some thoughts about what they might bring. For Hugh Taylor and for Canadian archivists, his separation from, but not dismissal or rejection of, "the ould sod" turned out to be hugely significant. Emigration took Hugh far away from his old work experience and showed him the value of new perspectives being grafted to old stock. In thirty-five years of thinking, talking, and writing about archives, Hugh would also draw his new colleagues far away into different perspectives on their work.

Others have discussed the particular substance of Hugh Taylor's contribution to archival thought, as will the following essay by Terry Cook. My purpose is to offer a personal view (Hugh might well call it "quirky") of the impact his presence has had on being an archivist in Canada during the last three decades. It says nothing about his administrative and managerial experience of which I know very little since I never worked as an archivist in any of his programmes. I did try to persuade him to come to the Archives of Ontario at one point—it needed his vision—but he wasn't having any of that! This is not, of course, to suppose that had he not been in Canada much of what has changed would not have occurred. Rather it is a means of saying *because* he was in Canada, Hugh Taylor can be identified in special ways that have affected what we do as archivists. With a nod to David Letterman and the proclivity we have to list, I'll identify ten ways in which I can recognize Hugh in the fabric of the Canadian archival world—a sort of Taylor's Top Ten, in no particular ranking other than those conjured by my own whimsy.

AS TEACHER

The gift of teaching is an idiosyncratic asset. It comes in different cloaks and fashions, but is detectable most of all when something catches fire between teacher and taught. Hugh Taylor has that elemental power. You could hear it in the inflection of his presentations to school children at the Northumberland County Archives more than thirty-five years ago. I remember feeling that persuasiveness in his elucidation of documentary analysis at the (then) Public Archives of Canada training course for archivists in 1973. He took his students into the documents and made them relevant, understandable, and alive by revealing their context. Barbara Craig has rightly emphasized that the records themselves must be the fuel of the archivist's engine, and Tom Nesmith has shown how Hugh Taylor was a central figure in the Canadian "rediscovery" of provenance.

In my sights, it is the rapport and sensitivity that Hugh Taylor brought to the materials—the documents, the records—with which he worked as a regional archivist in the document-rich "muniments" of En-glish life that nurtured the archivist as craftsperson and communicator. Listening to Hugh and watching his behavior in front of a class or group, the gestures and mannerisms, you sensed the authority and immediacy of the teacher. Hugh imported to the—as yet—unformed Canadian archives community in the late 1960s a pedagogic quality that, if hidden, was badly in need of airing—a relationship he later referred to as "the master and the apprentice." By the mid 1980s, after retirement from Nova Scotia, first at the University of British Columbia and then at the National Archives as a guest director of its training course for archivists, he had moved away from this relationship toward a more philosophical exegesis of the archivist as interpreter of recorded communications and the culture of the record.

AS EDITOR

Hugh's arrival in Alberta as its first Provincial Archivist in 1965 rapidly introduced him to the professional trappings of the archivist, such as they were. In those days, the archivist was still handmaiden to the historian and had met somewhat collegially, for only two years previously, at the behest of the Public Archives of Canada as a "section" of the Canadian Historical Association. A few stirrings in the archivist's breast led to the birth of *The Canadian Archivist,* an infrequent newsletter designed to give some shape to the comings and goings of archivists and a vehicle for addressing matters of some significance to archivists. Hugh became its editor and set about fashioning something with a bit more bite. Though he had written a little in England on mostly historical topics, *The Canadian Archivist* would be the first manifest sign of Hugh Taylor's interest in a voice for Canadian archivy. It also provided him with a print vehicle in which to wrestle with the mix of training and experience gained among records stretching back centuries from boroughs and estates in the North of England amid the novelty of a prairie government barely half a century old. Thus appeared his "Impressions of an Immigrant." The contrast piece comparing archives in Britain and in Canada seems in retrospect to have been a sort of clearing of the head and, as they say, all the rest was history. In fact, it was quite the reverse. Just about all the rest was *archives.*

The first article he wrote in the *Canadian Archivist* as editor became an unwitting touchstone for much of the intellectual enquiry about archivists and archives that he sparked in subsequent years. As Hugh himself now recognizes in retrospect, there was talk of understanding how and why records were created, of the significance of "documents that move and speak," of the records of cultural diversities, of linkages between artifacts and documents, of orality in society, of the archivist who functions as "historian of the record" as Tom Nesmith so adroitly observed in another decade. Much of this came from the two years he spent in Alberta, where he encountered the freshness of records bearing superb photographic imagery and the mystical symbolism of memory among its native peoples. His nurturing of the *Canadian Archivist* in subsequent years, shared with Ian Wilson, prepared the way for *Archivaria*, which he greeted on its first issue in January 1976 with enormous pleasure and concrete support. Hugh published a number of important articles in *Archivaria*, but stayed clear of its editorial activities. I recall too his strong advocacy for that journal in 1981 when its editor was under attack from disgruntled members of the Association of Canadian Archivists (ACA) at its annual meeting in Halifax, Nova Scotia.

AS PROGENITOR OF THE ACA

The Association of Canadian Archivists marked its twenty-fifth anniversary in June 2000—in Edmonton, Alberta, where Hugh began his Canadian archival career and where the ACA was officially born ten years later. At a party following a long day of constitutional wranglings in 1975, Hugh literally bounced onto a sofa beside me with the widest grin I had ever seen and declared that we had come a long way. It didn't seem the moment to question his meaning but, in reflection, I can see that the occasion was a bit of a watershed all round.

Hugh Taylor's part in the emergence of the ACA deserves recollection. When the Archives Section of the Canadian Historical Association (CHA) met one scorching week in 1973 at Queen's University, Kingston, Ontario, there were glimmerings of dissent, among the younger Ontario archivists including Ian Wilson in particular, about the continuing and indistinct marriage with the academic historians. The next year saw a grandly titled "Committee of the Future" chaired by Hugh Taylor with the objective of developing a movement that would lead to the extinction of the Section and optimistically to the birth of a new archivists' constituency. It was Hugh's enthusiastic and overt support for the idea, and total confidence that it could be done, which buoyed the travels of Marion Beyea, David Rudkin, and myself (dubbed affectionately by Hugh as the "Young

Turks") across Canada in 1974 and 1975. To build momentum for a brand new organization, we did the very Canadian thing of trying to build a consensus from region to region. It couldn't have been accomplished without Hugh Taylor's involvement and foresight and, I suspect, his chairmanship did much to convince at least Ontario's Provincial Archivist that he could allow two staff archivists to spend public time on such "frivolities."

I recognize Hugh so clearly, too, in a personal footnote of memory from 1977 when he sprang up to back my declared indignation at an annual meeting of the Society of American Archivists in Philadelphia that Canada was indeed a foreign country. American colleagues, some as close as Massachusetts, had long learned to think of Canada as an American archival region. We are still such a region within the Association of Records Managers and Administrators! Hugh, of course, was more gracious than I who, in those days, could hardly believe my ears.

AS ADVOCATE OF PROFESSIONAL EDUCATION

Quite aside from his personal teaching style and skills, Hugh Taylor lent his weight and persuasion to an emerging consciousness, in Canada at least, that archivists should have university-based professional education at the graduate level. Until the mid-1970s, the pattern for archivists appointed to archival agencies—because they were history, or sometimes library science, graduates—was to dip them in a series (if they were lucky) of short courses, institutes, or workshops on matters archival. Some of these were useful indeed, but they tended to be practice-oriented and ran the risk of showing colleagues merely how things were done in their "shops." What was clearly absent was the time and the scope to study such broad questions as to why societies have kept records, how information has been communicated through records, and what records-keeping practices can reveal about ourselves through time. Hugh Taylor specifically envisioned in 1973 that a postgraduate course in archives "should be essentially academic and philosophical." He joined with an old English friend and colleague, the late Edwin Welch, to fashion a curriculum for a master's degree in archival science.

The first members of the ACA Executive Committee gave a high priority to this mission and got Hugh Taylor to lead the Education Committee. Much talk ensued among administrators at the Public Archives, and the University of Ottawa, with historians at Carleton University, librarians at the University of Toronto, and both historians and librarians at the University of British Columbia. There were the usual regional jealousies, institutional competition, individual egos, fiscal concerns, and uncertainties about what a graduate curriculum for archivists would look like. In the process, which continued off and on until the University of British Columbia quietly went ahead in its library school with approval for a programme, Hugh got sidelined.

In retrospect, he might well agree that the curriculum was fairly slight—it was also labeled graduate archival *training*—but the guidelines were novel and carried some considerable influence. Frankly, nothing of this kind had been articulated in anglophone Canada or in the United States, and the guidelines acquired a kind of monumental appearance and symbolic importance, though Hugh would not have seen them in this light. Despite his unflagging promotion of the graduate archivist concept in the United States, culminating in his Society of American Archivists' presidency in 1980, it was with some dismay that he realized he could not entice the Society at that time to so radically conceive of archival education.

AS McLUHAN-ITE

"The medium is the message" assertion of Toronto's Marshall McLuhan clearly captivated Hugh Taylor. He has written: "I ran into Marshall McLuhan's *Gutenberg Galaxy* and *Understanding Media* and began to grasp their relevance for archivists." These works had emerged in the early 1960s and were "discovered" by Hugh later in the decade. During the next few years at the Public Archives of Canada, he increasingly devoted attention to the media of the record, convinced that archivists had given insufficient thought as to the full spectrum of communication processes through time and the flood of records they generated in many media. McLuhan's electrifying observations marvelously focused Hugh's mind on what nontextual records had to say and how they said it. The medium affects the record. Creation of media divisions in the archives where he worked was a striking expression of Hugh Taylor's conviction, prompted by his reading of McLuhan. The Ottawa example tended to be emulated to some extent in other archival agencies. He has always justified these changes as necessary to redress the imbalance of resources typically given over to care of and access to written records in archives. Critics would counter that concentration on media can obscure or at least distort the provenance or context of records that should be linked in a unified way for every medium to their creator and not divided into little media empires within archives. Of course, Hugh didn't intend that, for he always had a holistic vision of archives, but he perhaps naively trusted that archival managers would share his vision rather than being more intent on protecting their turf.

Nevertheless, the McLuhan fillip to Hugh Taylor's thinking about what archives are and how they should be understood was a most important provocation. It certainly contributed to several addresses and articles in the next decade that drew on his exploration of language, communication theory, and philosophy—always with an archival tilt. He was energized and encouraged by the leaping connections and phrases of McLuhanite literature, a little too quick perhaps at times to embrace utterances of disciples such as Barrington Nevitt and Derrick de Kerkhove, but ever keen to search for different ways of looking at life. Complacency, a state of mind that can be only too common, was stricken from Hugh Taylor's lexicon. The McLuhanites clearly gave him every opportunity to think outside the box, and Canadian archivists were often the better for it.

AS ECOLOGIST

For archivists, one of Hugh Taylor's less easily recognizable attributes is his love of life and life forms. More than any other archivist in my experience, he has been able to suggest vibrant parallels between biology and archives, not in drawing Foucaultian parallels between archival indexing and Linnaeusian classification, but as a means of understanding how organisms function in different contexts. Barbara Craig has referred to this in the 1992 festschrift to Hugh, *The Archival Imagination,* as the "genetic wealth of living things."

Doubtless some of this springs from his experience of wartime devastation and proximity to death as a young man, yet I believe it has been fuelled too by the rare pleasure of being an archivist. The effusions of human activity in daily life are so full of diversity that to be able to reach back through their ages in a spirit of respect and humility is nothing short of a privilege. Hugh's delight in this environment has always been evident and made the more attractive by extrapolations and predictions about how we treat our planet, acknowledge our humanity, and achieve self-knowledge. His involvement in various phases of the international peace and environmental movements, especially in the 1980s, which as the "me decade" has rightly been labeled one of the more narcissistic periods of the past century, was entirely in character.

Hugh's move to Nova Scotia after seven years with the Public Archives in Ottawa was, I suspect, quite a relief. It allowed him to return to what he liked best—a kind of "archival regionalism." By this he would not mean being narrow-minded, but rather in touch with the fabric of community record keeping in a way that being at the Public Archives could not, by virtue of its function, so easily provide. In the close-knit Maritime society, Hugh saw opportunities to foster family and neighbourhood connections that gave him great personal and professional satisfaction. Nova Scotia also allowed him to think more about bioregions instead of political regions.

The years in Nova Scotia as Provincial Archivist, and afterward as an archival consultant in semiretirement, were archivally extremely productive for Hugh Taylor. He was able to mastermind construction of a new provincial facility, an archivist's crowning tangible accomplishment. He delivered a series of seminars on society and the documentary record at the University of British Columbia. He began coordinating a number of the annual month-long archives courses offered at the National Archives of Canada, spoke at numerous conferences, and issued a spate of archival articles, including two of his most memorable in 1988: "Transformation in the Archives" and "My Very Act and Deed." Both of them were redolent of Hugh's restless urging to archivists to recognize what he first called the "information ecology" in 1984. This was a theme he returned to a few years ago in his "Archivist in the Age of Ecology" lectures in Australia, reworked into "Recycling the Past" for *Archivaria* (1993).

AS WORDSMITH

Most readers of Hugh Taylor are struck by his coining of arresting phrases, which tickle the memory. I have to admit that, as Hugh Taylor began to write about archives in Canada, I looked for Taylorisms. They weren't difficult to spot. Who can forget imagery like "the heap on the floor," "sea changes," "paper archaeology," "totemic universe," "cloistered archivists," and "dust to ashes," to mention a few. And those memorable titles—"Clio in the Raw," "The Media of Record," "My Very Act and Deed," and "Chip Monks at the Gate" (my favourite). Hugh's metaphors are arresting: my co-editor's favourite has Hugh viewing dogmatic archivists as busily arranging the ship's logbooks, while the band plays its final tune . . . on the *Titanic*! Hugh designed his prose, in his words, to offer "a range of insights in mosaic form, analogous to synchronic discussion rather than diachronic research." He resists "tedious modifiers in an ambience of suspended judgment, as thoughts swarm over the subject in a nonspecialized way to let the light in and perhaps reveal some fresh approaches. This is not the path of painstaking research, which has its place, but rather of 'organizing ignorance for discovery.'" More than for most writers, and perhaps again reflecting McLuhan, Hugh's prose reflected his message—perhaps sometimes was his message. Words and phrases, like ideas and strategies, are to be played with rather than enunciated as rigid ideologies, thereby permitting the ambience of fresh light to fertilize the archival ecology rather than seal it in darkness.

AS SPEAKER

I once made the mistake of introducing Hugh Taylor at a speaking session with a long rendering of his positions and accomplishments. My intent was to prepare the gathered throng with a drum roll buildup for the eminent archivist. He turned to the audience when I had finished and apologized with a straight face for not recognizing himself.

Yet most living Canadian archivists cannot fail to have seen or heard Hugh Taylor on one occasion or another. His English speech cadences alone seemed mellow and engaging to North American audiences. His distinctive orality (a term often used in his writing) was, to my ears, quite unforgettable. There was no mistaking who it was. A hush usually fell on any room in which Hugh had agreed to speak as the audience waited eagerly for his "opener." His style was ruminative but curiously assertive at the same time. It was as if he wanted his audience to see the intellectual foray he had been through and then to persuade them that he had reached workable conclusions—effective tactics indeed in oratory of any kind as Tommy Douglas demonstrated on political platforms. Hugh, in quite different circles, was a natural just like Douglas; you were never conscious of any preening or dissimulation. As in writing, speaking, or in person, what you saw or heard was what you got. He invariably took his listeners to a new level of insight or understanding—by "probing," a favourite Socratic tool in his exploration of ideas.

Above all, Hugh almost always spoke with the freshness of discovery, and the excitement of ideas, whatever the topic—making the "been there, done that" young cynics in the back row later, upon reflection, feel shamed and envious. Some of them became admirers. Two became the editors of this book.

AS ARCHIVAL PHILOSOPHER

Hugh would resist this label out of real modesty. It is deserved. If philosophy can be seen as investigation of the principles and processes underlying reality, Hugh is indeed a philosopher. If you doubt it, read him.

Time after time, he has deliberately challenged the archival status quo in thought and practice by raising questions, suggesting connections, overturning conventions, looking the other way, being imaginative. True to the philosopher's mettle, Hugh does not usually offer solutions or methods. He occupies no stout positions, takes few stances, confronts all absolutes, and constantly searches for relationships. One of Hugh's most noticeable traits, frustrating and engaging at the same time, has been his unwillingness to become rooted in time or thought, preferring instead to retain the instinctive flexibility of the sparring boxer who will slip sideways to avoid being pinned. "We have," wrote Hugh some twelve years ago, "to see the elastic, inexact character of truth, and symbolic interpretation rather than literalism, that allows us to err, to change, to adapt." That is what he constantly strove to do in his excursions into the archival forest. It had a decidedly postmodern ring to it long before postmodern ideas began to enter archival discourse.

AS GALACTIC TRAVELLER

Writing and discussion on topics of archival practice can be leaden and prosaic, too much rooted in institutional procedures and "our shop" exposition. What a difference there has been since we have begun to ask why records are the way they are and how such knowledge helps us to understand the human condition.

We talk bureaucratically these days about "managing change" as if there is a prescription for the future if only we can grasp the true nettle. Hugh didn't manage change; he provoked it. He asked us gently but passionately to ask ourselves who we are and why we do what we do across the aeons of time. Canadian archivists have felt the winds of change blown by Hugh Taylor and have been energized by them. In his inimitable and idiosyncratic manner, he injected much cerebral vigor into Canadian archival life when it was most needed. As James Burrows and the late Mary Ann Pylpchuk commented, in their 1992 review in his festschrift, Hugh "transcended comfortable notions of logic and linearity to entice archivists into contemplating multiple realms of communication . . . local, national, planetary, and tribal; acoustic, literate, electronic, and mythical; holistic, humanistic, scientific, and organic."

Hugh Taylor would be the last to see himself as pilot of the archival "good ship *Enterprise*" going boldly where none before have travelled. He is both too personally modest and too little deterministic in setting direction. Yet there is a whiff of an "out of this world" dimension to his utterances and writing that distinguishes his contributions to Canadian archivy. Hugh came to Canada from far away, and he has taken many who were open to travelling with him on splendid ventures far into the distant galaxies. These essays—a fine legacy indeed—Hugh would hope might inspire "the next generation" to imagine similar voyages for the archives of tomorrow.

Chapter 2

Hugh Taylor: Imagining Archives

Terry Cook

Imagination is synonymous with Hugh Taylor. I picture Hugh sitting at conferences or quietly talking over tea, attentive always, yet looking off dreamily to some distant point. Perhaps he is trying to focus through those ever-smudged glasses on some approaching person. But he is not distracted at all, simply allowing his mind to soar in flights of imagination. Suddenly, he alights, exclaiming a new idea: "Why not look at it this way! Let's see this anew. Just imagine!"

Yet none of Hugh's insights are delivered as Olympian pronouncements. Hugh plays with ideas, words, images; he neither dictates nor prescribes. There is no sense of the oracle coming down from the mountain with ideas carved in stone for the masses. He treats the young student with all the attention given to senior colleagues. He asks probing questions rather than giving firm answers. He encourages, he mentors, he nourishes. Of course, for all his politeness and shyness, Hugh certainly has opinions and voices them fearlessly. Yet his interjections, in my memory, are usually phrased about looking, about seeing, about exploring, about imagining *together*, rather than about wanting people passively following in his footsteps. By this approach, Hugh opens vistas rather than closes them. He visualizes more than he analyzes. He creates mental pictures, uses metaphorical juxtapositions, paints collages of meanings, more than he employs conventional linear thinking and logical critiques. Ever adventuresome, he reaches out to innovation, rather

Note: I am very grateful for the generous and helpful commentary that this essay received, to its significant improvement, from Gordon Dodds, Verne Harris, Candace Loewen, Tom Nesmith, Jean-Stéphen Piché, and Joan Schwartz. These friends are, however, blameless for any errors that remain and may not share all of its interpretations.

than defensively erecting monuments to consistency, ego, or tradition. "We are builders of bridges, not castles, as we cross from the assurance of 'now' to the uncertainty of 'new.'" By such probing, Hugh continually imagines what could be, what should be, the character of recorded communication, the function of archival institutions, the identity (and education) of the archivist, the nature of memory, and the deeper societal, even mythic meanings of archives. And for the past three decades, he has done it all more imaginatively than anyone else.

* * * * *

One meeting with Hugh remains vivid in my memory. In Banff, Alberta, in late May 1991, at the annual conference of the Association of Canadian Archivists, in the heart of the majestic Canadian Rockies, the mountains topped with fresh late-season snow, Hugh and I happened to meet crossing the parking lot at the conference hotel. We had somehow both managed to miss our dinner engagements. We stood and chatted awhile, until thoroughly chilled in the crisp twilight air, then retreated to a nondescript cafeteria, sat at a corner table, and talked, really talked, for hours. It was a transforming evening for me. To that point in my career, I had written about the historical context and record-keeping systems of the Canadian North, national parks, and the settlement of the prairie West, which were my areas of archival specialization, and was starting to publish pieces addressing such archival issues as the virtual fonds, electronic record keeping, and macroappraisal. I remember being pretty full of myself, and certainly regaled Hugh with the new ideas I then had swirling around in my mind.

Hugh as always listened patiently and supportively, but he also kept pushing gently and insistently. It is all well and good, I remember him suggesting, to have better ways of appraising or describing archives, better strategies for articulating our processes and procedures for electronic records, but for what purpose? Better methods and better concepts to do what? And why? What connection, for example, do we archivists have to the splendid cosmos that almost overwhelms any reflective visitor in the Rockies? What relationship is there between the patterns of Nature's memory seen in the massive rocks and trees around us and the traces of human memory enshrined in documents stored in archives? Between the strata in rocks, the DNA code in humans, and the lines on parchment? What connections might there be between the fragile global ecosystem(s) so evident in the mountains, and the system(s) of human and societal organization that we strive to document? Is there kinship (or at least holistic analogies) between them, or should there be?

Further yet, I think Hugh and I were inspired alike by the spiritual presence many others have also felt in the mountains—these "sacred places" in Aboriginal culture. And so we pondered the spiritual dimensions implicit in the preservation of memory, these very "acts and deeds" of remembering, and the whole "remembrancer" function in society. Are not these archival impulses to remember profoundly spiritual, a *de facto* witness to transcendent faith in humankind and its continued shared existence on this planet? Do they not signify at a fundamental level that there indeed *will be* a future, when having documents from the past worth remembering will actually matter? And if so, wondered Hugh—for the dreamer could always bring things down to the "coalface" (as he liked to call it) of workplace reality—should we really be spending so much effort amassing kilometres of official records of "bureaucrats talking to one another," rather than records of lives lived; of art, music, emotions; of struggles for justice and human rights; and of the planet itself—those right-brain artistic, intuitive, symbolic, emotional, and holistic sides of humanity so often ignored in archives in favour of their left-brain rational, linear, analytical, scientific, and logocentric opposites? And so on and on we went, until the stars twinkled over the dark silhouettes of the mountain ranges.

That evening changed my perspective on archives. In the previous couple of years, I had been in a reading group with three close friends, where we would discuss recent works in feminism, history, philosophy, and cultural studies, and mull over tentatively their possible implications for the archival endeavour. And, now, here was Hugh, the *doyen* of Canadian archivists, not only legitimizing such private speculations, but taking them to new heights. Hugh gave me that night the confidence to embolden my own explorations, and no small part of my subsequent work owes much to his inspiration.

I discerned then that Hugh was really the first philosopher of archives. I saw—imagine!—that there *actually could be* a philosophy of archives. This philosophy goes far beyond the familiar archival "theories" of provenance or *respect des fonds* in which the profession prides itself; these concepts are primarily generalizations from past practice for certain media in certain times and in certain places. An archival philosophy involves digging deeper into the meaning of archives, looking at what they signify, searching their mythical and emotive dimensions as much as their rational and artifactual ones. Such a philosophy investigates, as Gordon Dodds has said, "the principles and processes underlying reality," and not just archival or record-keeping reality, but social, cultural, technological, and historical realities integral to record keeping. More, philosophy underpins living the examined life—and the examined profession. Hugh ever wants to shake us from our "comfortable state of complacent narcosis." He invites a questioning of orthodoxy, distrusts rigid formulae, and opens us to internal creativity and cross-disciplinary fertility. Hugh asserts that archives should be "an intellectual discipline based on the philosophical study of ideas, not an empirical discipline based on the scientific study of fact." Not surprisingly, he urges archivists to avoid "the trap of a scientific reductionism and technological structures inappropriate to archives. . . . We can and must think at times in terms of ideas, abstractions, metaphors, paradoxes, hypotheses, and the like, as one means of sharpening our perceptions."

Of course I had read Hugh's works before, but that night in Banff, I understood for the first time the remarkable nature of Hugh's re-imagining of what archives were all about. Up to then, I had confused the meaning of archives with their value. To be sure, archives retain valuable documents (financially, administratively, symbolically, culturally); many researchers find valuable information in these documents for a plethora of uses; modern democracies find value in archives as sources of accountability and collective memory; and archives by their existence demonstrate the value that the state or private sponsor places on history, heritage, and culture. And, thereby, the archivist indirectly becomes a valued professional in society for facilitating all these endeavours. Yet "meaning" is different from "value." Meaning is more direct, and much deeper, than just indirectly facilitating or reflecting the value that others find in archives. Archives have meaning in part, of course, because they are valuable. But archives also have meaning—as records, institutions, profession, activity—because they are an open window on our common humanity. They link human beings, as Hugh asserts in several of the essays in this book, to the psychological need to remember and to forget, to our animating stories and deeper myths. They collectively offer a sense of identity and a tangible connection to community. They let us belong. More yet, archives are (and represent) a foundational desire for justice in human affairs, a potential safeguard for our vital interdependent relationship with ecological systems, and a hopeful symbol of our spirituality as human beings—a means for transcending this mortal sphere. Archives touch our souls.

In this meaning-making or perhaps meaning-opportunity, in Hugh's imagining, the archivist is no passive instrument of Jenkinsonian archival mythology, no neutral—or neutered!—guardian of historical truth. Rather, the archivist is an active mediator in interpreting and documenting social phenomena to find and reflect these deeper meanings. Hugh's whole corpus is a clarion call to archivists to engage the many issues he raises in his essays, figure out their archival implications, and develop strategies and methodologies to address the gaps in our perceptions and our practices that he has highlighted so well. The main thrust of Hugh's "imagining archives" is challenging archivists to have some imagination! Get out of your complacent custodial cloisters, he repeatedly urges, and engage the world, directly, actively, and imaginatively.

If "imagining archives" is the essence of Hugh Taylor's contribution to our profession, he would be the first to agree that imagining has many meanings. Dictionaries tell us that *imagination* is the mental faculty for forming images or concepts of external objects not present to the actual senses; and it is the ability of the mind to be creative and resourceful. *Imagine* as an action verb carries the additional connotations of educated guesswork, supposition, and evocation of surprise ("just imagine!"). Hugh displays in rich abundance all these dimensions of imagination in the substance and style of his essays that follow.

Imagining Archives, as used in the title of this volume, takes on an additional meaning in light of recent scholarship. Benedict Anderson led the way with his influential *Imagined Communities: Reflections on the Origin and Spread of Nationalism*. "Imagining" in this sense is about creating a shared view of some phenomenon that its adherents or members can embrace as their own, whether as citizens of a nation or members of a profession. Anderson says of the nation as an imagined community, "It is *imagined* because the members of even the smallest nation will never know most of their fellow-members, meet them, or even hear of them, yet in the minds of each lives the image of their communion." He continues that "it is imagined as a *community*" because, despite inequalities and difference between internal regions, components, or individuals, all members feel an overarching "comradeship" of belonging. These imaginings are naturally historical in part, but also must have an "emotional legitimacy" in the present. Imagined communities were initially "the spontaneous distillation of a complex 'crossing' of discrete historical forces; but that, once created, they become 'modular,' capable of being transplanted, with varying degrees of self-consciousness, to a great variety of social terrains, to merge and be merged with a correspondingly wide variety of political and ideological constellations."

In *Imagining the Law: Common Law and the Foundations of the American Legal System*, Norman Cantor notes that there are traditionally two ways of addressing our shared imaginings. One is narrow and internal: write simply about the law in the past, and how the law has changed from its origins to become what we have today, by studying the thoughts of great jurists. The result is an imagining that is "highly technical," with a "focus on the operations and techniques of the legal profession." The other approach, and the one Cantor favours, imagines the law "interactively with present-day concerns and within the contexts of past culture, society, and politics. . . ." While he concedes that this might be dismissed pejoratively as "social constructivist or relativist," Cantor sees the approach more positively as "sociological and cultural," offering that these imaginings may best be seen as "historical sociology." In *Lincoln and Davis: Imagining America, 1809–1865,* Brian Dirck agrees that the process of answering "imagination questions" requires exploring "the psychological, social, cultural, and political factors that shaped . . . national imaginations. . . ."

Hugh Taylor "imagines archives" in the very same way. He seeks to articulate those deeper meanings and shared identities that might allow archivists to feel part of a community, whether they work in the public or private sector; with photography, maps, or government records; in a large national or small local institution; alone, with other archivists, or in alliance with librarians and museum curators. He searches for the inspirational bonds and intellectual possibilities that give meaning to our community. Archivists are not archivists because they do the same things in different places (appraise, acquire, describe), or because they or others find what they do to be "valuable," but because what they do has its own significance, its own community of meaning, its own transcendence.

In so imagining archives, Hugh very much adopts Norman Cantor's second analytical approach. Hugh ranges with erudition across archival and media history; stresses the social, cultural, and political factors that determine archival choices; explores the philosophical, psychological, and mythical concepts relevant to remembering and forgetting; and links these to present-day concerns around technological determinism, media power, public accountability, Aboriginal consciousness, environmental spoilation, and spiritual ennui. Reading Hugh's work offers the profession nothing less than an opportunity to seize the moment of Benedict Anderson's "spontaneous distillation" that provides definition, emotional resonance, and deeper meaning for members of any "imagined community." "Only by exploring and extending our professional reach to the limit of our integrity," Hugh asserts, ". . . will we escape that backwater which, though apparently calm and comfortable, may also be stagnant with the signs of approaching irrelevance." Hugh ever sought to turn that complacent backwater into a dynamic community of social meaning.

* * * * *

Believing that archives should reflect the society that creates them, a few archivists began in the 1980s (in English at least) to explore various "societal approaches" as the basis for archival theory and subsequent strategies and methodologies. This perspective represented a shift in the archival discourse from one based on the state to one reflecting the broader society that the state serves. In this vein, Eric Ketelaar of the Netherlands asserted that archives should now be of the people, for the people, even by the people. As the illegal destruction of records has graphically demonstrated in the past decade alone, from the White House to Queensland cabinet, from

Ottawa to Pretoria, from Enron to Big Tobacco, archives must be more than creatures of the state and similar powerful interests, where only the elites' self-serving memories may be preserved for posterity. Similarly, archives should not exist only for the convenience of special clienteles, especially the traditional one of academic historians, and therefore collect records primarily of value to specialized groups of users. Rather, as Germany's Hans Booms wrote, "If there is indeed anything or anyone qualified to lend legitimacy to archival appraisal [or any other archival activity], it is society itself, and the public opinions it expresses—assuming, of course, that these are allowed to develop freely. The public and public opinion," Booms noted, ". . . sanctions public actions, essentially generates the socio-political process, and legitimizes political authority. Therefore, should not public opinion also legitimize archival appraisal? Could it not provide the fundamental orientation" for all archival activities? The key insight of this group of thinkers was that society, not state administrators and not specialized users, should animate the core values of archival decision making.

No one better represents the "societal" rather than "statist" paradigm for archives than Hugh Taylor. He was a key architect of the "total archives" concept (and practice) at the National Archives of Canada—and earlier in England—that broadened understanding of the range and media of archives. Shortly after coming to Canada from England in 1965, Hugh was much influenced by the communications and media theories of two Canadians scholars, Harold Innis and Marshall McLuhan. Beginning at that time his long series of speculative essays, Hugh blended together an acute awareness of the transforming character of new audiovisual and electronic recording media and the immense power of worldwide communication technologies, with deep historical, ecological, and spiritual perspectives. With this potent mixture, he urged archivists to get out of their "historical shunt" of looking after old records primarily for historians and to embrace the age of electronic records, global communications networks, local community heritage concerns, and bioregional imperatives. While not diminishing the work done from archival sources by academic historians, and while repeatedly extolling the need for archivists to conduct scholarly research into the history and character of their own records, Hugh saw archives as a rich societal resource for many other professions and community interest groups, if archivists would but imagine anew their professional calling.

In all his essays, Hugh explores a revitalized sense of the contextuality (or provenance) of records in the complex interconnections between society and the documentary record, between the act and the deed. His historical analyses reveal fertile connections in the evolution from ancient to medieval to industrial to information society, and the parallel evolution from oral to written to audiovisual to electronic records (and related record-keeping practices). In our brave new world of interactive electronic transactions and instant "real-time" communications, Hugh discerns "a return to conceptual orality," that is to say, a return to the medieval framework wherein words or documents gained meaning only as they were "closely related to their context and to actions arising from that context." In that oral tradition, meaning "lay not in the records themselves, but [in] the transactions and customs to which they bore witness as 'evidences.'" For Hugh, it is always this connection between the broader social and cultural context of record keeping and the actual document that gives meaning to archives, and more broadly to societal remembering.

Hugh advocates that the heart of the archivist's work should be "a new form of 'social historiography' to make clear how and why records were created. . . ." This would provide a deeper understanding of contextuality, or provenance. Hugh's approach is virtually the equivalent of Norman Cantor's commendation of an "historical sociology." Faced with incredible information overloads, archivists should not see their work "as essentially empirical, dealing with individual documents and series to be arranged, controlled, and retrieved as ends in themselves," but rather be "concerned with the recognition of forms and patterns of knowledge which may be the only way by which we will transcend the morass of information and data into which we will otherwise fall." These contextual patterns must be right-brain as much as left-brain in conception and articulation. Furthermore, the search for holistic patterns of knowledge, as his essays in this book make clear, is not based merely on internal archival knowledge, although Hugh values that clearly enough, but animated primarily from external knowledge: social, cultural, philosophical, historical, epistemological, planetary. We need, Hugh urges archivists, to "submerge our professional insularity, but not identity, beneath the waters of holism." We need to link the human, natural, and spiritual worlds, with record-keeping contextuality in all its phases.

Imagining archives also means casting off some of the central myths masquerading as truth inside the archival pantheon. In his last essay, his parting *cri de coeur* to his beloved profession, Hugh criticizes those who fall into "the trap of literalism," who see universal theories underpinning the archival endeavour, who fail to "recognize the illusory nature of archives as repositories of truth waiting only to be uncovered." Archivists, he warns, tend to perpetuate "the status quo in the name of neutrality." That is the profession's central illusion. It amounts to little more than continuing "to arrange and describe the ship's logs on the *Titanic* while others rearrange the deck chairs." Clinging to such an illusion stifles creative imagination and renders impossible relevant social engagement. Drop the illusion, he counsels, to "avoid an archival fundamentalism which refuses to recognize that new forms of communication, both technically and semi-otically, change the meaning of the content. Not only that, but our assumptions about our own practices may need reassessing followed by the abandonment of 'dead certainties.'" In this legacy statement, Hugh exhorts archivists to embrace deconstructive energies to let in "a kind of meditative light and space where . . . new insights may occur." Focus on the spirit, not the letter, for "the letter killeth, but the spirit giveth life." And so Hugh's imaginings have given life to those archivists willing to listen.

*   *   *   *   *

Hugh Taylor's ideas led North American, and especially Canadian, archivists to what Canadian archival educator Tom Nesmith has called "a rediscovery of provenance." Until the late 1970s, North Americans limited their use of the concept of provenance to a narrow range of arrangement and description activities. Even here they allowed compromises, such as the "record group" concept, to weaken the deeper contextualizing power of provenance. While lip service was always paid to provenance, all too often in practice it was either ignored or actually undermined. Knowledge of the historical subject content of the records replaced provenance as the animating force in most North American archival appraisal, description, and public service—and education.

Under Hugh's continuing inspiration, this older approach has changed radically in Canada over the past two decades. At the National Archives of Canada in the 1970s, Hugh was dean of what current National Archivist Ian Wilson has called a "faculty of applied archival studies at the NA in those years." Hugh encouraged archivists there, educated as historians, to apply their historical skills and research methodologies not, as before, to the subject content of records, but to researching and understanding, in Nesmith's words, "the evidential context which gave them birth." In this regard, Nesmith was himself a leader, calling for a "history of the record" similar to Hugh's "new form of 'social historiography.'" Responding to Hugh, I then wrote that, by focusing on the "provenance, *respect des fonds*, context, evolution, interrelationships, order" of records as the heart of our professional discourse, archivists could move from an "information" to a "knowledge" paradigm, and thus to renewed relevance in the era of electronic records and networked communications. Rather than rejecting such archival contextual approaches and adopting those of information management or computer science, as some commentators were then forcefully suggesting, or remaining locked in the historians' content-centred cocoon, many Canadian archivists began discovering (or "rediscovering") the intellectual excitement of contextualized knowledge that was their own profession's legacy—and its future hope. A whole range of research into archival records was undertaken across Canada to explore provenance-centred knowledge about the functionality of records creators, the administration of records and record-keeping systems, and the history, forms, functions, and physical characteristics of various archival documents in all media.

From this Canadian tradition of discovering anew an enriched contextuality for records and for their creation processes, it was not a big leap, as Hugh himself points out in his last article and in several of his new "reflections" in this book, for Canadians in the 1990s to lead the way internationally in thinking about archives in a postmodern world. Because Hugh imagined such a community, some archivists have actually started to live there, with pleasure and renewed hope.

Of course, as with any thinker, Hugh has his blind spots. The strong patriarchal dimension of the archival endeavour, historically and now, and its consequent marginalizing of women, curiously does not draw his attention—at an intellectual level, save a couple of passing comments. Personally, he was gender-blind, and treated women as equals. But in his writing, he overlooks the feminist revolution of the exact same period when his archival career was flourishing, rarely citing any of its leading authors. Yet a good deal of such feminist scholarship very much complements his own holistic and ecological perspectives, and injects a powerful storytelling dimension into memory preservation that he might have welcomed. On another front, Hugh's ambivalent views about academic history and historians—and about archivists working in an "historical shunt" allegedly shirking their responsibilities for managing current records—seem based more on stereotypes than reality, or, perhaps more fairly, on the assumption that "history" was still focused on the traditional political, legal, and economic topics he had studied long ago at university in England. But when Hugh was thus tweaking historians in the 1980s and 1990s, many were, in fact, looking at the very issues—memory, identity, mythmaking, the environment, the marginalized—that Hugh was then extolling to archivists. Valuable allies and important sources of knowledge for archivists were driven away by this wedge—or shunt—placed between archivists and historians. Hugh was quite right to fight for and then celebrate the professional and associational independence of archivists from historians, but he never quite worked out the relationship of historians and archivists, or archival knowledge and history. But Hugh's scope of thinking is so vast, his interest so wide-ranging, that it is not surprising that some missteps occur, or that some trails remain unexplored. The measure of the man must be what he accomplished, and by any yardstick that is very considerable.

Hugh's ideas have also occasionally been criticized for not explaining the better merits of two opposing viewpoints that he seems to present to his readers with equal praise. In his writings, a positivist universalist is cited side-by-side with a postmodern relativist; the need for guarding the evidential quality of documents with the imperative of actively promoting cultural memory; the local, particular, and bioregional with the macro, global, and planetary. Hugh did this very consciously, adopting a prose style increasingly rich in metaphors, paradoxes, humour, and juxtapositions to reflect his deeper convictions about the nature of professional discourse. He was critical of the "fragmented approach common to all professions that . . . tend[s] to polarize points of view. All this is done in good faith defending the 'right.' But . . . are we striving for synthesis or supremacy?" Ever the synthesizer, never the supremacist, Hugh thought that "both polarities around the broader issue of classic philosophical rationalism *versus* post-modern analysis recognize the value of use, but not necessarily in the same terms. Wisdom grounded in an understanding of social change which incorporates accountability at the local level should be recognized as an element in macroscopic realities." The macro and micro need to join hands, the bottom-up and top-down, the mind and the matter, if archives are to flourish. Hugh asked rhetorically: "As in the natural world, can we settle for a 'balanced turbulence'? Perhaps this is an issue requiring a holistic solution beyond opposing points of view which are so much a part of our literate culture of individualism." Hugh's "balanced turbulence," which well describes his own writing and ideas, could lead, he hoped, to a creative tension between professional polarities, rather than defensive posturing and personal animosities. In several essays, he cites approvingly Stéphane Malarmé's dictum, "To define is to kill: to suggest is to create," and Barrington Nevitt's approach to scholarship as "organizing ignorance for discovery." What we do not know may be more important than what we think we know, especially in the face of multidisciplinary "paradigm shifts" and a "new cosmology" leading to "a holistic, planetary renaissance. . . ." In that new universe, there must be room and respect for many professional viewpoints.

Hugh joked that his all-embracing perspectives would cause some archivists to argue "that I've stood back too far . . . and toppled over into outer space." But I think he rather hoped not. As he once remarked, "I have purposely played around with some outrageous archival possibilities which will tease and infuriate the more traditionally minded. We should not be afraid to dance a little with the absurd from which insights may emerge." No one has danced better, or generated more insights.

* * * * *

By combining in his own person the European and North American archival traditions, by enhancing rather than diminishing the archival customs of his adopted country, by ranging imaginatively from medieval oral society to the postmodern global village, by embracing into "total archives" the audiovisual and new electronic record, by offering numerous practical and tactical suggestions to complement his imaginings, by searching for patterns and connections in place of fragmentation and compartmentalization, and by linking archives to their social, cultural, technological, and philosophical contexts, Hugh Taylor demonstrated, again and again, that archivists can serve society as its new electronic "chip monks," rather than simply as minions of the powerful (in the state or corporations) or as "handmaidens" of academics. More than any other writer, Hugh has charted pathways in which archives cannot just survive in the years ahead, but really flourish.

A favourite metaphor for Hugh contrasts the traditional jigsaw puzzle of his youth with the new transformer toys popular with children a decade ago. The jigsaw could only be put together in one way, within defined borders, with always the same result—very much like the goal of traditional archival practice to take that heap on the floor and make it right. There is only one option, one solution, one order, one methodology. The transformer toy, by contrast, can be twisted into a myriad of shapes, colours, views, "ambiguous constructs filled with options ranging from robots to rockets to racing cars; the pattern changes, the meaning changes, the information changes, but the data—the given 'bits'—remain the same." There is no right answer, but many answers. Hugh noted that, like most traditional archival concepts and practices, the jigsaw is a product of the Industrial Age, whereas the transformer mentality of ambiguity, diversity, and multiplicity, is what animates our virtual and postmodern era. Hugh is absolutely convinced that archivists must focus less on controlling those atomistic "bits" and more on understanding these ever-changing patterns and broader holistic meanings. By such imaginative thinking, Hugh has transformed us in ways that we may not yet fully appreciate. Perhaps we have been *his* transformer toy these past decades!

As the international archival community reacts to the challenges posed by electronic records surrounding us on all fronts and to the sometimes unsettling postmodern ethos in which we live, Hugh's wise, graceful, and persuasive vision is needed more than ever before. Always the humanist, never the technician, Hugh's gift to us in these essays and reflections is nothing less than imagining what the future of archives can be.

Part 2

ESSAYS AND REFLECTIONS
BY HUGH A. TAYLOR

Chapter 3

Archives in Britain and Canada: Impressions of an Immigrant

As immigrants, we decided to enter Alberta by the traditional route from Europe, that is by sea and railway, and for us as for so many thousands of others, Quebec became the gateway to Canada. I think this is an important historical experience, for there is a danger that those who travel by air may feel that they are landing in some distant territory which is out of context with its surroundings, an island in a sea of land. We were conscious of Quebec as a most ancient and beautiful gateway to Canada, and we will not forget our very warm welcome on the threshold by the Immigration authorities. In our journey across Canada, we soon appreciated that there was a historical, as well as a physical distance to be covered, for after all, even English archivists are historians, at least to some extent!

For most immigrants there is always a problem of language, or at least terminology, and I soon found that I had to tread warily when using the archival terms to which I had grown accustomed. I soon found that "Archives" was usually descriptive of a repository of documents and not of the documents themselves. I would like to suggest that the English terminology is perhaps a little more logical in this respect, if only because we have introduced the term "Record Office" into general use, which enables us to reserve the word "Archives" for administrative documents of all kinds, and use the description "public," "semi-public," and "private" for the three principal subcategories. The term "manuscript" can then be reserved for documents which are handwritten and not be forced to cover private collections as a whole. I note that Bernard Weilbrenner, in

Originally published in *Canadian Archivist* 1, no. 7 (1969): 22–33. Reproduced with the kind permission of the author and the (successor) publisher, *Archivaria*.

an article on the Public Archives of Canada, refers to a proposal by the Historical Commission for a Canadian Public Record Office in 1914 as an extension to the Public Archives, so you very narrowly missed the perfect solution to this thorny problem.

On reflection, this term "Record Office" perhaps lies at the heart of the difference of outlook on archives in England and this country. Most of the public archives of England grew out of the courts of law which were also courts of record, where the evidence of public transactions, whether legal, financial, or testamentary, were filed and kept as a service to the community. Thus, the Public Record Office in London, which was established in 1838, was for many years mainly concerned with the preservation of the records of the medieval courts of England, and significantly enough was placed under the supervision of the Master of the Rolls who was the head of the Court of Chancery. It is important to remember that most public administration in England stems directly from the courts of law, and this is also true of local government. Parliament itself originated in the Court of the King (and here we have another interesting association with this word), and the full title of one of our most venerable institutions is the High Court of Parliament. Sometimes an office of administration turned itself into a purely legal court such as Chancery, which began as the principal executive arm of the Norman Kings.

Similarly the local record offices of England based on the counties and principal cities were set up primarily to preserve and arrange the records of the Courts of Quarter Sessions and their equivalents. All these offices had in origin one basic consideration, i.e., the preservation or keeping of the public record for the service of the community.

The historical origin of his office has greatly influenced the preoccupations of archivists in England. Most of his energies have been devoted to those centuries before the nineteenth when the conduct of law and administration were not usually separately defined, and the early records were given first priority because there was this obligation to maintain their existence as public documents. I should hasten to add that soon after the creation of a local record office anywhere in England, collections of documents from private sources began to pour in and were given detailed attention according to their merits until now the bulk of private collections may surpass that from the public sector.

I would suggest that the cumulative effect of this tradition has been to make English archivists more record keepers than historians, and many would hold that this is the true role of the archivist. The records have in general been kept most faithfully in this sense, but there were times when I felt that we were a little too concerned with the *minutiae* of the records at the expense of their general historical implications.

The interests of the users of record offices have changed radically over the years, but to some extent the training and duties of archivists have not kept pace, for the historical reasons that I have suggested already. Yet I would maintain that no one can make much of the archives of England unless he is a historian. We are not just manipulators of dead medieval files.

Another factor which greatly influences the archivists' work is that there are only four Land Registries in England covering a very small part of the area of the country. This means that much of the archivists' time and most of the records accumulated from private sources are concerned with land titles and the ancient forms of conveyancing, which are unbelievably involved. Imagine the situation in this country where all the Land Titles Offices were destroyed and the only evidence of occupation was to be found in copies of documents in the hands of the owners of property, or their attorneys. Most English record offices are bursting with the records of land titles, whose bulk is often out of all proportion to their value, besides being extremely laborious to catalogue.

The fact that land has not been registered by law has meant that much of the English archivist's skill—and because of his skill, his interest—has been directed to problems of land tenure and consumed a great amount of his time and energy. So, what with the records of the courts and the accumulation of title deeds constantly challenging him to set them in order and interpret them correctly for the public, the marvel is that so many English archivists have achieved such a richness and variety in historical scholarship and archival insight. Perhaps it is the historian in them. Again, the accounts and correspondence from the great landed estates which accompany the title deeds are rich and varied but they reflect only the hereditary, politically conservative governing body in England, throwing the total surviving evidence of society out of balance. This is not the fault of the archivist.

By contrast, Canadian archivists have, as I see it, a totally different background. The first accumulations of public records were made by the provinces in the conduct of their affairs, but the provincial archives which were subsequently formed were not set up primarily to "keep" these documents in the English tradition but to accumulate the raw material of history.

The Public Archives of Canada owes its creation to the Literary and Historical Society of Quebec, and Douglas Brymner, a journalist, was appointed Archivist in 1872 with "three empty rooms and very vague instructions." You can see at once that here is a totally different point of departure which is both limiting and unfettered; limiting because the archivist of that time had no powers to restrain the destruction of many ancient series of documents by his being appointed specifically to keep them, and unfettered because his terms of reference were so broad that he could range into Europe in search of historical material relating to Canada. The great microfilm project which has resulted in the copying of so much material in the Public Record Office and Beaver House during recent years is in direct succession to the nineteenth-century transcripts made in Paris and elsewhere. As far as I know, this international concern for the sources of history is not echoed to the same extent in England, but perhaps it is because we believe all our history is made at home!

I can now see why there in an emphasis in some Canadian repositories for archivists to be primarily historians, and I greatly respect this point of view, although not brought up in quite the same tradition. One of the basic assumptions of this doctrine appears to be that Canadian archivists shall seek out information on the records of their country wherever they may be, and inform the student accordingly. In England, I believe there is an overemphasis placed on the self-contained nature of the record office, and I have known many archivists with the very vaguest knowledge of the contents of record offices other than their own, even within the same city. The splendid work of the National Register of Archives in London is helping to change this but the process is a slow one. Yet the time may come when Canadian archivists will develop attitudes of mind similar to those bred in their colleagues in England as they come to receive more and more of the departmental records of government and the courts of law. An increasing amount of their time will be spent in "keeping" these records (and destroying them), and less and less of it will be occupied in the search for historical material wherever it may be, unless the staff can keep pace with the work involved. The appointment in Ontario of an Archives Liaison Officer reveals an interesting development and a possible solution. This makes the Union List of Manuscripts prepared by the Public Archives of special importance at this time.

The paper which was read to our section by Professor Lewis H. Thomas five years ago, reviewed the machinery of archival legislation in Canada and some of the problems of its application. Since that date, several more statutes have been passed into law, and it is clear that most archives have now considerable responsibility for the records of government and that their bulk and impersonal nature will mean that the researcher will have to be increasingly aware of administrative history and that the archivist will be unable to come up with information on persons and places which is more readily obtained from records in the private sector, or from the correspondence of public figures.

This shift of emphasis in holdings of records in Canadian archives may well have a profound effect on historiography in Canada, which has had its counterpart in England already. My impression is that Canadian historians are still deeply concerned with national politics, especially as it is reflected in the great series of correspondence of Prime Ministers and others in Public Archives of Canada. Local historians are at present concerned with the history of their own locality, which tends to be generally biographical in nature, and this is particularly valuable when impressions of founders of the communities are being recorded while they are still alive. But a time will come when more attention will be paid to administrative history as the point at which legislation and political policy became effective, or not, as the case may be. Much of the history of this country lies within the records of its administration, especially as this administration was quite highly developed even in the early years; I am thinking here of Western Canada in particular. The counterpart of this movement in England may be of some interest because it was during the latter part of the nineteenth century that a great deal of work on the constitutional and political history of England was accomplished, based on the publication of the Rolls Series of Public Documents and Chronicles, and the early calendars of the Public Record Office. These gave way around the period of the First World War to an intensive consideration of administrative history, both nationally and locally, which still continues partly due to the increasing sophistication of modern administration and appreciation of its problems, and partly to the fact that the records of administration are becoming more readily available in record offices.

There is, however, a danger of overemphasizing the importance of administrative procedure, which is rather different. Professor T. F. Tout, who virtually founded these studies with his six volumes of *Chapters in Medieval Administrative History*, has been criticized as tending in his later volumes to write a history of England through the standpoint of administration, which a critic has said "is rather like trying to command a warship from the stoke-hole." The records of administration are arranged in such a way that it is all too easy to write a history of the administration or administrative procedure, but this is not the same thing as writing a history of the administration as it affects individuals or extracting information from administrative records as raw material for other historical projects.

Because of his control over the preservation of administrative records, the archivist has immense influence on the writing of historians, especially through the suggestion of subjects for M.A. and Ph.D. theses. The tendency nowadays is for professors to inquire about suitable subjects available in the archives, rather than for students to ask initially whether there are papers relating to a subject in which they have a particular interest. We should, I think, ensure where possible, a balanced use of our collections in this way, although we all know the temptation to recommend neat, self-contained groups of papers on perhaps rather a limited subject which seems to suit everyone's convenience.

In England, the relationship between the Public Record Office in London and local record offices has for many years been rather difficult to assess. The Assistant Keepers of the Public Records are the custodians of the records of central government, which far surpass in completeness and span those accumulated locally; they are Civil Servants who become archivists through extensive in-service training but I think the difference lies more in the fact that the records of the central government differ radically in kind from those created locally, and the Public Record Office has rather different problems, or at least had until recent years. Individually, the staff have always been most kind and helpful, but in my own experience, our paths rarely crossed. I think it is worth recording that the Public Record Office has worked closely with London University on the Diploma Course for Archive Administration since about 1948, and that there has been a good deal of rivalry between the University of London and the University of Liverpool, which ran a similar course more specifically related to local records and the local archivist. Most of us who were at Liverpool, and many who were not, felt that this course was in many ways better suited to our needs. In brief, the attitude of the Public Record Office in general has been rather paternalistic towards the local offices, though this is now changing. By contrast, one of my earliest impressions on my arrival here was the close and friendly relationship between the Provincial and Public Archives. Dr. and Mrs. Lamb personally entertained me and my family during our short stay in Ottawa, and my only moments of apprehension were when my three small and boisterous daughters disappeared out of sight in the Lamb's lovely home. I feel that one of the basic reasons for this accord may lie in the fact that the older provinces antedate the federal government, and government departments were developed in a similar way at the federal and provincial level. Besides this, as I indicated earlier, the Public Archives always had a more outward-looking view of its role than its English counterpart. I am sure this relationship will long continue and will make possible the resolution of certain problems that might arise when a professional body such as the doctors or architects of Canada might decide that they would like to recommend that the Public Archives make collections of manuscripts in their respective fields. The provenance of these manuscripts may well be provincial in origin, and there would be an argument for retaining them in provincial archives, but at least the alternative could be placed clearly before any organization considering such a project. I have found this relationship with the Public Archives very helpful when it comes to considering federal records which have been passed for destruction as of no value from a federal point of view being retained in provincial archives where the provincial interest might well be greater and merit their retention. I have never so far heard of a similar approach to the Public Record

Office in London on this matter by English archivists, although there has been a valuable arrangement by which the records of nationalized private industry may be retained at approved repositories locally; and Mr. Collingridge, the liaison officer of the Public Record Office, has been appointed to deal with problems such as these, showing a distinct change of heart from attitudes of some years back.

The separatism of the Public Record Office is further emphasized by the fact that the care, arrangement, and publication of manuscripts in the great private collections of national importance came within the terms of reference of the Historical Manuscripts Commission and not of the Office. The early years of the Commission's work were concerned mainly with publishing, correspondence, and other papers of a political nature, together with summaries of the contents of the Muniment Rooms of the major landed families of England, which have for so long been immersed in political life. In more recent years, the National Register of Archives was set up under the Commission to gather information on the smaller collections covering every kind of archival activity. The fact that the Public Record Office was never involved in the work of searching out manuscripts in the tradition of local offices has further tended to isolate it from the mainstreams of archival development in England. I am very glad that the Union List of Manuscripts is being prepared within the Public Archives of Canada, thus further strengthening the links with repositories at the provincial level. While I am on this subject, you should know that the Public Record Office in London closed daily at 4 P.M. and weekends, while the PAC offers round-the-clock service. I know there are good reasons for this difference, but you will see how the amateur historian has been virtually excluded from the Round Room in the PRO unless blessed with a private income. I would like to pay tribute to Roger Ellis, Secretary of the Historical Manuscript Commission and President of the Society of Archivists, as the man who more than any other has sought to make local and central archives an indivisible entity in terms of our profession. I am sure he will always be remembered for this.

I suppose the most obvious difference between the two countries we are considering lies in the time span of historical evidence, and you may feel this is so obvious as not worth dwelling upon. Many people have asked me how I can possibly find interesting the records of Alberta which, for the most part, date from the 1880s, which is a point at which most English archivists begin to feel that they are treading on the heels of modern records managers. The answer is that this time span is purely relative. There is just as much excitement in locating a cache of documents 80 years old in Alberta as there is of locating a box of medieval charters 800 years old in England; perhaps even more so since these charters are more common than most people imagine, and probably contain a good deal less information. But the most important difference occupationally is that the archivist of Western Canada cannot help being almost immediately involved in the problems of records management. The English archivist enjoys an *embarras de richesse* and finds it difficult to become enthusiastic about the records created during the last 80 years of an 800-year span. In Western Canada, however, the evidence of the earliest settlements still lie within the files of departments which may be lost by default if the Provincial Archivist is not active in securing them. In Alberta I am most conscious of the fact that what may seem a trivial set of records, taken individually, such as the series of chattel mortgages in court houses, may provide information on credit facilities and genealogy unavailable elsewhere, especially if the courthouse is in a rural area, which, by the nature of things, will not be heavily documented. One must also, I think, bear in mind that a complete run of trivial records may furnish information of value over and above the sum of their parts, and that although too laborious to handle by present-day methods, may be scanned and digested electronically in years to come. This is not a problem which faces the keepers of nineteenth-century records in England where much more of a trivial nature can be safely destroyed.

It is stimulating and exhilarating to be forced to face squarely problems of records management and to make decisions on records disposal after considering the whole picture of documentary survival in a way which we English archivists are only beginning to do. One sees more and more clearly that the role of archivists and records managers is not simply as antiquarian, and the records manager understands that the explanation for administrative change lies always in the past, whether it is immediate or less immediate and that continuity of record should be maintained as it passes into the archives.

There is one point upon which my impressions are very hazy and that is what, in the Public Record Office, is called the Fifty Year Rule, by which documents are not generally made available to the public within 50 years of their creation. There has been a good deal of discussion about this in England, and I am wondering what the rule generally applied in Canada should be. As a local archivist in England, I tended to use my own judgment and refer to the owners of the records when in doubt. Perhaps this is on the whole the best solution.

Because provincial and territorial government in Western Canada was closely associated with the early waves of European immigration and settlement, the archivist is soon confronted with the importance and the problem of government publications. It would be interesting to know to what extent settlers relied on this kind of literature, but in any case, much of it forms a distillation of policy and statistics not easily located elsewhere. For the most part, government departments have not kept file copies of their publications, and most sets in legislative libraries I suspect are defective in many ways. There is, therefore, an important task before us to locate copies of this material and Alberta has a splendid example to follow in the case of Saskatchewan, where a most exhaustive handlist has already been produced. While recognizing the value of printed annual reports, I do not think that English archivists pay the same kind of attention to the more ephemeral productions which may be a serious omission in the future since a lot of these brochures are produced to meet a specific demand or a specific problem.

I suppose one of the great glories of Canadian archives lies in their splendid and massive photographic collections. Very few repositories in Britain have accumulations of this magnitude despite the larger number of photographers. Perhaps it is that there was a genuine widespread urge to record the pioneer period since this was clearly one of the great epochs in North American history and could be seen to be so at the time. One of the problems about history in England is its gradualness. Everything changes yet seems to remain the same, and it is gone before we realize it. It may be that these photographic collections will become the most prized and sought-after resources in the archives of Canada.

The foundations laid by these great collections must be built upon, and I have the impression that most archives are busy doing this, but there is a further aspect to the problem of topographical record. Until quite recent times, there has been a strong tradition of topographical painting by artists, some of whom are extremely good—others of only fair ability, but who were producing works which were of great interest historically for what they contained. I believe that the artist can make as valid a statement about the buildings or people he sees as anyone setting down the description in words and that this statement will in many cases enhance a purely photographic record. This is hard to define, but I am convinced that the artist can express a certain attitude of mind toward the subject he paints in the manner in which he paints it, which it is important to know. The tendency nowadays is for a great many art galleries to be preoccupied with abstraction at the expense of much that is intrinsically interesting, if not of great artistic worth. I shall not quarrel with this point of view, but would like to emphasize that it may well be the role of the archives to continue this long tradition of topographical painting, and I am finding myself that I cannot ignore this field. I am well aware that many institutions such as the Glenbow Foundation have done good work, but I am not sure how fully the new trends in the art galleries are appreciated by archives generally. This is a problem which has to be faced in England as well.

Finally, I would like to say a word or two about the Indian population who leave very little that can be classed strictly as manuscripts, apart from a few faded photographs and the remarkable Winter Counts which have in some cases been written up in Syllabics. For all the artifacts and ceremonial material that still survives, much of the Indian way of life may be permanently lost if the background and explanation of these objects is not recorded in time. I know that I am treading perilously near the edge of anthropology at this point, but with so few anthropologists available I feel that the archivist must urge and undertake some of this recording. In Britain we would dearly like to know the songs, religious ceremonial, and the chronicles such as they were remembered by the Iron Age folk who inhabited Britain during the Roman occupation. I had the fortunate experience of being able to assist at a recording of a medicine pipe bundle transferral last year on the Blackfoot Reserve, and it is an experience that I shall not forget. With so much record of Indian affairs being generated by church and government, it is vital that the world of the Indian as it is buried in song and ceremony be preserved, for within a generation it may well become extinguished forever. I feel that the archivist has a responsibility to ensure that a proper balance is struck between the earlier settlement of the Indian and the later settlement of the European, if justice is to be done to the true history of Canada.

In conclusion, I believe that the role of the archivist, in both our countries, is likely to undergo a profound change which will iron out the differences between us. The electronic scanning of written records, perhaps a generation away, will enable the archivist to control the personal side of government accumulations by the construction of detailed indexes to persons and places, which at present is impossibly laborious. This will redress the balance toward the personal aspect of modern records which is so far lost to view.

A time may come when there will be no more documents produced in the form we know them today, and even in Canada it will be hard to call a "manuscript" the magnetic tape generated by a private individual. More and more the hard record will come to be kept on tape and the paper printout will be used mainly for answering questions. I am omitting consideration here of printed books and letterpress products of the computer, which is not primarily our concern. May I conclude with an example of the way in which the new, gleaming electronic world is inching its way into at least one provincial repository?

The Attorney General's Department of Alberta has set up a Central Registry containing electronic microfilming equipment designed to handle more than 4,000 documents a month by Miracode, which stands for Microfilm Information Retrieval Access Code. The system will handle chattel mortgages, lien notes, and similar documents produced in vast quantities, but at the same time, the earlier records in the Court House in Edmonton are being filmed and their retrieval built into this modern records process. Information can be exchanged on a telex network and copies of documents produced very rapidly as required. I believe one can see in this the beginning of the end of original paper documents, although it is extremely important to make sure that a proper sample is retained. A Provincial Statute was obtained to enable microfilm copy to be produced in courts of law as evidence, and this destroys one of the principal and ancient reasons for keeping legal records. I realize that none of these techniques is new, but the increase in automation and speed at which answers to questions may be obtained is a matter that we should ponder well. I can almost (but not quite) foresee a time when records and manuscripts which have survived in the form we know them today will have been electronically drained of their information to become mere artifacts of interest for their texture, form, and colour. They may provide a valuable visual experience, but will no longer contain any new facts for the historian. The problem of storage space will disappear as the information distilled from a hundred years of administration is packed within the confines of one filing cabinet. Binary bits can now be etched onto tape by laser beam within a fraction of the space occupied by the magnetic method! I expect that several such bits would sit on the point of a needle, but these latter-day angels have the power to banish into limbo the steel shelf, the cardboard box, the files, bundles, and packages, and even ourselves as a profession, unless we encourage our successors to master this new technology and continue to "keep the record" as we have always done.

May I turn from this Orwellian nightmare to glance at my favorite keeper of records, William Prynne (1600–1669), very much an archivist, although he flourished three hundred years before the word was coined, and a man who would be quite at home in our company. I introduce him as a witness to the antiquity of our profession, since we have been so busy renewing ourselves of late that we have almost forgotten those predecessors who have been thinking archivally for centuries and fighting in the same kind of battles as ourselves.

William Prynne spent the greater part of his working life as a politician and was one of the most successful writers of pamphlets and tracts in his day. If he were alive now we would probably call him a journalist, and I would like to remind you that the first Dominion Archivist of Canada practised the same profession. As an indication of his success between 1634 and 1636, the Establishment marked its disapproval by fining him $15,000, cropping his ears in the pillory, and branding him with the letters SL (for seditious libeller) on both cheeks. We can only assume that he was somewhat mellowed by age since he was appointed Keeper of the Records in the Tower of London shortly after the restoration of the monarchy in 1660. John Aubrey tells us that, "his manner of study was this: he wore a long quilt cap which came two or three inches at least over his eyes which served him as an umbrella to defend his eyes from the light; about every three hours his man was to bring him a roll and a pot of ale to re-focillate his wasted spirits; so he studied and drank and munched some bread; this maintained him till night and then he made a good supper."

After a while, like all good archivists, he submitted his report on the state of the records, which he says "through negligence, nescience and sloathfulness had for many years then past layen buried together in one confused chaos under corroding putrifying cobwebs, dust and filth in the darkest corners of Caesar's Chapel in the White Tower. . . . I employed some soldiers and women to remove and cleanse them from their filthiness; who soon growing weary of this noisome work left them almost as foul as they found them. Whereupon I and my clerks spent many whole days in cleansing and sorting them into distinct confused heaps in order to their future reducement into method, the old clerks of the office being unwilling to touch them for fear of endangering their eyesights and healths by the cankerous dust and evil scent." You can see that he was a man of unquenchable spirit and enthusiasm who had not lost his gift for the telling phrase at a time when the career of archivist was not as respectable as it is today. We may not have to cope with London grime of the seventeenth century but those "distinct confused heaps" are very familiar.[1]

REFLECTION, 2000

The first paragraph in this the first paper which I prepared in Canada contained the word "context" which would be used and discussed in detail several years later by my colleagues. There is always a very strong sense of context in Britain where ancient patterns of community life changed so rapidly from one shire to another as does the history and the evidence in the record which survives.

The second paragraph dealt with archival language on both sides of the Atlantic in a very superficial way, a constant reminder of differences in culture and tradition. When terms are juxtaposed in this manner we begin to examine them for meaning and cease to take them for granted. Thirty years later Eric Ketelaar was to begin his paper with a quote from Charles Dickens and to draw attention to "the risks of archivists using a metaphor or borrowing a term from another domain and giving it a special archival meaning, a meaning which moreover can change over time."[2] An example is "life cycle." Ketelaar has juxtaposed terms with telling effect, and although I dared to gently suggest back in 1969 a little rationalisation as a new boy on the block, I would now agree that the difference is indeed best postponed. When different cultures use the word for "bread" the material substance is quite different. In years to come will we still be trying to define "archivist" for the same reason? We are always best identified by what we do rather than who we are.

Pondering over this paper for the first time since its publication, I can sense a restlessness in me about the role of the archivist in society. The very complexity of English textual documents kept our heads to the parchments! In addition we needed a sound knowledge of history to grasp their context and meaning. Even at that time I was looking up and beyond this emphasis toward other sources which would render the record more inclusive, stretching beyond the landed estates and courts of law which took so much of our time. I was not alone; we were all striving to be as comprehensive as we could in our acquisition policy.

Canada offered geographically a much broader vision over more recent history. With manuscript material thinner on the prairie ground, I began to take a special interest in photographs conveying the early years of settlement, which were recognised as the great treasures of the West, together with topographical art, ephemera, and oral records, all of which I have tried to defend ever since in terms of adequate resources for their preservation. Some experience with the aboriginal people in ceremonies, required by them when medicine bundles were purchased by the museum but which I had to describe and record on tape, gave me some understanding of oral cultures that were so at odds with the immigrants from Europe.

Archivists in England saw themselves as professionals, well equipped with a number of archival skills learned on the postgraduate diploma courses following the Second World War. Those in Canada saw themselves as historians with the limited archival training available at that time. Postgraduate, preappointment training should help to establish effective archivists with less emphasis on purely academic history required for those involved in nontextual media. I never at any time saw the archivist as simply a records and information manager—but this is an issue for a later essay.

NOTES

1. This paper was read before the Archives Section, Canadian Historical Association meeting at Carleton University in 1967.

2. Eric Ketelaar, "The Difference Best Postponed? Cultures and Comparative Archival Science," *Archivaria* 44 (Fall 1997): 142.

Chapter 4

Administrative History:
An Archivist's Need

This is the age of "instant" archives. Government repositories are now set up and opened within a year, their shelves are filled with miles of paper, a records centre will probably feature in the operation, and an archives act will tie the whole package together and thereafter regulate the flow. The archivist, as he walks through his stacks, will see around him the minutes, registers, accounts, and correspondence of a dozen departments, and will probably be congratulating himself on his grasp of record groups and the completeness of the various series which he has managed to reconstruct. A stranger, or even a historian, would perhaps imagine that the archivist was a person of great learning, so familiar with the organizations that created the records in his care that he is able unerringly to place them row upon row as they would have been arranged in their offices of origin. Nothing could be further from the truth.

For one thing, the archivist might be an émigré Englishman, marvelously ignorant of Canadian bureaucratic structures, but with a certain animal cunning acquired during years in his profession for recognizing similar handwriting or simply reading the designations of officials at the foot of correspondence files, and stringing out each series in date order. This works well enough with a great deal of records, but inevitably there will be those odd volumes listed rather opaquely under the title "miscellaneous," which *someone* must have created for a purpose too obvious at the time to be entered anywhere. And there are those series of papers which once breathed and grew in live files but which are now so horribly

Originally published in *Canadian Archivist* 2, no. 1 (1970): 4–9. Reproduced with the kind permission of the author and the (successor) publisher, *Archivaria*.

dead and unbelievably mangled and dismembered on floors or tumbling from transfer cases, appearing to the archivist like bodies "half-moulderd in rotten coffins that would suddenly yawn wide open, filling his nostrils with a noisome stench and his eyes with the sight of nothing but crawling worms." (From an account of the Great Plague in London, 1665.) This kind of confusion is likely to make even the most seasoned archivist gently perspire, but again he attempts the same approach and frantically studies endorsements for a clue to provenance and purpose.

In New Brunswick, we had three large groups like this. The dockets of the Supreme Court, the Legislative Assembly, and the Provincial Secretary responsible to the Legislative Council. Apart from the Judgment Rolls, which were numbered in series and totalled about 20,000, the remaining Supreme Court records were in no sort of order and had to be bundled annually by type of instrument, which was basically a process of visual recognition by the part-time staff available for the task. As regards the purpose of the various instruments and their interrelationships, we were largely in ignorance. The papers of the other two groups presented a rather different problem, more like cutting out cattle on the hoof. The difficulty lay in distinguishing the "brands" in the form of archive marks which identified the owners and then steering these into the correct record groups with only a very uncertain notion as to which group any particular document might have ended up in originally. Take for instance a petition directed to the Lieutenant Governor in Council. It might be laid before the Executive Council and endorsed "in Council"; it might then be passed to the Legislative Assembly and be found there, or it might never leave the Provincial Secretary's office and be buried amongst his own departmental paper. Where, in fact, *did* it end up? Whole subgroups of records would also appear in this way, with no clear indication of departmental origin.

It could, I suppose, be argued that the records are now in fair shape. series have been re-created and chaos has been resolved through a sequence of more or less informed hunches by which a great deal of information is now organized in an orderly way. The trouble is that few of the records series are adequately articulated; the relationship between them may be largely unknown and their significance within the context of the whole record group may be lost. We need to know their administrative history, to be reminded that they were created by people to serve a particular purpose in the administration, and we should know the chain of command in any department and evaluate the records accordingly. In short, we cannot accurately arrange or assess the significance of a department's records until we understand thoroughly how it works. Many of our neat, archival reconstructions should be treated as hypotheses to be modified in the light of further knowledge. Too often, they may reflect all sorts of emphases which could deceive the unwary and even be taken for granted as an accurate representation of the administrative structure.

The study in depth of a department's records may perhaps be approached in two ways: as a history of the administration, in which the works are taken apart and the entire operation analysed in relation to its parts; and as administrative history, in which the impact on the politics, power struggles, and the public at large is considered. This is often much more difficult and would have to include a great deal of time spent at the grass roots amongst the general correspondence. Both approaches are needed. The second is far more difficult; the first would be of greatest assistance to the archivist. Together, they might result in a number of historical revisions of, for instance, the efficacy of all sorts of major constitutional and statutory reforms. It is one thing to proclaim a statute, but it is quite another to expect that it will necessarily operate as intended. The administrative record will provide the answer. Again, there is the big question of departmental initiatives by civil servants in relation to their ministers and the politicians generally, but I need not dwell upon this point here. Rather, I would like to turn for a moment to the English scene, and show how the study of administrative history has affected our whole concept of government in the Middle Ages. This conveniently distances the problem by a few hundred years, and the position has been admirably summarized in a most lively way by Professor V. K. Galbraith in his *Studies in the Public Records* (Oxford, 1948).

Before about 1900, popular medieval English history had been written from the evidence of chronicles, common law, and parliamentary statutes; historians tended to write a commentary on the past in terms of their own world in which heroes and villains trod the stage in that apparently dark and barbarous era which preceded renaissance and enlightenment. King John was a bad king both because the chronicler, Matthew Paris, said so shortly afterwards and because he appeared morally bad to our great-grandfathers. All the elements of today's parliament were identified in the days of Simon De Montfort as democracy struggled with tyranny. It just wasn't like that.

Let us consider for a moment the medieval sources for this kind of history and their modern counterparts. For medieval chronicles we can substitute newspapers, political correspondence, and a great deal of parliamentary debate, all of which is essentially a commentary, one man's view, in which material is selected, presented, and sometimes distorted for the purpose of entertaining or persuading an audience. There may be no modern counterpart for the study of common law, but as I have said earlier, statutes have their limitations as evidence of what happened and often embody a good deal of wishful thinking.

As for the administrative record, it had always been there but, then as now, the bulk was prodigious. Scholars first began to use this source in a search for constitutional niceties and that old chimera, absolute or scientific history. These men, the products of late nineteenth century thought and learning, were themselves surrounded by an increasingly sophisticated bureaucracy and were developing a growing respect for the civil service which in turn produced a sympathy for its medieval counterparts.

A massive publishing programme produced calendars of the Chancery Rolls from 1199 in a hundred volumes in addition to many other series of government records. This kind of source material recorded formal grants by the king, decisions of the courts, and financial transactions of the Exchequer through which the impact of government on ordinary folk could be studied for the first time, since the chronicles were concerned almost solely with the more colourful and prominent figures of their period.

What did the historians find? Much of the answer lies in T. F. Tout's *Chapters in Mediaeval Administrative History* (1920–1925), which ran to six volumes and took 20 years to produce. He showed us that medieval government was efficiently and flexibly organized around the king. In Galbraith's words, "the dynamic energy of the Royal household, whose administrative pressure set all in motion and whose direct activity, exercised through the Privy Seal and Signet, was the most persistent force in government." Apart from the substitution of a few terms, this could just as well apply to the Colonial Governor in pre-Confederation Canada. Medieval people required, above all, strong government and not freedom in an abstract sense, for they had extensive rights in custom and common law. For the king, good government meant efficiency and profit, but he was expected not only to reign but to rule, to take initiatives, to act. The complaint of the baronial opposition to King John was not that he governed badly or wickedly but that he refused to take the initiatives expected of him as King. Weak government usually results in administrative oppression. In every age, people are more governed than they like to admit. The impact of government, then as now, is not so much via the politician as via the bureaucrat, and their record is fully documented in the archives.

It must also be remembered that modern government bureaucracy emerged not only from the royal household but also from the royal courts of law, administering common law and statute. The lawyers of both canon and civil law were the top civil servants, and one cannot grasp the true value of their records until this is understood. The petition, the writ, the judgment, the warrant: these are all embedded in later bureaucratic practices, no less in Canada than elsewhere. This is because all law and its implementation stems from the King in Council, or the Lieutenant Governor in Council, which is its direct successor. Crown

Land Office procedure reflects this ancient origin very well with its petitions, warrants for survey, and grants by a Committee of the Council. It constituted, in effect, a court of record. Parliament itself was not in origin a democratically elected debating and legislative body but a court, "the High Court of Parliament," presided over by the king and petitioned by those with grievances. The members of this court were all those from whom the king wished to seek advice or gain support. The decisions of the court would be implemented by the clerks in the royal household. Early colonial government can again clearly be recognized as being along these lines, and, had its opponents been aware of this, how they would have loved to have described it as medieval!

Then, as now, the administration was subject to "Parkinson's Law" and the king, as the chief executive of government, was forever seeking to get out from under the various departments which grew up from his increasingly varied activity. At first, he used only the Great Seal, held by the Chancellor, but when this became a cumbersome office of record, then he devised the Privy Seal, but that in turn "went out of court" as the saying is, and he then used the Secret Seal from which we get the word "secretary" today. Finally, as the secretary built up his own office and was concerned with state papers, the king used his signet or his signature as the most direct form of authentication and authority. This process of "going out of court" is still very much a part of the administrative process as departments spawn subdepartments and branches, which in turn become departments in themselves.

The need of the chief executive to be preserved from routine encumbrances is met in this way. The Provincial Secretary has, in most cases, moved some distance from being the servant of the Executive Council, which was his original role, but he still keeps the seal of the province and thus becomes linked with very ancient tradition.

One of the valuable disciplines implicit in a study of medieval administrative history was the obligation to follow the threads of individual persons and problems and unravel them from the immensely technical and complicated procedures of the royal household and the courts. Such a study became identified with the impact on individuals outside the government as part of the whole historical process. It is significant that Tout, after volume one of his *Chapters*, ceased to separate administrative from general history, and this was instinctively sound on his part. Moreover, medieval historians have always had to study most carefully the diplomatics of their sources as they grappled with the medieval mind. And I think this is a lesson which should be borne in mind today. Administrative phraseology is important and so its implications; as Professor Galbraith put it, "roughly speaking, the official mind, then as now, was concerned to minimize any elements of unusualness; to deny as far as possible the facts of change and to preserve at all costs the appearance of legality." This leads to a continual search for precedents and for the "official" version of events as recorded in annual reports, and this legal approach of the administrator runs far back into history. It is therefore essential to know the status of any document, who is writing what and for whom, if we are to assess its historical value.

Unfortunately, it is becoming increasingly clear that the archivist of today, unlike his learned colleagues of a generation ago, will be unable to spend a lifetime of intensive study on a few basic series of papers. In "instant" archives, this is impossible. Yet, without a critical approach to diplomatics and a careful analysis of the administrative structure, we will not be able to assess with confidence the historical implications of our holdings for the historian. A well-planned M.A. programme in which a series of theses is written on the various departments of government in any one province could help a great deal, as archivist and historian work closely together on the problem. This discipline would be an admirable one for both parties, and in no sense parochial, since structures of government and administration have a universal application.

So far as I know, very few studies of this kind have been made, and the lack of them may be reflected in two outstanding works on the subject: Leonard B. White's administrative history of the United States government in four volumes, and his pupil, J. E. Hodgett's, *Pioneer Public Service* (1955). I do not wish in any way to belittle these works which cover a very broad field and have been most carefully researched. In Professor White's volume, the emphasis for the most part is on the politics and power struggles behind the evolution of United States' departments of government, the extent to which political theories are practised, the constitutional implications—almost a political history of the administration, which although immensely important, is not the whole story. A brief examination of sources revealed in the footnotes reinforces this impression. A great many are from the private papers and diaries of politicians who became administrators and the official House reports to Congress, with almost no reference to departmental records at a lower level.

Professor Hodgett's book makes a similar approach to the United Provinces administration and again the footnotes reveal very little use of departmental material below the level of annual reports. Admittedly, he writes more from the standpoint of the political scientist than the historian. He explains in his preface that his aims are first "to provide a description of the evolution and structure of the administrative machine" including the "contributions of the public servant to the welfare of a pioneer community"; secondly, to examine "certain basic administrative issues" which are still with us; and thirdly, to show that responsible government was won politically before it was recognized at an administrative level.

These are broad issues and they are finely handled, but there is, I maintain, a genuine need for a study of the administrators themselves biographically and relative to their social background; to see how they viewed the provision for public servants; what promotion they received; and how they organized and modified their departments to meet pressure of work arising out of obligations to the citizen on the one hand, and policy changes at the ministerial level on the other.

Perhaps these two examples will have made my point. The active cooperation of historians and archivists in this field is essential. The archivist's ability to give a more informed appreciation of his resources will be greatly increased. It is high time for departmental records to be studied from the "consumer" point of view. We have "consumed" (or been consumed by) a great deal of administration since the early days of government in Canada. It is now time for us to take a closer look at the product and stop taking the label for granted.

REFLECTION, 2000

In this essay, I felt as if I was turning the pages of an old photo album. Here was an archivist from England who had set up the last county archives to be established there, and then had come over to Canada to start the last two provincial archives, which took me to Edmonton, Alberta, and then Fredericton, New Brunswick. No wonder I saw the 1960s and 1970s as an age of "instant archives," which had its origins following the Second World War. I was reminded again of the phrase, "organising ignorance for discovery" coined, I think, by Barrington Nevitt. I had a great deal of ignorance to organize, with practically no formal knowledge of Canadian history. While taking History 101 at the University of New Brunswick, I conducted tutorials for my fellow students—an exercise in hounds chasing the hare, who somehow had to keep ahead!

By this time, I had over 15 years experience as an archivist under my belt, but I soon realized that while analysis with English public administration could be helpful, I could all too easily take for granted a structure which was superficially familiar, but in detail very different. This also was the age in North America of the "lone arranger" who brought order out of a chaos of parchment and paper and was rather pleased with the result, which suggested a kind of arrogance arising from ignorance. At the same time, this was an opportunity to open up the subject of administrative history which, in contrast to England, had not received a great deal of attention in North America, especially Canada with its concentration on the history of nation building, so necessary at the time.

And so I rather obviously "strutted my stuff" as an English archivist with one or two metaphors from cowboys in Alberta thrown in. A huge attic several feet deep in paper and parchment over the Legislative Assembly in Fredericton had obliterated paper trails, provenance, and all the usual archival fenceposts. This forced me to fashion an arrangement of the crudest kind prior to the reassembly of dockets which was achieved so well by others several years later. When public records had been kept more or less in their original order, Canadian archivists did not usually have to think too deeply about a structure which could be taken for granted. I was forced by circumstance to question this and to begin to differentiate between "administrative history" and "the history of administration," which can mean the same, but which I used to differentiate these approaches. In short, public records, in contrast to papers from the private sector, required less physical attention and arrangement, which was all to the good; but their contents, structure, and meaning never really challenged us in those days; consequently they were relatively less approachable to users, as to some extent they still are.

Administrative history has never really caught on here, but then it seemed to be a dry, academic, and unattractive subject with little appeal to postgraduate studies, which might have helped us. A number of archivists at that time, especially in the then Public Archives of Canada, strongly insisted that archivists should create their own history of the various public records fonds in their care. In reality, they could manage, for want of time, little more than introductions to the structures within the fonds. Remember that this was an age during which Hilary Jenkinson, Margaret Cross Norton, and T. R. Schellenberg still held sway over a kind of archival logical positivism based on the arrangement of series of registers and files, not on their history.

Since then, there have been signs of a major change as content expands to context and function, as in "My Very Act and Deed" appearing later in this volume, and Terry Cook's extensive writings, along with the work of many others. Terry's concept of macroappraisal lifted us out of our attachment to the series and the file to an appraisal strategy requiring an estimate of purpose behind the creation of the material record. Thanks to scholars like John Ralston Saul,[1] we now have a much clearer picture of the impact of bureaucracy upon parliamentary and local government which may cause us to revisit files that contain evidence of citizen involvement in the democratic purpose, which is my "history of administration," especially in relation to nongovernmental organizations and "citizen science" as it challenges all manner of professional assumptions in the environmental scene.

All in all, I believe we are as archivists indeed organizing ignorance for discovery, which may change the way society contemplates its memory. However clumsily and crudely we appraised what we deemed of lasting value, much has survived; we could have done a lot worse.

NOTE

1. See, for example, John Ralston Saul, *The Unconscious Civilisation* (Concord, Ont., 1995).

Chapter 5

The Discipline of History and the Education of the Archivist

You may wonder why, at such a time as this when you are once more celebrating the solemn festival of *Clio Americana Invicta*, I should presume such a thoroughly domestic subject as what may appear to you as the care and feeding of handmaidens (or should I say handpersons?).

However, I make no apologies, for I believe that you should consider where the profession of archivist may be leading us and how best we should be equipping ourselves to serve our clientele, in particular scholars of American history. The opinions expressed are my own, and if I sound too dogmatic I intend to probe rather than preach and do not offer proof for all my assertions.

For archivists as for historians, these are troubled times. For over five millennia the archivist, in one guise or another, has shown a remarkable instinct for survival. Society has always tolerated, usually respected, and sometimes honoured the faithful keepers of its memory. We can boast a lineage back to the households of priest-kings, where the scribes made the entry, kept the record, and presumably devised and designed the format on the physical base, the "medium of record." These media have not only carried messages but, by their physical nature, have transformed society. Cheap, durable clay when soft allowed the stylus to make its rapid indelible uniform impressions well suited to the inventory and the stock in trade of Sumerian commerce; papyrus accepted the sophisticated brush strokes which could extend over long continuous rolls the *volumina* of libraries for a literate elite or the registers of the Mediterranean armies;

Originally published in the *American Archivist* 40 (October 1977): 395–402. Reproduced with the kind permission of the author and the Society of American Archivists.

parchment, rough and durable, could survive the climates of Europe and the attentions of public servants and ecclesiastics over long periods, but its cost and texture predicated the set hands, abbreviations, and formal entries of the registers, rolls, accounts, and charters. Paper, on the other hand, was much cheaper and could take the hard-driving pens of secretaries chasing depositions like modern tape recorders and amassing correspondence in the state papers of nationalism. All these developments overlapped and had their counterparts in what we are pleased to call "the private sector."

Today we are back to an earlier format of rolls for film and magnetic tape, and we as archivists are the heirs of all these media and communication systems. Meanwhile our mandate has come to extend over every facet of society and over the very recent past. We can no longer be content with the old and the arcane. For one medium alone we have gathered in a paper mountain, itself only a fragment of the total output of public or private bureaucracy generated during the industrial age in which the repetitive format of ledger, letter book, and box file parodies the mass production and fragmentation of the assembly line. We also collect pictures, photographs, maps, and film; and our traditional record-keeping role has been shaped both by the media of the records described above and by the media of communication (pictogram, ideogram, phonetic alphabet, manuscript, or printed page with all their attendant iconography). Add to all this the output of radio, TV, the computer, and the satellite, which can be recorded more or less permanently; no wonder that appraisal and selection pose tremendous problems. At present, the sheer cost of preservation imposes its own constraints and prevents us being drowned in a sea of record. But more and more is being generated and preserved at relatively less cost, and we are fast approaching an age when information becomes the principal staple and we will perhaps achieve our professional apotheosis.

Our predecessors kept the memory of literate societies usually for the purposes of law, rights, customs, personal identity, and resources. For most of that time, their training was an apprenticeship within the bureaucracies large and small that supported them, they became specialists in a rather narrow clerical sense, and they even wrote in hands that visibly distinguished them from their fellow civil servants in other departments. Their *raison d'etre* was largely administrative, and they were a part of the organism of which their records were the secretions. There was a comfortable security and identity in that.

The modern archivist, and to some extent the manuscript curator (although this latter activity has origins in ancient and famous libraries), is coterminous with "scientific" history. As the study of history became self-consciously fragmented and professional, so the archivist accumulated around him the records of bureaucracies whether public or private (and large families were often petty bureaucracies) together with the papers of individuals. The ties of the *creators* of the material became tenuous, brief, and sometimes nonexistent; the modern counterparts of the keepers of the records, or guardians of vellum-filled libraries, floated free upon uncharted seas with only administrative history and a few basic principles as guides. The *contents* of archival repositories were brought together in an entirely artificial way (unless they contained the records of the parent body). This is not to say that the collections themselves were artificial; in most cases they were not, and archival principles preserved or re-created their original order. However, the specialization in industrial society has required that if records and papers are to survive they must be wrenched out of their environments and placed in the care of a person who is not a historian, not a librarian, or not a museum curator; we were reduced to defining what we were *not* and that is not helpful to a sense of identity. Many people became archivists because they did *not* wish to do other things. We are museum curators in that we deal with documents as handcrafted artifacts removed from their environment; we are almost librarians when we handle the printed ephemera that comes our way; and some of us divide our hearts with the historians in that our unique, organically created material has a relevance to specific instances in time (and, we are increasingly aware, to time series) and place which we describe as "historical." We have tended to make common cause with other professions—librarians, curators, others—only in the field of conservation. Mould is a great leveller. In parts of North America where the tradition of institutional record keeping is not so strong, the historians have often taken the initiative and archivists have, in a sense, become their handmaids. However, we are learning to serve a wider public, and what seemed a comfortable "upstairs-downstairs" situation is changing. We are once more adrift and here may lie our strength as we cultivate a kind of creative nonalignment.

Ironically, it is just at a time when the old fragmentation and specialization of "jobs" is collapsing in our postindustrial society that the archivist, having remained free so long, is seeking the right of other professionals to a recognized and recognizable pigeon hole. We may be the last to do so but, for a number of reasons, it seems that, in self-defense, we must. Society deserves professional value for its money and requires from us a recognizable badge.

However, one of the dilemmas which faces modern society is how to reconcile the specialized "professional" with the interdisciplinary "implosion" of knowledge that Marshall McLuhan seems to have identified correctly. In a world where information is becoming the universal staple, we who move it must contend with the old, historically valid, fragmented professions, buttressed by professional associations, examinations, and standards which are often by nature intensely conservative in outlook. Creativity is often won in spite of professionalism; many of the great inventors had a minimal education, and artists in particular are aware of the problem.

This will, I believe, be only a transient phase in the long run. A generation from now will probably see initial training in the basics and groundwork of library/information/archives science leading to specialization in archives during the second year. There is a new, universal information grammar to be devised and learned. We are dealing here less with techniques than with language and communication circuitry, and it is in this context that the craft of the archivist will be practiced. We should thrive in this new environment for we have always worked within a field theory of information derived from the organic nature of archival originals.

In the light of this future and because, essentially, we practice a craft, we must seek to preserve our oral tradition of instruction, our empiricism and flexibility, and our holistic approach to the archival scene, so that we enter the whole information field from a position of strength and not as a desperate leap onto the bandwagon of information science.

First, we should recognize that preparation for the role of archivist in society may be much more varied than we are usually prepared to accept. There is an archivist in Canada who holds a Ph.D. in chemistry and gave up a career in that field. He thrives. One of the pioneer archivists in England who established the first County Record Office was a biologist who devised an organic taxonomy of quarter sessions records which is still in general use. One of the first to receive the archives diploma with distinction at the University of Liverpool was a nongraduate. An experience of, and reverence for, life and knowledge relating to the organic nature of society, in whatever way this is obtained, will be of great value. It may take the form of a university degree, and in the present state of society it probably will. There is likely to be a preponderance of history degrees, and the whole study of history is itself undergoing responsive change; but we should never exclude those who show excellence in the craft of archivist and do not have a degree. Again, higher degrees do not necessarily make for better archivists; but they often do, and this should be recognized. There is even a danger that specialization arising from excessively specialized historical research may blind the prospective archivist to potentials in archives which those with a broader educational base may perceive. But there will, of course, always be a need for specialists having custody of specialized collections. Next, since the journeyman archivist needs a badge, we should hasten to pin one on him as soon as possible.

The Council of the SAA is at present considering a draft scheme for the voluntary certification of archivists and institutions offering archival education by which the certified archivist may be recognized as having reached a basic standard of competence according to an approved set of educational guidelines which cover very briefly the following ground:

1. The nature of archives, including principles, methodology, terminology, legislation, administrative history, palaeography, and diplomatics.
2. The acquisition of archives in the public and private sectors, including techniques, strategies, appraisal, and acquisition strategies within various "universes."
3. The processing of archives, including arrangement and description, finding aids and indexes, conservation, workflow, and building design.
4. The use of archives, including reference and extension services, access, security, and public relations.
5. The administration of archival repositories, including program planning, budgeting, and staff management.

To which must be added substantial laboratory *practicum*.

This should, however, be seen only as a beginning which will recognize the better archives course offerings as they exist at present in whatever department or faculty they are to be found. As Frank Burke has said, we have concentrated too much on techniques, too little on philosophical perception. We should, I believe, be working now toward the establishment of an institute for advanced archival studies where research up to the Ph.D. level may be carried out and where ultimately there may emerge a postgraduate degree in archival science which will become the norm for entry into the profession. I would like to suggest the following as some of the areas for advanced research: we need to develop our pioneer but rudimentary archival networks so that they become responsive to pattern recognition and the demands of regional history in all its forms; we who are now senior archivists will have to learn to supplement our "mental sets" derived from our own historical training and learn from those now entering our profession with more recent perceptions.

The historians have already helped us a great deal in our task, and we must learn to respond to their insights. We now see time less as a continuum than as an influence constantly reshaping our present in subtle ways that often escape us; as archivists we are constantly trying to discern patterns rather than impose them, and we are desperately trying not to mistake the parts for the whole. We have come a long way from the viewpoint of the New Brunswick historian who confidently wrote a "definitive" history of the province from the transactions of its legislative assembly, to the definition of "historical social research" as perceived by Samuel Hays, which underpins so much regional history. He identifies two main elements:

One is a concern for the broad structural characteristics of society and the long-term changes in those characteristics . . . a discontent with the narrow range of vision of limited segments of space and time, and a desire that the frame of reference be a set of articulated concepts of social change. The other is the accompanying desire to bring into the study of the past the whole range of society . . . the non-people and the non-events, not simply the mass of people as a mass but all segments of the social order, from top to bottom, as an interacting whole.[1]

Kenneth Thibodeau has posed more specifically the question of whether this is an age of profound or superficial change. To answer this we will need: "Masses of data, first, coherently and appropriately organized. Secondly, objective and unambiguous measures of change. Thirdly, the ability to extract from the data the information needed to apply the measures of change and perform the associated tests."[2]

We should be much more conversant with the technique of quantitative research and pattern recognition which help to overcome the problem that the fragmentary survival of the papers of elites (let alone the rest) colour our view, especially if the writer is more voluminous than typical—cases in which you might say the squeaky quill gets the space!

What is attempted in quantitative research is not full knowledge of reality but an increasingly closer approximation to it: what has been described in a mathematical metaphor that is entirely appropriate, as the asymptotic approach to truth.[3]

We must learn to respond to historical social research which is systematic rather than intuitive, whereby the historian no longer gets the feel by immersion in the evidence but tests historical descriptions and hypotheses, probing in a tactile way through the computer. However, the technical aspect of the numbers game should not overshadow concept and method. A preponderance of quantitative studies in political and urban history in the United States are a direct response to the appropriate records being available, mostly through the computer; but unrealistic expectations of what can be achieved through quantification should be avoided. The archivist, like the historian, has learned to become wary of the computer.

These techniques employed should be studied by the archivist because in the drive for greater objectivity the records become central, the historian's gloss more peripheral. It is becoming increasingly unacceptable to speak of a "typical" entrepreneur or politician in a particular field; dichotomies and homogeneities ("blacks and whites," "national character") become less prominent, as in the archives themselves, suggesting that in our cataloguing techniques we should be very careful how we classify and categorize information out of context. We recognize the need for a rich variety of disaggregate descriptions and records from all levels of society.

It is within this context that the uniform but individually insignificant pieces of data in central and local records become so important, especially at the level of the record series (specific operational activities of departments of government), case papers, and legal papers. These are precisely the series which archivists in the past have found to be so intractable, partly because they defy retrieval by subject, partly because of their bulk, and partly because of their insignificance at the item level, given manual retrieval only. We have sometimes taken comfort in aggregates and sampling, but neither route is giving much comfort to our clients. Most of us are sensitive enough to have a bad conscience about this destruction, but in the face of space shortages and hitherto little indication of a user demand, we had no choice. Even archives have to be reasonably cost-effective or, more correctly, use-effective. Sampling is no help to block-face analysis when relating the census returns to tax records, for instance.

We need to reexamine constantly our philosophy of appraisal and selection. In public records, do we keep too much that is evidentiary, too little that is informational? A great deal may be just bureaucrats talking to each other to very little purpose. We become what we behold, and we must learn to shape the administration and management of our media of record accordingly. Regional and thematic history, for instance, is essentially interdisciplinary and multimedia in the documentary sense. The nonlinear, spatial nature of urban and geographical studies draws on maps and photography, including the time series of topographical maps and aerial photographs. Alterations to dwellings, as revealed in photographs, can also be linked to changing family fortunes and lifestyles. "The rhetoric of a geographer is the rhetoric of the map," and the photographic aggregate provides a gestalt which is hard to perceive in any other way. A further development which the archivist should study is record linkage as a kind of microbiography. Just as the antiquary has passed down to us a love of the document as an artifact to be appreciated for its own sake, so the genealogist has kept alive the notion that we are all part of a great chain of being, a kind of universal double helix; but whereas so much of genealogy is the rather bland compilation of a family organization chart within a fixed hierarchical structure, it could become immensely revealing about specific people, and not just aggregates, within the context of a wider study.

We for our part must learn to perceive more clearly and articulate our interdependence with our professional neighbors. First, we have to recognize that the days are past when archivists could run their repositories (or even divisions within a repository) as little fiefdoms from which they looked out with no little suspicion at their professional neighbors and carved out spheres of influence as best they could. This is, of course, a caricature since archivists, by the nature of their calling pragmatic and adverse to systems, learn to be tolerant of eccentricity among their colleagues. We do not need a highly articulated system of archives in this country; but it is time that we examined together the "universe" of our archival responsibility as it exists, using Buckminster Fuller's definition of a universe as the aggregate of all consciously apprehended and communicated experiences. For archivists these are the experiences which survive on record and much of it is still "out there." We have in the past assumed an infinity of acquisition potential in our bailiwick, to be harvested on specific fishing expeditions or by deposit of riches on our doorsteps. This has worked well enough in an era when the researcher/historian was prepared to infer the whole from the part, often snatched at random from destruction by the archivist. If we are to achieve true pattern recognition, we should develop the art of survey and identification and try to select more systematically from the total existing record what should be preserved, and establish priorities among ourselves, with the aid of the users; although this is much more easily said than done, for we operate within a jungle of mandates.

If the media of record are and always have been "change agents," and I believe H. A. Innis and Marshall McLuhan have made the case, we as custodians should pay more attention to what the media theorists are saying. We need not go all the way with technological determinism to recognize the profound effect of media on society, and we should be able to contribute our own insights through, for instance, the study of diplomatics. Such an approach would move this somewhat esoteric though valuable pursuit aimed, for instance, at the dating of early documents and the unravelling of the more arcane administrations of the Middle Ages, to a more fundamental level of the relationship of form to content in the media of record as a whole. Official documents are devised in specific ways to achieve certain administrative effects irrespective of content. In every age, people are more governed than they like to admit. The impact of government then as now is not so much via the bureaucrat, and their record is fully documented in the archives. We need to know more about process and impact, less about results, when we research administrative history at the grass-roots level.

The device of the letters patent over the royal seal being read out and shown in court to a preliterate audience has a powerful audiovisual effect, using a technique of "show and tell" which every kindergarten has now learned to adopt. The words of command are brief and dramatic, the royal iconography majestic and powerful, the impact as telling as a modern TV commercial (which is yet another form of broadcast message). Before this parallel is dismissed as archival *lèse majesté*, we should consider the impact of commercials which reflect and create the folklore of our society and are heeded more than we are aware. They are documentaries of the first importance, and as documents the form of their presentation as opposed to their content deserves careful study.

The study of diplomatics is in a sense the study of the cliché deployed for administrative and other purposes of persuasion. Combinations of clichés capable of endless variations formed the basis of preliterate rhythms, as in chess, and our eyes are once again being opened by their power.

We should perhaps work to ensure that those who draw sustenance and insight from archives feed on a balanced diet of media and are aware of the effects; we should be more conscious of the power of the media hybrids, especially in the field of conversion to microimages; if we have the mandate, we should ensure that our repositories have good media balance and, since we must be selective, develop the insight to choose the medium of record which is most appropriate in a given situation. There is a great deal to be learned about the popular enjoyment and appreciation of archival materials for their own sake as something comparable to, but distinct from, popular history. Above all, we must learn the "languages" of media without the benefit of syntax and with the grammar still uncertain. Only then will we be able to do full justice to our documents and our profession in the twenty-first century.

Archivists, as I have said, have developed out of a rich variety of experience, and I would like to end by introducing you to my favorite colleague who has, alas, been dead these 300 years. William Prynne was very much an archivist, although he flourished in Stuart England long before the word was coined, and he was a man who would be quite at home in our company. I introduce him as a witness to the antiquity of our profession since we have been so busy renewing ourselves of late that we have almost forgotten those predecessors who have been thinking archivally for centuries and fighting in the same battles as ourselves.[4]

William Prynne spent the greater part of his working life as a politician and was one of the most successful writers of pamphlets and tracts in his day. If he were alive now we would probably call him a journalist, and I would like to remind you that the first Dominion Archivist of Canada practised the same profession. As an indication of Prynne's success between 1634 and 1636, the Establishment marked its disapproval by fining him $15,000, cropping his ears, and branding him with the letters SL (for seditious libeller) on both cheeks. We can only assume that he was somewhat mellowed by age, because he was appointed Keeper of the Records in the Tower of London shortly after the restoration of the monarchy in 1660. John Aubrey tells us that "his manner of study was this: he wore a long quilt cap which came two or three inches at least over his eyes which served him as an umbrella to defend his eyes from the light; about every three hours his man was to bring him a roll and a pot of ale to refocillate his wasted spirits; so he studied and drank and munched some bread; this maintained him till night and then he made a good supper."

After a while, like all good archivists, he submitted his report on the state of the records which he says "through negligence, nescience and sloathfulness had for many years then past layen buried together in one confused chaos under corroding putrifying cobwebs, dust and filth in the darkest corners of Caesar's Chapel in the White Tower. . . . I employed some soldiers and women to remove and cleanse them from their filthiness; who soon growing weary of this noisome work left them almost as foul as they found them. Whereupon I and my clerks spent many whole days in cleansing and sorting them into distinct confused heaps in order to their future reducement into method, the old clerks of the office being unwilling to touch them for fear of endangering their eyesights and healths by the cankerous dust and evil scent." You can see that he was a man of unquenchable spirit and enthusiasm who had not lost his gift for the telling phrase at a time when the career of archivist was not as respectable as it is today. We may not have to cope with London grime of the seventeenth century, but those "distinct confused heaps" are still very familiar.

REFLECTION, 2000

I have, it seems, always had problems with historians in a kind of ambivalent relationship and I am not clear why this should be so. On the one hand I am grateful for their scholarly wisdom while I was at Oxford and have had a high regard for the profession since then. On the other hand, I was ambitious for the archival profession to develop its own scholarship on equal terms with historians with its own intellectual content and opportunity for discovery, not only of content for scholars and the general public, but also the riches which lie within the cultural and contextual dimension of the record in all its forms.

I was a member of the Society of American Archivists' Committee of the 1970s,[5] which was mandated to plan the future of the Society in all its aspects. The assumption was that archivists should all be graduates in history who, with a little practical help and apprenticeship, could become effective practitioners. I was the odd man out with dreams of postgraduate degrees. This was the period all over North America of short courses in History Departments and Library Schools, thanks to a generally held belief that the archival discipline lacked sufficient "intellectual content" for a postgraduate degree. Shortly afterwards, another English expatriate, Edwin Welch, and I put together guidelines to counter this position, the first of its kind in North America.[6] Our American colleagues argued that no University would support an archivist as professional director of the programme—and this in a country with a population ten times the size of Canada! Consequently, I had nothing but praise for the University of British Columbia for entertaining just that very idea and appointing Terry Eastwood as its first director. Our guidelines have since been revised, but the SAA acknowledged its debt to Canada in this regard by approving a similar approach some years later.

On this matter of historians and archivists, Canadian archivists struck a Committee of the Future, in the early 1970s, with myself in the Chair, which resulted in the creation of the Association of Canadian Archivists. Before this archivists met professionally as a section of the Canadian Historical Association, which had itself been fostered in its early years by the Public Archives of Canada, as it then was called. This is in contrast to the United States, where it was the historians who lobbied for the creation of a national archives. Indeed, this paper was given at a conference of the American Historical Association.

This sequence of events and the success of Archivaria *were to set Canadian archivists on a course that would lead us to deal with the problems of postmodernity in a period of very rapid change, perhaps bringing us full circle back to historians addressing similar issues of memory, the nature of the past, and the role of the archive—but now a relationship of professional allies rather than master and servant. I want to stress that there continues to be a need for short courses, workshops, and apprenticeships for postappointment training, but that they alone are now generally insufficient for preappointment education given the complexity of archival knowledge.*

NOTES

1. Samuel P. Hays, "The Use of Archives for Historical Statistical Inquiry," in Meyer H. Fishbein, ed., *The National Archives and Statistical Research* (Athens: Ohio University Press, 1973), p. 60.

2. Kenneth Thibodeau, "Machine Readable Archives and Future History," in *Computers and Humanities*, vol. 10 (1976), p. 91.

3. W. C. Aydelotte, A. G. Bogue, and R. W. Fogel, *The Dimensions of Quantitative Research in History* (Princeton: Princeton University Press, 1972), p. 11.

4. My concluding passage first appeared in Hugh A. Taylor, "Archives in Britain and Canada—Impressions of an Immigrant," in the *Canadian Archivist*, vol. 1, no. 7 (1969), 32–33 [see the first of the essays by Hugh Taylor printed in this volume.]

5. Philip Mason, "The Society of American Archivists in the 1970s: Report of the Committee for the 1970s," *American Archivist* 35 (April 1972): 193–217.

6. These Welch-Taylor guidelines are later reproduced as Appendix 1 in Terry Eastwood's "The Origin and Aims of the Master of Archival Studies Programme at the University of British Columbia," *Archivaria* 16 (Summer 1983): 44–51.

Chapter 6

The Media of Record: Archives in the Wake of McLuhan

Societies have always been shaped more by the nature of the media by which men communicate than by the content of the communication. . . . It is impossible to understand social and cultural changes without a knowledge of the workings of media.

Marshall McLuhan, *The Medium Is the Message*

Until comparatively recent times archives as institutions have been regarded essentially as repositories for the public records of government, and for manuscripts from the private sector. The very terms used by archivists have their origins in the administration of handwritten, textual documents on papyrus, parchment, and paper. If typescripts are added to manuscripts, then the overwhelming preoccupation of our profession has been with these "media of record." The writing of history and indeed our whole view of the past has until recent years largely depended on such sources made available in the original, in copies made by hand, and in published versions. For centuries the written, textual record was regarded as the only respectable source for scholars with surviving architectural remains, paintings, and other artifacts serving more as illustration than evidence. Myth, being largely misunderstood, was dismissed as totally unreliable evidence and a product of barbarism. Omar Khayyam's moving finger wrote, and some of our most powerful images have resolved around holy writ, the tablets of stone, and the book of life. In short, civilization became dependent upon and equated with literacy.

Originally published in *Georgia Archive* 6 (Spring 1978): 1–10. Reproduced with the kind permission of the author and the Society of Georgia Archivists.

Modes of communication in literate terms have made a profound and continuous impact on civilization, but archivists have given little consideration to this subject, central though it is to the study of administrative history. We have taken our records very much for granted: while we have respected and sought to preserve their physical nature, we have regarded them simply as the neutral "carriers" of messages or pieces of information, despite the fact that the nature of each medium does shape administrative systems. The interplay between the medium and the receiver creates a communications environment over and above the content of the message and thereby becomes a message itself. Information and the medium of record must together be confronted by the reader, at which point they both become a communication and pass from a static to a dynamic state.

The foundation for this study of the relationship between the medium and the message was laid by two Canadians: Harold Adams Innis, an economic historian who may be almost unknown to American readers, and Marshall McLuhan who is very well known indeed. Studies by Innis on the fur trade, the cod fisheries, and the Canadian Pacific Railway had impressed on him the extent to which the movement and processing of staples altered the lives of those involved. The staple itself became a medium of communication as it passed from hand to hand, much as with money to which it is closely related. Equally important was Innis' stylistic rejection of narrative from a fixed point of view in favour of the generation of insights through interface, as in dialogue. This approach can be a stumbling block for readers accustomed to a logical and orderly presentation by an author. Innis for this reason has sometimes been condemned as unreadable, and yet this surely is the reaction of only one part of the brain! We are rapidly learning that insight may be gained by other than rational literate means: by interface and symbolism, for instance, and by the deployment of space, intervals, and silence. All of these elements of thought are much easier to depict in fine art, conversation, and literature than in the writing of history, which traditionally and classically has received a linear, narrative, cause-and-effect treatment. We know that this view of past activity and process is an illusion. Perhaps that is why it took a Tolstoy to penetrate and record the confusion of a complex military engagement.

Marshall McLuhan, who greatly admired Innis, places great stress on insights arising out of the interplay of suggestive fragments of information at different levels, in contrast to the approach from a "point of view" where the detached "gaze" of the narrator magisterially, but perhaps superficially, describes the scene. For McLuhan, "an insight is a contact with the life of forms. Students of computer programming have had to learn how to approach all knowledge structurally. In order to transfer any kind of knowledge to tapes it is necessary to understand the form of that knowledge. This has led to the discovery of the basic difference between classified knowledge and pattern recognition. It is a helpful distinction to keep in mind when reading Innis since he is above all a recognizer of patterns."[1]

This capacity to develop insights is part of the archivist's skill in the appraisal or selection and the arrangement of disordered material. We understand well this "contact with the life of forms," which distinguishes us from librarians who of necessity must classify, if only so that we can browse through the bookshelves! Classification as an instrument of retrieval has fallen on hard times among archivists and others.

Innis believed that the source of social change was to be found in technological innovation, which extended man's physical capacity, particularly in communications technology, which could be considered an extension of the mind of the sender. He examined the characteristics of the various media, including the media of record as they affected the Ancient World and the Middle Ages. He then extended his study to the newspaper. He also developed a theory of limitation in time and space. Stone, clay, wax, and even parchment, while durable, were cumbersome and "time binding." They made for static hierarchical institutions and traditions within a culture built upon oral traditions in which custom grows out of consensus, and mutually acceptable roles identify status. Paper and papyrus, on the other hand, were light, yet sufficiently durable to be "space binding" and moved rapidly. Information and detailed commands could be conveyed accurately over great distances to the delight of generals, bureaucrats, and expansionists of all kinds whose records now fill the archives of today. Innis supported his findings with a wealth of references. As McLuhan put it, "each sentence is a compressed monograph. He includes a small library on each page, and often incorporates a small library of references on the same page in addition."[2]

It is not surprising that another Canadian, Marshall McLuhan, should take up the study of media where Innis left off. Canada perhaps more than any other country owes its life to staples such as fur, fish, timber, and grains and to communication systems such as railways, the telegraph, the telephone, radio, television, and now the world's most powerful communications satellite. On the prairies, where McLuhan grew up, all the communications of media of his generation came together in vital confrontation and interplay. Where Innis perceived the different media of record as affecting social organization, McLuhan sees them changing sensory perception and thought through a type of technological determinism even more complete than that of Innis. Like the sailor in Poe's *A Descent Into the Maelstrom*, one can recognize what is happening and survive through study of the vortex, the process, and not simply the contents. The *Gutenberg Galaxy* was written by McLuhan "as a footnote to the observations of Innis on the subject of the Psychic and social consequences first of writing and then of printing."[3] It was also a note of warning about taking media for granted. We as archivists should heed this warning and try to understand the characteristics of the media in our custody which are expressed in "messages" beyond their literary content and pass on this awareness to the user.

Before examining McLuhan's insights into the various media of record and communication which concern us as archivists, it may be useful to look first at his observations on media in general. McLuhan's major interest is in how the media affect the person, and this bias gives rise to one of his most important concepts. Each medium causes a different relationship between the human senses, a different "ratio." Much of this theory is presented in the *Gutenberg Galaxy* and rephrased in later works. It may be summarized at the risk of gross oversimplification as follows: Communication is not just a matter of logistics, but requires the involvement of the senses to receive the message. Short of ESP, which is not discounted, the earliest form of communication was oral/aural and involved all the senses in the full interplay of interpersonal relations. Oral man was also tribal man, who lived mythically and in depth with his neighbours. Myth was the holistic perception of a complex evolution that ordinarily extended over time. In tribal society, the individual was a role player rather than a specialist in the fragmented, industrial sense. Words had a power and a resonance in themselves which they were to lose with the onrush of literacy.

Among McLuhan's most important ideas concerning communication was the concept that "All media are active metaphors in their power to translate experience into new forms. The spoken word was the first technology by which man was able to let go of his environment in order to grasp it in a new way."[4] However, the phonetic alphabet traps words, without the benefit of expression, within a visual code of symbols unrelated to the object being described or communicated. The one-to-one relationship is broken, and the alphabet becomes a technological tool, an extension of the sense of sight, and a closed system, unlike the senses themselves which are "endlessly translated into that experience that we call consciousness."[5]

In this way, the media of record and communication, as extensions of the senses, create totally new human environments which are not passive wrappings, but active processes at war with previous environments. There is a constant interplay between media resulting in a fierce hybrid energy, for instance, telegraph and newspaper, photograph and movie film, film and sound. The alphabet made Gutenberg possible, but the technology of uniformity and repeatability exemplified by movable type was not new; it had been present in writing but was now intensified in print and standardized typefaces. Movable type, the first industrial assembly line, led to expansion, nationalism, specialization, detachment, and exploitation. It created the "public" and the passive consumer and brought about a fragmentation of life which separated content from media through a massive dehumanization of society.

McLuhan further posited that the content of one medium is another medium, for example, thought in speech, speech in writing, and writing in printing. He expressed the importance of this concept when he wrote "the 'message' of any medium of technology is the change of scale or pace or pattern that it introduces into human affairs."[6] The principle is particularly evident in the development of automation and its effect on information management.

Media can be divided metaphorically into those which are "hot," those of high definition such as the printed page, film, and radio, as opposed to "cool" media of low definition, such as T.V., comics, and automation. "Hot" media excite; "cool" media involve and invite participation through completion of the images. Electric technology, especially T.V. and automation, represent extensions of our nervous system. Instantaneous information has caused an "implosion" more violent than the Gutenberg "explosion." We now must live mythically and in depth in the "global village" of our new tribalism. The attribute "tribal" is used throughout in a strictly metaphorical and not in a pejorative sense. It is a shorthand description of those group-oriented characteristics of preliterate society which contrast with the intense individualism of typographic man.

If McLuhan's theories are brought to bear on early record keeping in North America, the following conclusions would seem to emerge. For McLuhan, the United States, in contrast to Western Europe, had no medieval particularisms to abolish in its transition to an industrialized society, and was in fact the first nation to be established on a homogeneous foundation of literacy and print culture. The Cartesian environment went unrecognized because there had been no other, in contrast to England, where ancient and medieval traditions and institutions prevented print culture from taking complete hold. The fact that there was no tradition of a permanent public agency keeping written records is explained partly by the poor record keeping in America observed by the DeTocqueville. Ernst Posner's suggestion in response to DeTocqueville that "Archives thrive best in regimented society; poor record keeping seems to be the price of liberty"[7] conveys much truth with gentle irony. Europe's oral, traditional culture may have been more significant, however, in determining the nature of their archival systems. In Europe, records were, in effect, "file copies" of the complex operations of common law, custom, and land tenure. In contrast, within the print culture of the United States, a record not worth printing was generally not worth keeping.

In this setting, it was the professional historian, that exemplary product and promoter of print culture, who sought to rescue manuscripts and create archives as centers for historical research. Contrastingly, in Canada, which inherited English and European orientations, it was the Public Archives that fostered the study of Canadian history and helped found the Canadian Historical Association. Canada, as a much less homogeneous culture, has perhaps experienced a more organic archival growth than the United States.[8] Canadian archivists are not so closely linked to the historians. It may be significant that in the Public Archives of Canada, the name "Historical Branch" has been changed to "Archives Branch" as being more encompassing. Likewise, the Association of Canadian Archivists has parted on friendly terms from the Canadian Historical Association. As archivists, our future lies elsewhere.

If McLuhan's insights into administrative history have value for us, he may also help us define our role as archivists in postindustrial, automated society. We may have to assume the shaman's role as keepers of the tribal memory in our global village. Using the McLuhan metaphor, we have already shown distinctly tribal tendencies despite our typographic and consequently linear acculturation. We are constantly involved with the mosaic of surviving records within our collections, and the mosaic of information spanning them. We constantly seek not an artificially imposed classification by subject, but authentic pattern recognition of media in their archival order. There are gaps in all these mosaic patterns, and the urge towards closure in which we fill and complete the relationships is immensely sense involving. This absorption is over and above our tactile involvement with a wide variety of media of record and our audio-tactile relationship with donors and researchers. We are not operationally specialized, and our work is not functionally fragmented. In short, we enjoy a healthy mix of experiences which embraces all our senses. Even when we become managers in a large archives, we resist fracture and specialization and encourage total involvement through matrix systems, task forces, and intermedia committees to further enrich the archivists still physically involved with the records themselves.

We publish relatively little and often feel guilty about this, but it is not in our nature to trap our science in print too often lest it fossilize there. We are constantly creative, pragmatic, and we instruct those under training through oral exchange and the use of classic texts in the medieval tradition. The archivist's training is an apprenticeship, and we are none the worse for that. We try hard to combine intellectual expertise with practicality. McLuhan expressed the concept by saying that

Professionalism merges the individual into patterns of total environment. Amateurism seeks the development of the total awareness of the ground rules of society. The amateur can afford to lose. The professional tends to classify and to specialize, to accept uncritically the ground rules of the environment. The ground rules provided by the mass response of his colleagues serve as a persuasive environment. . . .[9]

The "expert" is the person who stays put. In this sense we should all cherish our amateurism.

If we are to realize our role in the newly integrated tribal society of the electric age, we will have to re-examine the assumptions of the historical methods which have dominated our public service for a century. The emergence of "scientific" history and the pursuit of the definitive objective account, in contrast to myth, literature, and folklore, created the professional historian. He in turn evolved the modern archivist from those who kept records for purely legal purposes. We have diligently sought out material, but we have for too long concentrated our efforts at the center of our industrial world to serve the interests of historians of centrist political history. There are signs of rapid change here as we respond to other calls, but the "archival edge"[10] should be faced more boldly as we move into a society without centre or margin, one of regions, communities, neighbourhoods, families, and environments served by local repositories and networks and fostering local studies. The archivist, because he or she is more tribal than the historian, often acquires and saves material prophetically and uses prophetic vision in scheduling and appraisal, but how often? If we are to live mythically, the past becomes both yesterday and as one with the present. The archivist once more becomes keeper of the permanently valuable in the broadest sense with little separation between today, yesterday, and something we have learned to call "history." This is particularly true of the record in machine-readable archives.

Probably the most vivid analogy to implosion and mythicality is achieved by projects arising out of the "new" history. These studies collect massive data to be received and correlated by the computer, researched through a "field" approach, and made available through a number of outputs almost instantaneously. Their correlation and interface can only be achieved in measurable time by the computer as an extension of our central nervous systems and provide a kind of group memory and recall. This is particularly true of studies involving family history, case files, census, and tax returns. The process is again almost tribal in nature and much closer to oral tradition. It provides a marked contrast to the selective, detached point of view to the qualitative approach, or even to the individualists' orientation of genealogy concerned with specific ancestry in time and space.

The "new" history is largely dependent, again, on groups and teams and interdisciplinary involvement. Archival documents as aggregates of data are transferred to the new medium of magnetic tape where they retain a total validity in contrast to the old approach where each document is "mined" for information in support of a specific line of enquiry by an individual. Hitherto neglected series, especially in the field of municipal records, may yield unexpected insights. Unfortunately many archivists do not have the space to store bulky series of this kind while they await their possible automation.

Further evidence of this metaphorical tribalism and increased immediate awareness may be found in the program of the thirty-ninth conference of the Society of American Archivists in Philadelphia in 1975, which included the Society's first archival film festival. Sessions were also held on patterns in urban archives, which required a "field" approach closely related to McLuhan's "pattern recognition"; the right of privacy, an increasing problem in any retribalised society, since privacy is closely related to literate individualism; and archives, community, and the media as they related to outreach programs.[11] Other presentations discussed the preservation, use, and interpretation of photographs, and the linking of institutions through archival networks, particularly in Ohio and Wisconsin. Of course, this was not the first exposure these subjects had ever received, but their inclusion, as a group, in a single conference indicated an acceleration of important new trends. Add to this the intense activity of regional associations and "activist archivists" groups, and there emerges something approaching McLuhan's in-depth relationships resonance among archivists today.

Media study may also help us with information control as we move from fragmented classification systems to exploring the concept of integrated pattern recognition. The development of PRECIS (Preserved Context Indexing System) by the British Library, with its emphasis on free language descriptors and context dependency, is in sharp contrast to the older classified indexes and is only possible on a large scale through automation. It is now being tested for use with archival materials. McLuhan has surely said something important about the nature of the retrieval process when he contrasts Sherlock Holmes, to whom every detail is important and instantaneously related, with the official, bureaucratic, segmented approach of the Scotland Yard stereotype. Fiction perhaps, but we have here a parable about perception. We cannot go on indexing archival materials as if they were finite, self-contained blocks of information. We may have to direct the researcher to patterns rather than specifics, and one day, perhaps, this is all he will require. Meanwhile, we are faced with the deluge, which McLuhan notes that: "The twentieth century, the age of electric information, instant retrieval and total involvement, is a new tribal time. If Gutenberg technology retrieved the ancient world and dumped it in the lap of the Renaissance, electric technology has retrieved the primal, archaic worlds past and present, private and corporate and dumped them on the Western doorstep for processing."[12]

It is therefore instructive and reassuring to see how pre-Gutenberg man coped with the media of record, to see ourselves reacting in a similar way, and to consider the media of the post-Gutenberg age, since all come within our responsibility. We greatly value printed books, but as custodians we relate more closely to scrabble society. We recognize our sense of involvement, both public and private, in archival affairs, and we are learning to react immediately. Failure to cope results in what McLuhan calls "rim spin," as technology speeds up process to the point of dislocation. Automation is producing more information than can be effectively managed by conventional programs as anyone in machine-readable archives knows. Traditional retrieval systems are breaking down.

As archivists we have always been less concerned with "shedding light on" the surface of our record from a fixed point of view than historians in the past have sought to do. We try to illumine the whole corpus of our collections and allow the light of relatedness to penetrate through our intricate archival reconstructions as through the interlace of an illuminated manuscript or a stained glass window. We have also re-entered an era of "light through" in a physical sense as we recognize the power of the film and the transparent slide, which may be just as involving as the stained glass window and the stone tracery. The printed book may once again become the visual aid to the other media that it once was, and not vice versa which has long been assumed as the natural order of things. If we believe that media exert such a powerful force we should understand not only the impact upon us as archivists, but also its impact on our clients, as they too learn to move more freely from one media of record to another and recognize the difference in psychic terms.

The classroom is only beginning to feel the full impact of postindustrial society and the new media: John Dewey the educator "wanted to get the students out of the passive role of consumer of uniformly packaged learning. In fact, Dewey in reacting against passive print culture was surf-boarding along on the new electronic wave."[13] The whole field of diffusion and outreach to all who appreciate archives, and not just our traditional clients, is only beginning to be explored.

It is becoming increasingly clear that we can no longer view the records of the past as totally distinct from the records of today. The media of record are presenting their challenges both to the records manager and the archivist, and solutions may affect our senses in ways we should know about. Micrographics is more than a "ditto" process. It involves a significant media change from "light on" to "light through" which may subtly alter our perceptions. As we become more involved with our media and our users, the professions of archivist, librarian, and records manager may become one at the point where the media of record becomes predominantly electronic and incorporates the principle of the video-disc as a near-permanent record. There is no wear since the laser scans in an almost tactile way the indentations of the encapsulated matrix or copy. Technology, by "throwing light on" information, is again turning metaphor into process, as yet another medium acting as a metaphor in an endless related chain of communication with the human consciousness, causing "closed systems" to disappear.

McLuhan does not preach instant salvation through electronics and media study. The mastery of the new languages is a tough and demanding discipline. We cannot short-circuit the effort required to assimilate them to our past, but success will enrich us all. Further study of media effects must be undertaken, but as Edmund Carpenter has warned us, "Knowledge of media alone is not sufficient protection from them. The moment Marshall McLuhan shifted from private media analyst to public media participant, he was converted into an image manipulated and exploited."[14] We should perhaps work to ensure that those who draw sustenance and insight from archives feed on a balanced diet of media and are aware of the effects. We should be more conscious of the power of media hybrids, especially in the field of conversion to microimages. If we have the power, we should ensure that our repositories have good media balance. Since we must be selective, we must also develop the insight to choose the medium of record which is most appropriate in a given situation. Above all, we must learn the "languages" of media without the benefit of syntax and with the grammar still uncertain. Only then will we be able to do full justice to our documents and our profession in the twenty-first century.

REFLECTION, 2000

I never heard Marshall McLuhan lecture, nor did I speak to him personally, but given the excitement of "discovering" him I would have been quite overawed, which is the last thing he would have wanted. My first encounter with McLuhan in print was a curious one. I had been taking History 101 at the University of New Brunswick in Fredericton, as my knowledge of Canadian history was almost nil. On one of the reading lists was The Gutenberg Galaxy, *which was removed the following year as being too difficult. I found the book absolutely compelling, and devoured a number of McLuhan's other works in quick succession. I found myself catapulted into the world of postmodernity before that term became common, and long before I knew what it meant!*

The breathless style of the first part of this essay reveals the uncritical enthusiasm of the convert, but I remain unrepentant! The session of the Society of American Archivists' annual conference in 1976 where I delivered the paper bore the title "The Media of Record: Change Agents or Carrier Pigeons?" This was my first attempt to present the media as a significant part of the meaning as opposed to concentration on its content as the sole source of information. No one was interested in publishing this paper until I was asked by the Editor of Georgia Archive *to offer a contribution as Vice President of the SAA. Space was found for a subject which at the time stirred very few hearts in our profession. I don't think "The Media of Record" was quite what was expected, but I was very grateful for the editor's courage. Shortly afterwards, I invited Barrington Nevitt, a colleague of McLuhan, to speak at the Association of Canadian Archivists' annual conference. He read a paper entitled "Archivist and Comprehensives,"[15] whereupon the lead balloon fell with a crash, and I was obliged to offer myself as a very amateur "translator" of his mystifying style and aphoristic language.*

Thereafter, I was more circumspect with my McLuhanisms, but I plugged away until they became archivally respectable, or at least tolerated as a means by which the power of the various media could be better understood and no longer taken for granted.

After a period of turbulent criticism, McLuhan has been reinstated as a voice to be listened to as the citizen strives to be heard through the barrage of media persuasion. The corporate world was interested in McLuhan as a guru of successful advertising and public relations. More seriously, he may be giving us confidence and the will to maintain our tribal, community memory enriched by a multiplicity of media and sources that speak for bioregionalism and informed democratic action in the face of corporatism and the citizen's passive silence. The Internet and World Wide Web very much reinforce the "global village" that he saw almost forty years ago.

NOTES

1. Harold A. Innis, *The Bias of Communication* (Toronto, 1971), p. viii.
2. Ibid., p. ix.
3. Ibid.
4. Marshall McLuhan, *Understanding Media* (New York, 1964), p. 64.
5. Marshall McLuhan, *The Gutenberg Galaxy* (New York, 1969), p. 14.
6. McLuhan, *Understanding Media*, p. 24.
7. Ernst Posner, *Archives and the Public Interest* (Washington, 1967), p. 162.
8. Hugh A. Taylor, "Canadian Archives: Patterns from a Federal Perspective," *Archivaria* 1, 1976.
9. Marshall McLuhan, *The Medium Is the Message*, p. 93.
10. Gerald Ham, "The Archival Edge," *American Archivist* 38 (January 1975): 5–13.

11. Hugh A. Taylor, "Clio in the Raw: Archival Materials and the Teaching of History," *American Archivist* (July–October 1972): 317–30.

12. Marshall McLuhan, *Culture Is Our Business* (New York, 1970).

13. McLuhan, *The Gutenberg Galaxy*, p. 176.

14. Edmund Carpenter, *Oh, What a Blow that Phantom Gave Me!* (New York, 1974), p. 166.

15. I might note that even the adventurous *Archivaria* did not publish it.

Chapter 7

Documentary Art and the Role of the Archivist

Not long ago I borrowed a book for our youngest daughter from the local university library. She was preparing an essay on the causes of the First World War, and I thought it might be helpful to allow some images to speak for themselves before we became lost among the great armies of words which tramp across the pages of histories. The work I had chosen was an unusually well-illustrated account with captions which not only described but also explained the photographs. Unfortunately I soon discovered that several pages had been cut up, presumably to adorn someone else's project. When I pointed this out to the librarian on duty, her reply was: "We often have this problem, but as long as the text is still there it isn't so bad, is it?"

This librarian should have been with us last year when President Rundell triumphantly broke with tradition and treated us to an absorbing presentation on photographs as records making their statements, supported by, and not in support of, the historian's text.[1] This year I will try to make a case for treating another form of visual creation as a document worthy of full membership in an archival family that now embraces not only records and manuscripts but also maps, photographs, film, sound, and that formidable nonrecord until recently, machine-readable archives. I wish to bring before you the watercolor and the oil painting, and I would plead for their legitimacy at a time when I believe many of you have grave doubts about these media, for are they not works of art altogether too wayward in conversation for their more staid companions, the record and

Originally published in the *American Archivist* 42 (October 1979): 417–28. Reproduced with the kind permission of the author and the Society of American Archivists.

the manuscript? Most of us have examples of these charming pieces in our repositories, but are not too certain how they fit into our scheme of values. If they are "good," should they go to an art gallery; and if they are not "good," what kind of rating can we give them? I think there is a small voice in all of us which says: "You can't really trust those painter chaps!"

Let us try to go back to the beginning of communication between adults in its simplest form. It seems fairly clear that if a message was to be conveyed in a form other than sound and gesture, its form would have been in some way representational of familiar shapes—humans, animals, birds, and the like—which could be scratched in sand or mud and later painted on rock. In recent times, Indian braves recounted their exploits and counted their coups by recording them on teepees and buffalo hides in just this manner.[2] In short, the first statements to survive the sound of a voice were pictures, not words. Out of these simple shapes emerged the pictogram, the ideogram, and the hieroglyph conveying complex information and ideas in brushstrokes still carrying the subtle suggestion of a pictorial origin and influencing the thought processes in a most distinctive way. The loss of this image base before the onset of the phonetic alphabet seems to have had a profound effect on literate society in the West, and the consequent linear stress was further intensified from the fifteenth century onwards by Gutenberg's invention of printing from movable type.[3] What became of the picture?

The craftsmen of ancient Greece, for want of a more flexible medium, executed some of their finest pictorial work on their black and red figure vases and painted miniatures on glass worked with gold leaf. We can trace a continuous line from this tradition to the illuminated manuscript[4] and the transcendent historiated initials in the psalters of the Middle Ages. These works were designed to be explored through touch, as the vase is raised or the page turned. They were used in elaborate ceremonies which engaged all the senses. Above all, they were not just to be looked at. Such images retained their central place in communication sacred and profane, from which text and voice were never far away. From earliest times the artists had accepted the challenge of building narrative into a basically static form of expression. Few secular examples remain, but the eleventh-century Bayeux Tapestry, protected by the authority of a great abbey church, has survived as one of the finest pictorial documents of the early Middle Ages, essential for an understanding of the Norman Conquest of England. Incidents are elided with great skill, as the narrative is developed in the manner of a strip cartoon.[5] Again, one cannot omit the mosaics of Byzantium glowing and flickering in their vaults, to be matched later by the stained glass of Chartres and York, enveloping the court and the church in total environments of color, design, and record.

Without this wealth of iconography we would know little of the appearance of things during those centuries. The biblical narratives and the lives of the saints were communicated in a mythic way, in "modern dress," and an all-at-onceness which can still be experienced in medieval churches to this day. This has been termed acoustic space, which we are now re-experiencing through the instantaneous communication of electronic media and the reaffirmation of all the human senses through both sides of the brain. This acoustic experience was to be totally at variance with Renaissance tradition in which text and image parted company and developed quite literally along their own lines. Paintings became works of art and have remained so. As such they were not regarded as documents in any sense, for documentation as we know it became the prerogative of such textual records as the printed book, the enrolment, the deposition, the letter, and the diary. Even seals, those wonderful, visual, tactile expressions of status which were appended to all medieval conveyances of land, lost their significance with the increasing use of signatures by the literate. In England, the symbol of the sovereign's authority through image and seal, rather than sign manual, was retained only for royal letters patent, a reminder of an ancient usage in a world of print and literacy.

In this harsh, geometric world of continuous space bound by the laws of Euclid and the philosophy of Descartes, which limited the spectator to a fixed point of view, the great machine of passing time slowly revolved. Historians prowled happily amongst the gears and levers, showing us more or less how it all worked, and used as their blueprints those textual records which by the end of the nineteenth century abounded in the archives of Europe and America. The more they found, the better the past could apparently be explained; but the cumulative effect was asymptotic. They never quite got there; scientific history proved to be a delusion, and we now turn to the more human disciplines of archaeology, anthropology, folklore studies, and the "new" history, seeking pattern and process within a field rather than cause and effect along a continuum. Textual records have been supplemented and at times even replaced by the whole range of oral and visual media, with which we have now become familiar. In an almost tactile approach to data, the electronic scanner of the cathode ray tube and the selective process of the computer become an extension of ourselves in our search strategy and have helped us to appreciate visual configuration in a new way, not just as illustration in support of text, but as a pattern of record in its own right capable of making statements far beyond the power of speech and writing. We must now examine more closely these visual media of record.

First, we should recognize that archival principles, as we know them, were formulated and developed by scholarly bureaucrats from a careful study of textual public records based on the registry and the filing cabinet, and this is reflected in our stewardship over the past century. Nontextual material showed little evidence of a time series and obstinately resisted an original order between inclusive dates. Repositories are filled with map collections, for instance, arranged by size and geographic area with little attention to provenance; the map record group is still comparatively rare. Likewise, photographs were long ignored as records in the archival sense, and collections were plundered for unusual illustrations or, more mercifully, allowed to gather dust pending more enlightened treatment. We now preserve the sanctity of the photographic collection and maintain the photographer's order based on his records, if this is possible. Photographs have joined the family. Film, on the other hand, preserves its original order at twenty-four frames a second. Although film archives tend to operate more like special libraries, the fundamentally documentary nature of a wide range of film, including some feature films, is now clearly recognized, and copyright laws enforce a meticulous record of provenance.

There remains one group of media for which no crisp generic term exists, which includes paintings, drawings, prints and occasionally posters, seals, and medals. The term *iconography* is sometimes used, and I might have included it in my title rather than *art*, which can be a rather loaded word. For the most part, we do not harbour works of art in our archives in the sense that an art curator or historian would use the term, i.e., as works important primarily as paintings in their own right rather than as documents. We give house room to documentary art or iconography, and we control it after a fashion, so that it can be retrieved, but do we really believe it to be archival? With archivists, like latter-day Noahs, welcoming documents of every kind, nature, and description into their arks, it is time that we gave some thought to the matter. I am limiting my paper to drawings and paintings in oil and watercolour, but much of what is said applies to the other pictorial categories.

Perhaps we can first agree that a picture is a statement in the same way as is an entry in a diary or a paragraph in a letter.

> No other kind of relic or text from the past can offer such a direct testimony about the world which surrounded other people at other times. In this respect, images are more precise and richer than literature.[6]

But this is also art, and at once we become nervous.

> If the painter does nothing but render exactly, by means of line and color, the external aspect of an object, he yet always adds to this purely formal reproduction something inexpressible.[7]

To those brought up on history written entirely from textual records, the written word has a certain respectability, a deceptive precision, a convincing plausibility that masks its limitations. In a similar way, "most of us regard print as the familiar, comfortable, rumpled dressing gown of communications. We take print for granted."[8] We still communicate with words, not pictures (unless we are nonsmokers looking for a washroom), so naturally we feel more at home with them. We believe we can depend on them, and our very literacy blinds us to other modes of expression, even speech itself. But historians and archivists are also very well aware that textual sources can be biased, inaccurate, selective, and downright misleading, but they have one great merit: their content is presented serially, within time, through grammatical statements and logical arguments. Likewise, our literary training has often caused us to "read" pictures "literally" without being aware of certain rules and conventions that are in sharp contrast to the rules of alphabet, grammar, and syntax. How then, should we as archivists approach pictorial art?

In early classical antiquity the Latin *ars* meant a craft or skill; the modern concept of art was a product of the Renaissance.[9] Nonliterate cultures have no art, they simply do their best. *Ars* in medieval Latin became book learning, the liberal arts. Fine arts emerged in the eighteenth century as *les beaux arts,* which in English became simply *art,* a century later. In short, art, as we know it, is of relatively recent origin, and as archivists we may do well to consider painting not as art in the nineteenth-century sense, since we will rarely deal in masterpieces, but as the product of a craftsman who has learnt the business as professional or amateur painter, much as fine writing was learnt from the writing master. For Malraux, these are "non-artists" who produce at best "a memory, a sigh or a story; never a work of art. Obviously, a memory of love is not a poem, a deposition given in court is not a novel, a family miniature is not a picture."[10] But all of these can provide reliable records.

Writing, with its origin in the pictogram, may be regarded as a highly stylized form of painting, and the word *style* is derived from the stylus of the scribe. Let me again be clear that I am not denying creative excellence as expressed by the term *work of art* or the creativity of the great artists who quite transcended their teachers. If we have to consider any of these works from a documentary point of view, we will need all the help we can get from gallery curators and art historians. However, that such a work is a masterpiece should in no way affect its status as a record; it may reveal insights on a level which a lesser artist could not convey, and so increase its value for us. (As an aside, I cannot resist reminding you that every M.A. thesis submitted is a masterpiece in its ancient but scarcely in its modern sense.)

Let us now see whether drawings and paintings meet the criteria we apply as tests of archival material. First, we must try to establish authenticity. As with public records, a continuous period of unbroken custody is valuable (but not conclusive) evidence, and over-painting is a real possibility. However, no one forges the second rate or tampers with laundry lists. We can take comfort in the relative obscurity of much that we hold.

A picture may be authentic, but how do we assess its evidential or informational value? If works of art are to be considered as documents, then we have to grapple with the concept of representation which lies at the heart of the problem. Many artists in our collections will imitate styles, especially those of their teachers, but there is no way they can imitate or provide a mirror image of their subjects.[11] We are dealing with an order of truth somewhat different from the compilation of an inventory. We can, however, usually reckon that the artist is not out to deceive by adding significant elements which do not exist in the subject. This does not mean that a painting will look exactly like its subject, but that it will convey and suggest truthful comment as perceived by the artist as observer, which is as much as we can expect from any observer. The caption may, however, be misleading, but this may not be the fault of the artist. We have to recognize that in all representational painting, as in correspondence or report writing, there is selection and omission. This is also how archivists appraise and select records for permanent retention. Even the camera is highly selective, especially in tonal range, and may omit color altogether.

To communicate in a representational manner, the artist must also use techniques acceptable to the viewer if an accurate report is to be conveyed. The language must be understood.

> Up to a point this is done by representing the object literally; but beyond that point it is done by skilful departure from literal representation . . . and thus . . . produces in one's audience the kind of effect one wants to produce.[12]

We have recently been reminded that the aesthetic of the picturesque, so popular with the early Victorians, was in origin more practical and realistic than we now tend to think and was closely bound up with the making of an accurate record. The Reverend William Gilpin, champion of the picturesque in England, once wrote: "Your intention in taking views from nature may either be *to fix them in your own memory* or *to convey in some degree your idea to others*,"[13] which is precisely the visual aid provided by the modern snapshot.

We must now ask ourselves whether, in the case of a streetscape, for instance, we can isolate topographical fact from the formal conventions of composition with which the artist unifies his work and communicates with the viewer. There are those who would still argue that art and fact are in conflict, but this is true only if one restricts fact to a mirror image of reality, a goal as unattainable as that of "what actually happened" in historical research. Many of the early views of Halifax, Nova Scotia, in the eighteenth century show Citadel Hill more pronounced than it really is, but that may be a way of emphasizing the importance of the hill for the inhabitants and for the military garrison stationed there.

If we are to admit the archival legitimacy of documentary art, we should make a study of those artists who left a record of the territory within our jurisdictions and become familiar with their artistic language and form. Nova Scotia, along with other parts of Canada, is indebted to the work of army and navy officers from Britain for much of the visual record before photography. For purposes of military intelligence they were taught to draw and paint in watercolours as part of their training. Their drawing masters at the military academies included David Cox (1783–1849) and Paul Sandby (1725–1809), who "created the norm for half of the watercolour painting of his time";[14] both were outstanding artists of the English watercolour school. A certain military precision was emphasized and, to aid the neophyte, definite drill sequences for making a watercolour were devised.[15]

The artists painted the world of colonial peace, order, and good government, which they knew best. A fair number of their neat sketches were subsequently published for the comfort and enjoyment of the upper classes. Trade, commerce, factories, and poverty were not fit subjects for art. By contrast, the tradition in the United States was much more down to earth, and commercial enterprise was often recorded by local craftsmen. Travellers, writing in their journals or in letters home, gave the lie to this over-tidy vision of Canada, as did one artist himself when he exchanged the brush for the pen.[16] In general, their work was not intended to deceive; it was simply selective in theme and content, and we must be aware of these limitations. An outstanding artist in this group was James Pattison Cockburn, whose record in watercolours of early nineteenth-century Quebec, is unrivalled. To enhance their accuracy he used a *camera lucida* and placed his buildings in their correct relationships.[17]

Whereas prose is created serially, artists put together their information organically as they build up their compositions. If one substitutes for brushstrokes pieces of information on paper, this is also how the documents of an organization accumulate in their groups, series, and subseries, like the secretions of an organism growing more complex and richer in information with the passage of time. We are trained to recognize this pattern of growth, and we should perhaps look at paintings in this manner, as we identify the various elements and their interrelationships to achieve certain effects, in much the same way as our institutions are, or should be, designed to perform a function and leave their paperwork in a configuration which reflects this function.

Artists develop their carefully learned *schema*, such as the shape of various trees or stock attitudes for figures, modifying them and integrating them into their work or, if they are exceptional, transcend these *schema* altogether.[18] In this sense they are using figures *of paint* rather than figures of speech to describe a scene, and this is particularly true of those topographical artists who are thoroughly competent but do not attain the first rank. In this regard Etienne Gilson distinguishes helpfully between painting and what he calls "picturing" or the art of "doing pictures" and goes on to say:

> We do not intend to minimize the importance of pictures or images. On the contrary, if one succeeded in introducing a distinction between pictures and paintings that looks so well founded, pictures would benefit by it as much as paintings. We need a history and an aesthetics of the art of picturing conceived in a spirit of sympathetic objectivity suitable to the importance of the subject.[19]

Rudolf Arnheim suggests that artistic activity and visual thinking can be thoroughly rational.[20] We conceptualize and organize our thoughts around categories, stereotypes, and well-established concepts, which act as comfortable pigeonholes for the initial rough sort of our ideas. This is much the same process as form-filling, and we use the same term, *form*, in art to denote the deployment of the various elements in a picture. Similarly, the term *form* is used with legal records in such phrases as "common form," which are in fact groups of standardized legal *schema* which help tell us (at great length) what the document is about. Likewise *formularies* were whole books of *schema* for those drawing up title deeds and similar documents. Forms management may reduce a multiplicity of *schema* to a common form; form letters are built up from common form statements to give the appearance of uniqueness and spontaneity. The study of diplomatics is the study of forms as a clue to the nature, purpose, and date of early documents.

Although the "life of forms" is a familiar concept in art, this comparison may appear somewhat forced, but I believe it helps us to recognize the documentary nature of works of art. So much of our seeing is a matter of habit and the expectation of the familiar: "The visual arts are a compromise between what we see and what we know."[21] We read the first letters only of a scribbled word and conceptualize the rest, a practise which is most useful in paleography or deciphering poor handwriting, as we all know.

Winston Churchill, a very competent painter who was as familiar as any man with public records and communication, spoke of the artist turning light into paint via the post office of the mind which directs encoded pigment onto the canvas in the form of a cryptogram; the pattern only becomes clear when all the paint is in place.[22] He uses code here as a metaphor, yet the halftone block, the "wire" photograph, and the television screen rely on the code of a pattern of dots from which to build up the image. Seurat did much the same, and so do many of the magic realists of today. If we are to use pictures as record, we must recognize the pattern and read the code correctly as we do in other media.

If, then, art is conceptual, documentary art cannot be true or false, but only more or less useful and reliable for the formation of descriptions. Information reaching the eye is so dense and complex that our awareness must in self-defense select in order to conceptualize, and the history of art is the painful development of conventions through *schema* and modification. "If we shed any instinctively or throw them out deliberately, either they are replaced before too long or we fall back into private universes, self-immured, incommunicado."[23] Without communication there can be no record.

Finally, we should consider whether the output or collected work of an artist has an organically related quality we can recognize as archival. Let us take some examples: sketches within or attached to correspondence or a report present no problem, largely because textual records are classically archival and lend their archival quality to their attachments, like the label on Jenkinson's elephant. Sketches in a notebook with captions by the artist are probably the closest parallel to a diary, and these too would be accepted in most instances as archival, especially if they are dated. With loose and perhaps unfinished drawings or sketches of a work to be completed in the studio, we leave familiar ground but they are statements just the same. And so we come to the easel painting itself, and I hope that what I have been saying will help us to see this too as a record whereby the finished works of an artist may be considered as documents. The fact that they have been sold and are scattered halfway around the world is irrelevant, provided they have been authenticated. Some public documents and many manuscript collections have been dispersed in this way, to be reconstituted on paper and by the exchange of microfilms.

For those archivists who have patiently borne with me up to now, this last paragraph may well break the back of their patience!

Are *all* paintings, then, to be regarded as documentary record? At this point common sense must prevail, but let it be the *sensum communis* which engages all our senses and faculties. Clearly we must try to distinguish between an artist's personal record expressed through the painting in nonrepresentational terms, or a work of art which has no point of reference with the world of appearances, and the kind of documentary art which seeks primarily to record, using this expression in its widest sense to encompass paintings which may only remotely look like their subjects but express other qualities, in particular the creation of profound generalized statements about their subjects.

For Malraux the final liberation of painting came when the artist was able to express his work and his subjects solely in paint, and not with paint subservient to a recognizable image or story.[24] Perhaps this is the point where art ceases to be a document that may be used for documentary content in the archival sense. In any case, documentary content may be quite irrelevant to the painting as a work of art. As with many administrative documents, it is to be used by the archivist for a purpose for which it was not created, but for which it is perfectly valid. We must, however, still be cautious, because the development of an artist as expressed in all of his work is obviously an autobiographical record, of a kind. Must we then take over all the art galleries; and anyway, why stop at painting? Why not sculpture and ceramics? The line is by no means clear-cut and points up the dilemma of a culture that distinguishes art from record in an uneasy dichotomy.

Sometime ago the Public Archives of Canada presented the retrospective of an artist who had emigrated from Europe to Canada many years ago. Here was the record by an artist of what it meant to be an immigrant in Canada, and so it was presented jointly by the National Ethnic Archives and the Picture Division, both of the Public Archives. There was not much explicit Canadian content in the pictorial sense, yet it seemed to me a valid record of an artist's experience in an entirely nontextual form. Not everyone agreed, but I believe the point was worth making, if only once.[25] The retrospective exhibit is, of course, a commonplace in art galleries; but it may also be seen as an archival occasion.

In practical terms we must take a more arbitrary, pragmatic approach to the problem. We accept thankfully that there are art galleries staffed by curators and historians whose concern is with art and excellence, but we, and they, must realize that galleries are rich in visual documentary material such as we have been discussing, and that, because content is not the primary concern of the curator, information retrieval of a documentary nature may be difficult. It is significant that the rediscovery by both curators and archivists involved with the military artists, whose record of early Canada is so remarkable, has resulted in much closer relations between the two professions. Perhaps each will take on some of the characteristics of the other, with the archivist identifying the documentary record wherever it may be and ensuring that this aspect of works of art is fully appreciated.

I have said nothing of genre painting, which is analogous to anecdote, narrative, and literature[26] and may also be designed as illustration. Despite the apparently accurate observation of place and period which may be displayed, the archivist should be very cautious in regarding these as documents in the same sense as topographical drawings. They are probably best regarded as the pictorial counterpart of literary manuscripts.[27]

There is one category of documentary art which would seem to have all the attributes of public record, yet scarcely ever finds its way into an archives. Governments in two world wars have commissioned war artists to prepare records in their own fashion of this most intense of national experiences. There is ample evidence that, despite vast photographic coverage, the artists' contributions were appreciated, if only, at worst, as an arm of propaganda. In general, these artists were permitted a free hand and the total output was quite naturally somewhat uneven. Yet once the wars were over, most of this material found little response anywhere and was bundled into the vaults of reluctant galleries and museums, there to be neglected for years; because, good or bad, it was identified as art before it could be processed as document. Was it because archives laid no claim? This example is cited not to point the finger, but to point up the problem.

It may have struck you as rather strange that I should have spent so much time discussing iconography in classical archival terms, based on textual record. The reverse procedure might provide some interesting observations on manuscripts, which must wait for another time. Sufficient that our increasingly multimedia view of archives is already modifying principles, especially those based on the serial nature of archives. Machine-readable records cannot be viewed in this serial way, and the storage of this information in the computer, when it periodically leaves the tape, is chaotic by human standards.

We must look to future technology, such as the video-disc, for the simultaneous retrieval of multimedia information in the televisual mode with a wide range of "hold" and "browse" capabilities. Picture as record will then be available with text and sound to provide us with a balanced media fare. Meanwhile, I believe closer attention should be given to the reproduction of documentary art through increasing use of slides and microfiche. In this way the *fonds* of an artist's output can be assembled through adequate reproduction. This is what Andre Malraux is saying in his concept of the "museum without walls," by which we may study the entire work of an artist and make comparisons with all styles and all ages, in a manner once totally impossible, with some surprising results. The coloured microfiche series, published by the Public Archives of Canada, of the works of the artists in its collections are a means to this end and are the direct counterpart of a microfilm edition of a manuscript collection.

We can catch a glimpse of how records, both textual and pictorial, may be used as evidence and woven into a nonlinear presentation by studying the precepts of Jacob Burckhardt who writes that only "long and intensive exercises in viewing, the constant parallelizing of facts, the laborious steeping in best sources can develop the all important sense of style and awareness of the typical."[28] Because he sought to make general statements, he refused to use concrete images merely as illustration, and yet his command of words was such that "he could teach art history and lecture on painting and architecture, when projectors and other 'visual aids' were still largely unavailable."[29] Like Burckhardt, many of the so-called new historians are now presenting their history without heroes in a similar way, and increasingly they need the records of pattern rather than of achievement for their findings. We archivists should spend more time looking at pictures if we are to become what we behold and grasp the true nature of record in all its richness of form, substance, and texture.

In this brief survey, I have only touched on the problem. We need to explore the nature of documentary information in the context of all media of record and to realize that in iconography we have a great deal to learn from our colleagues, the art curators. At the same time I would suggest that the present methods of identification and cataloguing of works of art by curators are curiously literary and oriented toward externals. Entries tell us a great deal about the physical nature of the painting as artifact, the exhibits in which it has featured, and (if possible) its impeccable record of provenance, yet there is often little about the work itself beyond its title or caption, which may be less than helpful. Of course, it can be argued that the researcher should then view the original or a good copy. But what if the line of enquiry is, for instance, concerned with form or detail not related to the information on the catalogue card? We must all learn to describe pictorial content in words if we are to retrieve it.

Estelle Jussim, a library school teacher by profession, in an invaluable article on the subject,[30] uses the term "visual information" to describe the visual content of documents and, following Bernard Karpel, argues for descriptions taken from the language of art theory and from those who are accustomed to describe art in words. This whole subject is, of course, even more urgent in the context of automated systems of retrieval.

Again, we must try to define more clearly the roles of the archives and the art gallery as repositories, for it makes little sense if galleries are to retain, by implication, the privilege of creaming off all that is excellent and leave archives to deal with the second rate. In fact, and to our credit, archivists have assiduously cultivated the acquisition of the second rate on the correct assumption that in documentary art Oscar Wilde's aphorism that "if a thing is worth doing, it is worth doing badly" holds true; their subsequent discovery by galleries has sometimes left near masterpieces on our hands as the bad turns out to be primitive or folk art. I offer no solutions, but hope you will see that we have a problem here.

I would like to end on a more general note. Barrington Nevitt, a management consultant with a background in communications and a colleague of Marshall McLuhan, challenged the Association of Canadian Archivists last year by asking a number of searching questions which he believed we should face, including the following:

> Has the archivist as communicator yet learned to anticipate the effects of media on his publics?

and in reference to McLuhan's comment that "ever since Burckhardt saw that the meaning of Machiavelli's method was to turn the state into a work of art by the rational manipulation of power, it has been an open possibility to apply the method of art analysis to the critical evaluation of society":[31]

> Has the archivist as art critic yet learned to recognize the 'text' which evokes the context of their times—what to keep and what to destroy?[32]

The study of documentary iconography will not only help us extend our range, it may also enable us to develop the faculty of the artist to program effects and recognize new patterns within an information environment, where process and change have eroded old rules and verities. Only then will we assume once more the role of shaman, which the ancient keepers of records knew so well. To perceive, by projection, the future patterns of our documentary galaxy, and to act in the light of this knowledge, must be our awesome task.[33]

REFLECTION, 2000

This was my presidential address at the 1979 Society of American Archivists' Conference in Chicago before a gathering of several hundred archivists in the Palmer House. The previous year my predecessor as President had used black-and-white photographs most effectively. Since images had invaded this presidential moment, probably for the first time, it seemed right to consolidate the black-and-white nontextual element with the colour of "documentary art" by Canadian artists. So far as I know these innovations have not been repeated.

Once again I found myself reaching into the past and recalling briefly the development of iconography through time as I had done with early textual records. Iconography as an element in an acoustic worldview claims the attention of archivists as a contrast to linear, textual traditions. Historians are becoming aware of value and meaning of images in a postmodern frame. While an archivist working in Liverpool Public Libraries, I had taken care of a large collection of watercolours covering the city and dockland. Here were artists making their statement and exhibiting their point of view in paint with all the intensive insights which a good diarist might record in words. During the Summer Agricultural Fair, I would take the old glass "magic lantern" slides of early photographs of Liverpool and display them in an insufficiently darkened tent. Nevertheless, the audiences were delighted. Such images were to become commonplace on television but did not focus on local communities at that time. I even put together an illustrated history of Liverpool using these old slides and a reel-to-reel tape recording in sections, which lasted five and one-half hours in all! I also attempted a spontaneous "voice over" with music. This crude production by any standards was not a success, but I wanted to absorb public attention by sharing with me an enthusiasm for these early paintings and photographs.[34]

Such small beginnings prepared me for the photographic riches in Alberta and New Brunswick, so that later both documentary art and photographs in the Public Archives of Canada had my full support in my crusade for administration in terms of "media divisions," which were quite successful in the 1970s. Times have changed since then, and I have no knowledge on how things stand now twenty years on in terms of respect and space accorded to media archives. But I cannot praise too highly those archivists who were determined to bring images into the mainstream of archival activity as they developed theoretical bases which came to justify their archival nature whenever this was possible. An excellent example is Joan Schwartz's case for the validity of some aspects of diplomatics in relation to photographs. A few years ago this kind of archival thinking would have been unthinkable.[35]

NOTES

1. Walter Rundell, Jr., "Photographs as Historical Evidence: Early Texas Oil," *American Archivist* 41 (October 1978): 373–91.

2. Barry Lord, *The History of Painting in Canada* (Toronto: New Canada Publications, NG Press, 1974), pp. 12–13.

3. Marshall McLuhan, *The Gutenberg Galaxy* (Toronto: University of Toronto Press, 1968), passim.

4. Ibid., p. 78.

5. Otto Pächt, *The Rise of Pictorial Narrative in Twelfth-Century England* (Oxford, England: Clarendon Press, 1962), p. 10.

6. John Berger, *Ways of Seeing* (Harmondsworth, England: Penguin Books, 1976), p. 10.

7. J. Huizinga, *The Waning of the Middle Ages* (London: Edward Arnold, 1970), p. 253.

8. Donald R. Gordon, "Print as a Visual Medium," in Lester Asheim and Sara I. Fenwick, eds., *Differentiating the Media* (Chicago: University of Chicago Press, 1974), p. 34.

9. R. G. Collingwood, *The Principles of Art* (Oxford: Oxford University Press, 1938), p. 5.

10. Andre Malraux, *The Psychology of Art*, Vol. 2, *The Creative Act* (New York: Pantheon Books, 1949), p. 73.

11. Collingwood, *Principles of Art*, p. 42.

12. Ibid., p. 53.

13. As quoted in Michael Bell and W. Martha E. Cooke, *The Last "Lion" . . . Rambles in Quebec with James Pattison Cockburn* (Kingston, Ont.: Agnes Etherington Art Centre, 1978), p. 12.

14. Graham Reynolds, *A Concise History of Watercolours* (London: Thames & Hudson, Ltd., 1971), p. 55.

15. Paul Duval, *Canadian Watercolour Painting* (Toronto: Burns & MacEachern, Ltd., 1954), text unpaginated. Duval quotes one of these systems.

16. See Mary Sparling, "The British Vision in Nova Scotia, 1749–1848" (unpublished M.A. thesis, Dalhousie University, Halifax, N.S.) for an excellent study of this theme. For a well-illustrated survey of early Canadian topographical art, matched with contemporary textual description, see Michael Bell, *Painters in a New Land* (Toronto: McClelland & Stewart, Ltd., 1973).

17. Christina Cameron and Jean Trudel, *The Drawings of James Cockburn: A Visit through Quebec's Past* (Agincourt, Ont.: Gage Educational Publishing, Ltd., 1976), Introduction.

18. E. H. Gombrich, *Art and Illusion* (Princeton, N.J.: Princeton University Press, 1972), chapter 5, "Formula and Experience," pp. 146–78.

19. Etienne Gilson, *Painting and Reality* (London: Routledge & Kegan Paul, Ltd., 1958), p. 261.

20. Rudolph Arnheim, *Visual Thinking* (Berkeley: University of California Press, 1969), p. v.

21. Bernard Berenson, *Seeing and Knowing* (London: Chapman & Hall, Ltd., 1953), p. 14.

22. Gombrich, *Art and Illusion*, p. 38.

23. Berenson, *Seeing and Knowing*, p. 11.

24. Malraux, *The Psychology of Art*, Vol. 1, *Museum without Walls*, p. 73.

25. Public Archives of Canada, *Karl May Retrospective, 1948–1975* (Ottawa: Public Archives of Canada, 1976), 62 pp.

26. Sacheverell Sitwell, *Narrative Pictures: A Survey of English Genre and Its Painters* (New York: Benjamin Blom, Inc., 1972), p. 1.

27. What appears to be the only paper ever published by the *Canadian Historical Review (CHR)* on historical iconography is "The Visual Reconstruction of History," by C. W. Jefferys (*CHR* 17, no. 3 [1936]: 249–65), who discusses the whole question of accuracy in Canadian historical painting and illustration. As a competent artist and illustrator himself, his observations are particularly valuable.

28. Karl J. Weintraub, *Visions of Culture* (Chicago: University of Chicago Press, 1966), p. 153.

29. Ibid., p. 155.

30. Estelle Jussim, "The Research Uses of Visual Information," *Library Trends 25*, no. 4 (April 1977): 763–78.

31. Marshall McLuhan, *The Mechanical Bride* (New York: Vanguard Press, 1951), p. vi.

32. H. J. Barrington Nevitt, "Archivist and Comprehensivist," unpublished paper, 1978, pp. 3, 6.

33. Since most of the examples of documentary art which have been discussed above are Canadian, I would not like to close without special mention of Robert V. Hine whose *Bartlett's West: Drawing the Mexican Boundary* (New Haven: Yale University Press, 1968) and *The American West: An Interpretive History* (Boston: Little, Brown and Co., 1973) strongly emphasize the pictorial record.

34. Hugh Taylor, "Local History: An Experiment with Slides and Tapes," *Archives* 5 no. 27 (1962): 142–44.

35. Joan M. Schwartz, "'We make our tools and our tools make us': Lessons from Photographs for the Practice, Politics and Poetics of Diplomatics," *Archivaria* 40 (Fall 1995): 40–74.

Chapter 8

Information Ecology and the Archives of the 1980s

Stéphane Mallarmé once wrote, "To define is to kill: to suggest is to create," and I hope you will not be disappointed if at the outset I fail to define "ecology of information." Ecology is something of a buzzword these days, but it suggests a nonaggressive stewardship, a sensitive interplay, and an ongoing enrichment of resources in contrast to those exploitive analogies with which we are all so familiar. I therefore make no apologies for using it, for it lies behind much of our work today.

The theme of this issue of *Archivaria* is "Archives and the Law," and I would remind you that, in the public sector, law as popularly understood generates bureaucracy and bureaucracy creates the record. Law and the evidence of government became locked into forms of words and language, but in preliterate societies it was the poet and the shaman, the Greek mnemon and the Celtic bard, who recalled and rehearsed the customs and traditions of their people "when the memory of men runneth not to the contrary," to use a medieval phrase. Words then did not have specific meanings, but were closely related to their context and to actions arising from that context. Speech and action, attested by witnesses if need be, constituted the record to be retained in the memory. With the emergence of writing and the creation of documents, the ancient practice gradually changed, though not without considerable resistance.[1] For the greater part of the scribal age, actions remained a part of transactions; the document was merely the "copy" of the event which might include deeds, gifts of crosses, and symbolic transfers of turf. Vestiges of this still remain in the

---

Originally published in *Archivaria* 18 (Summer 1984): 25–37. Reproduced with the kind permission of the author, *Archivaria*, and the Association of Canadian Archivists.

red spots serving as seals on title deeds, and in groundbreaking or rope-cutting ceremonies. The reality and importance of the *signum*, the act, over the document may be illustrated by the demand of bank tellers that your cheque be signed in their presence. We need to bear this principle in mind when we seek to answer questions concerning "originals" and "copies" which may involve two different media of record and communication as in machine-readable archives where we speak of the "memory" in which the original is stored over against the paper printout. These are analogies which must not be pushed too far but, as we shall see, the nature of the record has an important bearing on the role of the archivist and the centrality of that function to the conduct of affairs.

It is only in comparatively recent times that the document has come to be perceived as the original reality, the "instrument," tangible, concrete, and immensely powerful as evidence in a visually oriented society, the words trapped in the illusion that they have only one meaning—to the delight of lawyers ever since. So valued were these evidences under the law that records of royal administration came to be stored with the royal treasure, and the French *Tresor des chartes* in the *Archives nationales* reminds us of their ancient status. In England during the Middle Ages, the senior royal administrators were never far from their seals and rolls. The Keepers of the Record remained at the heart of the administration and their scribes developed their own forms of writing, now called "set" hands. The legal value of the material ensured its survival then and for centuries, long after the administration of national affairs had passed into other hands. Canadian land registries are the direct descendants of these rolls, and the term "Crown land" reaches back to the day when all land was deemed to be held of the king.

And so to the age of paper, printing, and extensive literacy. The bureaucracy of the Elizabethan Secretaries would have been quite familiar to us, and they and their successors stored their records in the State Paper Office, which was both a "records centre" and an archives. The medieval rolls entered a kind of twilight—still of some value at law, but increasingly the happy territory of the pamphleteer and the antiquary. Nevertheless, they remained within their departments of origin, shadowy though these had become. By the 1780s the records were scattered among hundreds of little repositories, where the keepers levied quite stiff fees and maintained their finding aids (such as they were) as their personal property.

Meanwhile, the "national memory" that was readily retrievable in the administration became much shorter. For the ruling elite, this reality of the English remote past had become distasteful and irrelevant, totally fractured by an age which patterned itself on an idealized classical model. The Keeper of the Record in many cases had been reduced to a clerical hack or an anomalous predator hired by a political sinecurist.

As is well known, the French Revolution had a profound effect on the perception of early records which, up to that time, had still been viewed as the evidences and records of the offices of origin and still been maintained by them—still, at least in theory, "active." At one stroke, the creation of the *Archives nationales* sundered the ancient records from their roots, placed them in common archives, and, in effect, labelled them "historical." The modern archivist was born and the historical archives emerged, essentially as a repository of raw material for the historian who, using von Ranke's model as a prototype, would mine their rich veins of documentary evidence and found one of the most awesome heavy industries to come out of the age of steam!

The English approach reflected a totally different set of circumstances, but the results were virtually the same. Insofar as there was renewed interest in the early records during the Augustan age, it was to illustrate the evolution of an incomparable British Constitution. David Hume's immensely influential *History of England,* first published in 1752, became the ancestor of the German historical school, and Whiggish constitutional history was to preponderate in England for almost a century. It was this kind of pressure which led to the passing of the Public Records Act in 1838 and the establishment of the Public Record Office (PRO).

In the best tradition of legal fictions, a seemly appearance of continuity was maintained under the Act: the old Chancery repository, The Rolls Chapel, was first absorbed and then demolished; the earlier contents of the State Paper Office were also deposited in the Public Record Office; the Master of the Rolls, as Keeper, presided over the new institution whose administrator remained only Deputy Keeper until 1958. Certainly the ancient rolls continued to maintain their legal value, and Jenkinson was quite right later to stress unbroken custody in this context as a cornerstone of archives administration. It must be remembered, however, that for many years the deposit of departmental records remained voluntary and, until the Grigg Report of the 1950s and subsequent legislation, largely at the mercy of the administrations concerned.

Thus, the documentary record became central to the writing of history; the multifaceted, rich life of the so-called Middle Ages stood revealed; something akin to a scientific approach to the methodology of history developed, resulting from time to time in a marvellous union with literature and creative writing. The partnership of archivist and historian helped to advance our knowledge of the complexity of human affairs and the uniqueness of the individual, whatever else might be discerned in the broader sweep of events. Yet we have always remained deceptively far from the reality of "what actually happened," as we always will if we continue to ask this kind of question.

Perhaps it was the apparent impartiality of this new history which traduced the old keepers of the records and their masters into believing that in some way they, the historians, would make the past once and for all as intelligible and interconnected as the present appeared to be, and that all would be elegantly revealed without perhaps any further recourse to the records save on points of detail. Was "scientific" history seen by some of the emerging new archivists of the nineteenth century as a kind of integrated "finding aid" to the past, developed on historical principles, much as we dream today of that great data bank in the sky where all is recorded and retrievable to reveal ultimate synthesis and wisdom as a kind of mythopoeic counterpart?

I suggest that in Britain, across Europe, and so too in the United States and Canada, the old record keepers were caught up in a vast "historical shunt" during which the best curatorial minds and intellects were devoted to scholarship and the historian. The results, as we have seen, were as valuable as they were inevitable.

In England, the Public Records Act legitimized the divorce of the mainstream of records administration from the historical legal records which, as "the people's evidences," were generally regarded as the only "public records," in contrast almost to what might be called the "private" records of government officials which were notoriously inaccessible, and it is interesting that Jenkinson used not only the phrase "in their own custody" but also the phrase "for their own reference" in his famous definition of archives. Government records were for the business of ministers and bureaucrats and for their eyes only.

Departments were, however, permitted to deposit material in the PRO and there were signs that they used the new buildings as a convenient warehouse, but the Master of the Rolls never ordered departmental records into his custody even when they were in the PRO since he could not exercise authority over ministers of the Crown. This was still true in 1954. There was even a move afoot to reserve the PRO for legal records only and place the rest in the British Museum.

Administrative historians are largely silent about the effectiveness of departmental record-keeping systems from the sixteenth century, although there have of course been descriptions of their process. Ministers conducted their affairs in a highly personal way and many of their papers returned to their private estates. I rather suspect that, as the state business grew, paper became less and less retrievable, policies were based on less accrued evidence, and the useful life of records decreased sharply. In time, ministers came to leave a great deal of general administration to their clerks and, with their increase in education and executive skills, the "mandarins" emerged—men who had sat at the feet of historians, who had in turn used the European archives in the service of the diplomatic history of earlier courts and periods, and who coloured their students' thinking accordingly with preconceptions of what diplomacy should be like. As William Irwin Thompson has reminded us:

> History, by definition, is a civilized, literate record of events; it is a conscious self-image of a society projected by an elite. In a sense, history is the self-image of a culture, the ego of a culture. History is controlled through education and tradition, and is monitored, if not manipulated, by elitist institutions, whether these are temples, academies, or universities. History is the story told by the elite in power and is a way of articulating human time so that it reinforces the institutional power of the elite. One of the ways the British maintained Ireland as a colony was through the writing of history. The actual role of the Irish monks and the Irish centers of learning in maintaining knowledge in the Dark Ages was blanked out, and on that blank slate even brilliant men like David Hume wrote that there was no culture in Ireland until it was brought in by the conquering Normans in the twelfth century. So historical consciousness is closely related to power and the ego of a society. For these reasons, Voltaire said that 'history is the lie commonly agreed upon.'[2]

Meanwhile, the record keeping in government departments seems to have remained generally adequate, though no studies have been made as to how effective this was. Policy and administration were based on the limited, fragmented, and classified information available, and the registry system which thus developed was to make a sharp impact on archival theory. The records were preserved when the system worked effectively, but to what extent was the information contained in the records retrievable by the administrator? This limitation would have had its effect on policy formation and the whole bureaucratic structure.

It might be argued that, of course, records management as conceived in the United States and elsewhere was the answer. Yet records management emerged more as an economical measure, linked with efficiency, often at the cost of effectiveness. The system dealt admirably with housekeeping records and operational records at the series level, but failed to secure control of deputy ministers' correspondence and those files which lived with the administrators and died when they left office, if not long before—perhaps after only two years. Not surprisingly, the wheel was constantly reinvented as new ground had to be broken. Many planning documents lacked sufficient depth to make them realistic.

The capture or initiation of control over records management by archival institutions did not solve this problem, because all that was added was a component called "historically" (or more recently "permanently") valuable material being scheduled for preservation for research purposes once it arrived in the archives. There was no way in which archivists could enhance the record's effectiveness while it was still active with the administrations, beyond ensuring that appropriate filing systems were in place through records management. Archivists were clearly viewed by everyone as being at the far end of the continuum, as "historical research officers" or whatever the term might be. In an age when present and past could be clearly distinguished, no one expected the bulk of records to yield more than a limited amount of information without a vast amount of research, only possible when the records become historical; at best, the system works tolerably well.

The electronic revolution and, in particular, automation are rapidly changing all this as we move out of the hard-edged sequential and linear visual space to once more the much older acoustic space of preliterate man. Barrington Nevitt has written:

> Visual and acoustic space structures not only represent contradictory aspects of existence, but also opposite psychic preferences of literate and nonliterate people. Visual space is a sanctum created by civilized man, just as acoustic space is a habitat inherited by natural man. For example, when a preliterate Eskimo draws a picture, he draws not only what he can see, but also what he knows is there. When asked which side of his drawing is up, he will laugh. For preliterate people have inclusive awareness, but no exclusive point of view. When a Canadian geologist accompanying a band of Indians on a survey once remarked 'We're lost,' they burst out laughing and said, 'We not lost. Wigwam lost.' Although the geologist got lost by losing his bearings, tribal people are never lost in their own environment. The preschool child has similar space perception, even in strange environments, as did the little girl who was crying because she had lost her parents while wandering about in city streets. When asked by a sympathetic adult: 'Are you lost, little one?', she insisted, 'I'm not lost, I'm here.'[3]

This is not for a moment to suggest that we will somehow dispense with reading, writing, and print, but rather that we will become truly literati, that is "learned," in our perception and understanding of other media of communication and recover those insights lost to us through an emphasis on textual literacy.

A world which is exchanging relatively static centres and margins for centres everywhere and margins nowhere, has also become very dangerous as vast issues, such as national sovereignty and security through force and threat of force in the nuclear age, are called into question. To return to our own field of interest, archivists are not faced with cooperation or annihilation in the physical sense (though this may be true professionally if we are not careful). We see all our comfortable verities dissolving: the autocratic (or just fatherly) national archives with its preponderant resources staking out national perspectives, to some extent in competition with a welter of little fiefdoms in the provinces going it alone with all that vigorous independence which we once so much enjoyed; our delightfully

idiosyncratic and persistently incompatible finding aids, and even our notion that all our records are in every sense "unique" in contrast to printed
books; and our self-satisfaction with our service to the user without really
being aware that users (who are a patient and grateful lot by and large)
get what they want or know what they can get despite our finding aids
which barely scratch the surface of the potentially retrievable and valuable information in our custody. Instead, the Wilson Report reveals belea-
guered whales and stranded minnows struggling to survive in a new environment where national archives are only first among equals
(depending where you stand), networks are replacing sturdy independence, information cries out to be moved and merged, and the popular
emphasis is no longer on history but on heritage with all its multimedia
implications. Meanwhile, automation continues its inroads into government, industry, and even the home; rapid and accurate information is essential and the competition to provide increasingly cost-effective hardware and software is fierce. What is the archivist's role in all this?

It seems to me that this is our opportunity to enter once more the mainstream of record keeping and move out of the "historical shunt." We will
always have to care for and service our inheritance of permanently valuable documents which will continue to be used in a greater or lesser degree for the writing of history as we know it, and there must always be
what I will call "scholar archivists" to meet this demand and carry out research in such areas as modern diplomatics in support of both archivists
and historians.[4]

At the same time, we must be prepared to abandon the concept of
archives as bodies of "historical" records over against so-called active
records which are put to sleep during their dormant years prior to salvation or extinction. Records are active in direct proportion to the relevant
information that can be retrieved from them, and dormancy is closely related to the inability to retrieve information. This is particularly true of
correspondence files, case papers, and of many separate routine transactions incapable of an aggregation which might enhance their value. On
the other hand, machine-readable records can be analyzed by administrators, historians, and other academics with equal facility and on equal
terms. The archivist as intermediary preparing intractable historical
records, long since abandoned by administrators, for painstaking and
protracted research by the scholar with the help of manual retrieval systems, is no longer required for the automated record. (Although, of
course, data archivists have to appraise, validate, and document the automated record among their duties.) Now is the time for archivists to be
present at the creation of documents, to ensure that they are designed not
only to serve immediate administrative ends, but also administrative/
historical research for policy planning and development.

It may be necessary from time to time to recognize quasi-archival functions within administrative departments of government where the nature of the records resists public access over long periods or where there is prolonged administrative use in situ, often as a result of effective retrieval systems. This becomes increasingly true where machine-readable archives are concerned and presents challenges to traditional archival concepts which have to be carefully examined. In all these circumstances, the archivist should play a creative and supportive role close to the administration.

I would like to give an example of what I mean by examining archival values at the time of creation, although in this particular case archivists were not involved. In the early years of Medicare in Saskatchewan, doctors were able to claim expenses dating back to the beginning of the scheme, with no cutoff date for submitting their accounts. In consequence, the automated record had to be kept "on record" and a valuable resource for the pattern of medical treatment of all kinds could be aggregated and analyzed for years to come. I do not know whether these tapes are still preserved. When I later raised this question in Nova Scotia, no such regulations were in force and consequently the tapes were erased.

We should then, by the nature of our training, be thoroughly equipped not so much with a knowledge of academic history as with a knowledge of automation, communication theory, records management, diplomatics, and the use of records in administration—a vast and little explored intellectual field with historical dimensions of great importance. Good archivists are not, and never have been, limited to those with extensive historical training. I suspect this may become increasingly true.

If there are to be archivists within departments, what then is the role of the central archival repository and how will the user be affected? First, departments should be prepared to hire persons with archival training to function primarily as communicators of the record and its contents to administrators in need of information, even on a long-term basis. When such records cease to have even this extended use in departments, they would be transferred directly to the central archival repository, and the departmental finding aids (far more sophisticated than at present) would be shared with the repository if this was not already the case. Housekeeping records and those with small research value, which have to be retained for a term, would continue to go to the Records Centre. The head of the repository would retain a veto on all destruction as is usual at present.

The object of this arrangement would be to prevent information potentially useful to the department from lying dormant, and at the same time be in ultimate danger of destruction for want of a thorough understanding of its subsequent value, both short and long term, which departmental archivists would perceive.

Records received at the central repository would be for general public use, but researchers might well have improved access to records still in departments where archivists rather than clerical personnel would be in a better position to serve them perhaps under more liberal freedom of information guidelines. There would have to be a very close relationship between all archivists within such a network; departmental loyalties and priorities would have to be respected, but resources to aid research for both academic pursuits and government policymaking could be considerably enriched. Is this an impossible dream?

Given the changed information environment, we should increasingly encourage major institutions in the private sector to make use of the archivist not just as resident historian and custodian of the historical records, but as one versed in the whole nature of documentation and its implications—capable of supervising archives and records management, forms analysis (which is a modern concept of diplomatics) and information management generally, or working closely enough with others in these fields to achieve the desired results whereby legal, administrative, and historical values are enhanced.

If we can become overarching information generalists with an archival emphasis, we will be able to bring to bear what should be a deep and thorough knowledge of the documentary life-cycle theory to which we now perhaps rather glibly assent. It may be our most important asset in relation to (I do not say in competition with) our colleagues, the librarians and other information specialists, who in time are likely to become not so much separate professions as special skills within a larger and more encompassing occupational group which, in fact, may cease to be a "profession" as we understand the term. Centres, margins, and other demarcations will become a problem here as elsewhere.

This is not the place for a lengthy discussion of the heritage phenomenon, but suffice it to say that here is a grass-roots movement having much in common with other groups involved with the environment, participatory democracy, and personal identity. It embraces far more than literary history and, at its most perceptive, transcends genealogy and antiquarianism. It certainly requires of the archivist a more holistic approach to the past and a new relationship with museums and art galleries, which again is a move away from the traditional role of an archivist in the local context.

These grass-roots movements are closely dependent on freedom of information, and they have helped materially in extending the boundaries of "public records," which should be accessible to the public long before they reach the archives. The monopoly over certain information by government is being vigorously and quite properly challenged by interest groups who wish to join in well-informed debate requiring political decisions. Much of this information has been gathered at public expense and should be seen as the "people's evidences" of today but, if it is to be accessible, it must also be retrievable by the government as (if you like) the historical records of the most immediate past, which are no longer so easily distinguished from traditional (and older) historical records. For these first kinds of records are also the records upon which the public policies are formulated, and yet the information is not as retrievable as it should be.

To return to the public service administration, I would like to offer three quotations taken from *Optimum* and, therefore, having a Canadian context and relevance. Berliner and Bork wrote in 1977:

> Historically, little information has been available for making policy decisions. Therefore, the question might be asked—is this information really essential? Since policies are the vehicles through which individuals and governments try to achieve selected objectives and, since good policies are almost always based on accurate and complete information, the answer to this question must be a resounding 'yes.' Policies not based on this type of information often result in the implementation of decisions quite different from those desired. Policies based on incorrect, incomplete or disjointed data result in the wrong information being communicated to the wrong person at the wrong time. . . . Good information does not make good executives, but the contribution is enormous. With good information, they at least have a fighting chance, without it, they are reduced to exclusively depending upon luck.[5]

Two years later, Allan Cahoon wrote:

> The consensus of persons attempting to understand the environment of public administrators today is the recognition of an increasingly complex organizational and administrative environment. A rational approach to policy making under these conditions requires the building of administrative machinery capable of using up-to-date methods for the collection, computation, analysis and dissemination of information. Public administrators need to be capable of forecasting and projecting the requirements of government. Government can no longer function as a close-knit, in-house decision group; instead it requires an eclectic approach to public-policy management. There is an increasing concern for issue analysis as opposed to the more traditional specific program analysis. This produces a philosophical conflict between the public administrator's professional discipline orientation, and the need for system-wide organizational integration in decision making. . . .
>
> Because of the demand for more open government, public servants may very well be required to appear before parliamentary committees on a continuing and systematic basis. A main concern is that public servants, in trying to explain the relationship between the programs they are administering and the stated objectives of those programs, will simply not have a reasonable amount of relevant information arranged in a disciplined manner to discuss with parliamentarians. This could be disastrous.[6]

But the Treasury Board in a pilot project for the Task Force on Privacy and Access to Information found that

> One of the major problems identified from the project was the difficulty in associating groups of records with those administrators who have primary interest in their content. For accessibility to be effective, clear information linkages must be established. This difficulty with linkages raises a serious question as to *the inherent ability of government to respond to its own information needs, much less to external access requests.* Agencies with linkage difficulties will be required to spend significant resources to correct problems in and neglect of their information systems, policies and practices. These required expenditures do not result from ATI; rather, the problem has been forcibly highlighted in preparing for the access legislation.[7]

Surely this problem of "linkages" is familiar to archivists?

I would like to suggest that there is in reality no break between the "current" and "archival" record and that this is a fiction of the historical method. There is a pressing need by government and public alike for more effective retrieval and for an archival training which recognises this continuum and which could provide information specialists of appropriate calibre to work both in departments and in archives. This principle would equally apply to large institutions in the private sector. This action would take the profession out of the "historical shunt" and back into the administrative levels of departmental record keeping and among the policy makers where we belong.

As we become more secure in our perceived role, this would be a good time to examine the nature of the problems facing our colleagues, the librarians and information specialists, since some of them may have a commonality that deserves joint study. Certainly, we both administer (along with art museums) common media in printed maps and some aspects of audiovisual materials, such as paintings, drawings, prints, photographs, and film. Librarians are concerned about increasing levels of retrieval in monographs beyond bibliographical authorities and a few limited subject headings. Retrieval from full text descriptive abstracts in the manner of scientific serials or from chapter headings is being discussed. As David Bearman has pointed out, library catalogues deal with authorities rather than subject content and so does much archival description. Does the scope and content note of the so-called manuscript curator and the administrative/descriptive summary of the records archivist offer a parallel? Is this all too impressionistic, and do we need a hierarchical approach based on arrangement and carefully identified subgroups implying much subject content from their titles, as Richard Berner maintains? We may well have to seek formats which accommodate both approaches since the greater proportion of our descriptions is of the former kind. In any case, librarians and archivists should learn to speak a common language on this, even if solutions are widely different as we become increasingly literate in automation, and we must avoid disdaining this kind of literacy as jargon. Likewise, Estelle Jussim has drawn attention to her fellow librarians' failure to convey visual information through textual description, a problem which also faces us as archivists.

What then should we be doing at this time of scarce and sometimes shrinking financial resources? Some recent publications offer us admirable insights and guidelines: the Wilson Report, which is familiar to all Canadian archivists, and those reports issued by the National Information Systems Task Force of the Society of American Archivists written by David Bearman and Robert Lytle, together with the draft Data Elements Dictionary produced by the same Task Force. Both these bodies are notable for their clearly defined if sometimes controversial priorities, and both deserve our careful study. NISTF wisely moved away from its original mandate of trying to decide on one national system as between either the NARS 1 SPINDEX or the NUCMC model to consider the nature of the problem, the role of networks, and the need for standard communication formats between a multiplication of data bases. Bearman points out that networks (not necessarily automated) may be of value for sharing common needs, such as authority lists, in the first instance, rather than documentary content. In any case, the final step must be to define standard data elements and with this we may well agree. I remember how we set up just such a task force for the Archives Branch in the PAC and struggled with AACR2. Is there some further experience there to be shared? Certainly, Canadian archivists should grapple with standards of arrangement and description *now* if we are to fulfill our role in the electronic information environment.

I hope that the user is seen to be present in all that has been said so far. Whatever we may contend about custody, the other polarity of the archival dialectic is access and use, which makes for creative stresses and tensions as we seek resolution and synthesis. The move on the part of many archivists to distance themselves from any special relationship with historians has caused much concern to historians and "historian archivists"[8] and may be another sign that we are moving out of the "historical shunt." When Sir Hilary Jenkinson and Dr. Felix Hull declared that an archivist should not be an historian, they certainly did not mean that most archivists should avoid the study of history as part of their professional preparation. Most archivists have, and new recruits will continue to have, a background in history; few would agree, however, that it is exclusively essential.[9] The English Public Record Office has in the past recruited many classics graduates (Sir Hilary himself being an example) as an admirable preparation for the study of medieval records and diplomatics. What Jenkinson, Hull,

North, and others are saying is that there are professional archivists and professional historians with a profound difference of outlook which does not turn on techniques, but on the relationship to the record. The archivist is primarily concerned with the communication of the record to the user through preservation and all the subsequent processes with which users have become familiar. The historian (among other users of archives) exploits and interprets the evidence of the record for the user. The archivist must become aware of the documentary context of the record, both administrative and in terms of its form, which requires a study of diplomatics, ancient and modern, set within the larger frame of culture and society. Archivists have their time cut out performing these functions and their scholarly background, historical or otherwise, will help them in this task. Substantial historical writing should generally be restricted to the amateur part of their lives.

I do not deny that the first-class scholar archivist or "historian archivist" may bring a great deal of weight and insight to the record which we can all value, but I believe that the average professional archivist requires a "good second class" degree with evidence of skill in "archive administration" (to use an English term) which should not be confused with bureaucratic "management," although they are to some extent related. Experience with the *specific* records of an institution can be gained on the job. This is not an academic pursuit, nor is it a job for records managers or insensitive bureaucrats.

From time to time I have stressed my reluctance to "professionalize" the archivist because I believe certain forms of professionalism can be excessively conservative and restrictive. This should not be confused with standards of excellence towards which we quite properly strive. I must reiterate that the archivist, as keeper of the record, administers and communicates by means of insights which are not limited to those of the historian, and as time goes by the historical approach may itself seem more and more restrictive. This is no more crucial than in the field of documentary appraisal for preservation, which does not depend solely on historical principles.

I do not believe that historians now or in the future will have any more reason to be disappointed with archivists than we may be with our friends the historians. We all have our limitations. We will not have preserved all that their hearts and minds desire, but as always we will provide some surprises which may compensate as a result of an essentially extra-professional approach! Most archivists learn to be generalists, and their skill and judgement lies here as we deal with the whole spectrum of document survival. There will also be specialists in media or content (including historians with Ph.D.s). Our effectiveness will depend on a reasonable mix.

Perhaps the use of the term "ecology of information" in my title is now clearer. Both the records and the information they contain must be husbanded with the greatest of care if there is to be a fertile crop of knowledge and wisdom forthcoming. Last year I attended an absorbing lecture by Dr. Wes Jackson, one of the pioneers of sustainable agriculture. He spoke about the impact of agriculture on society as a form of quasi-industrial exploitation of the soil which is as old as civilization, and how the monoculture of highly specialized annual cereals, with the aid of chemicals as fertilizer and insecticide, destroyed and eroded the soil and may end by destroying us through starvation. In contrast, he described the marvellously variegated, flexible, mutually dependant, and self-sustaining grasses of the old prairie from which food crops were being bred to live and thrive together, in a similar way, to give a heavy perennial yield partly through a complex interchange of organic, chemical, and genetic "information." Specialized monoculture, fragile, vulnerable, and heavily dependent on external energy, Jackson described as "information poor." The sustainable counterpart was, in his words, "information rich." Are not archives, according to Jenkinson, the secretions of an organism? I cannot think of a better analogy to justify my title.

Other articles in this volume will develop the theme "Archives and the Law," and we use "the Law" in this way to mean the regulation of social practices by statute. We are quite right to concern ourselves with such matters, but we should remember that we are subject to laws of quite another order. We are part of all life on earth, subject to mysteries, rhythms, and cycles about which scientific discovery may be silent or misleading, but whose meaning may be revealed by the great myths distilled from human experience. This is the law beyond our control, but not necessarily beyond our understanding, which the archivist as shaman should seek to reflect and recognize in that which we preserve for the postliterate future:

Forms of knowledge change as society changes. Sometimes these changes are small and incremental; at other times the changes are transformations of the 'structures' of knowledge and not merely the 'contents.' From religion to philosophy, from alchemy to chemistry, from legend to history, the social organization of knowledge changes as a new elite comes in to challenge the old authorities. But this movement is not simply a linear and one-directional shift toward increasing rationalization and demystification; when the rational historian has come in to take away the authority from the mystical and tribal bard, the artist has returned to create new forms of expression to re-sacralize, re-enchant, remythologize.[10]

Perhaps "record keeping in a mythopoeic age" would be a good theme for a future conference of the Association of Canadian Archivists or a future issue of the journal.[11] I suspect it will be after my time.

REFLECTION, 2000

The context of this essay was an Association of Canadian Archivists' conference with the theme "Archives and the Law." I wanted to make the point that archivists should regard all forms of communication as technologies to be transcended if the role of the archivist was to be extended and capable of recognising meaning in all its forms, reached through hermeneutics, exploration, discourse and suggestion. The theme was also to serve as a counterpoint to recent statutory transactions by legislatures, and their administration and management by government bureaucracies, with the recent record as evidence, a commodity reaching the hands of the archivist in due course for public use which was believed to speak clearly and directly through text and image.

These records are normally in the hands of records managers who are primarily concerned with control and retrieval. There seemed to me a role here for departmental archivists who enriched the value of information in the records through a concentration on meaning, relevance, and relational understanding, the "extended memory" of legislators and administrators. All this was before the digital possibilities which we now enjoy, but I believe the principle still holds.

This raises the question to what extent do policy makers (as opposed to historians) depend on a memory of the past. Would access through the kind of archivist I had in mind be of value? I do not know the answer to this because, so far as I can gather, very little research has been done in this field. Critics of the essay were very perceptive, especially Terry Cook and Tom Nesmith who laid bare a lack of clarity on my part and resulted in my rejoinder,[12] which is itself a reflection on what I had written in the light of their comments. So far as I can judge we have now dispensed with hyphenated archivists as we recognise the immense possibilities of a truly holistic profession which still eludes simple definition and probably always will. Thanks to the writings of Brien Brothman, Richard Brown, Terry Cook, and others, we can now see much more clearly the limitations of archival material viewed from a positivist perspective and the subjectivity of appraisal techniques upon which our collective memory depends.

This was the kind of meaning I was groping for when I contrasted "information rich" with "information poor" and began to apply this analogy to our profession by using as an example the grasslands of the virgin prairie contrasted with the monoculture of agribusiness which ignores and destroys the information systems in the soil. Processing departmental records series approached in the traditional manner, out of context with the whole bureaucratic structure, and ignoring human bias in the process, creates an approach to information poverty. Going further, the records available for environmental studies, for instance, to be found in public records, and the fonds of NGOs and businesses involved in this field, which all taken together are becoming so essential for our survival, will require an approach by archivists that spans all media, as threads of knowledge are disentangled from a broad span of related sources, if the results are to be "infor-

mation rich." If we can do this then our value will be fully recognised and our services regarded as essential.

Corporate society usually abhors this past and looks only towards a developing and progressive future of ever-more wealth and power; and thus corporate memories will extend no further than a self-serving history. Consequently, available business archives are relatively scarce. The vital records of the citizen will also include those which will assist tomorrow's society and a culture which will value its natural organic past along with those pioneers who helped turn us from the present environmental abyss. We have a long way to go.

NOTES

1. M. T. Clanchy, *From Memory to Written Record: England 1066–1307* (Cambridge, 1979), pp. 231–57.

2. William Irwin Thompson, *Darkness and Scattered Light: Four Talks on the Future* (New York, 1978), p. 107.

3. Barrington Nevitt, *The Communication Ecology* (Toronto, 1982), p. 12.

4. For an excellent article on this role, see Tom Nesmith, "Archives from the Bottom Up: Social History and Archival Scholarship," *Archivaria* 14 (Summer 1982): 5–26.

5. Thomas H. Berliner and Cloene Bork, "The Role of Information in Public Sector Policy Making," *Optimum* 8, no. 2 (1977): 58.

6. Allan R. Cahoon, "The Modern Professional Public Administrator: From Monitor to Integrator," *Optimum* 10, no. 1 (1979): 54.

7. Timothy H. Reid, "The Failure of PPBS: Real Incentives for the 1980s (The past is not prologue)," *Optimum* 10, no. 5 (1979): 53.

8. For example, see George Bolotenko, "Archivists and Historians: Keepers of the Well," *Archivaria* 16 (Summer 1983): 5–25.

9. Michael Cook has also stressed this point: "A variety of first degrees provides a valuable base for a student group, and the expanding needs for archival management in specialist areas, particularly in science and research institutes, may mean that there will be some demand for archivists with a grounding in the natural sciences. More generally, it is an important requirement that archivists must emerge from their training able and confident in undertaking research which uses documentary evidence." Michael Cook, *Guidelines for Curriculum Development in Records Management and the Administration of Modern Archives: A RAMP Study* (Paris, 1982), p. 31.

10. William Irwin Thompson, *The Time Failing Bodies Take to Light: Mythology, Sexuality and the Origins of Culture* (New York, 1981), p. 34.

11. "Myth is not an early level of human development, but an imaginative description of reality in which the known is related to the unknown through a system of correspondence in which mind and matter, self, society, and cosmos are integrally expressed in an esoteric language of poetry and number which is itself a performance of the reality it seeks to describe. Myth expresses the deep correspondence between 'the universal grammar' of the mind and the universal

grammar of events in space-time. A hunk of words does not create a language, and a hunk of matter does not create a cosmos. The structures by which and through which man realizes the intellectual resonance between himself and the universe of which he is a part are his mathematical, musical, and verbal creations. Mediating between Nous and Cosmos is the Logos." William Irwin Thompson, *At the Edge of History* (New York, 1972), p. 191.

12. Hugh Taylor, "Through the Minefield," *Archivaria* 21 (Winter 1985–86): 180–85.

Chapter 9

Transformation in the Archives: Technological Adjustment or Paradigm Shift?

THE TRANSFORMATION OF CULTURE

If there is one symbol which epitomizes the relationship of the archivist to the automated record (whether document or finding aid), it is surely the transformer toy which presently delights young boys. The most ingenious are designed all of a piece as ambiguous constructs filled with options ranging from robots to rockets to racing cars; the pattern changes, the meaning changes, the information changes, but the data—the given "bits"—remain the same. Contrast this with the jigsaw puzzle fractured into a thousand separate pieces which has only one solution, one answer, one option. The jigsaw is also popular, but its form is very much a product of the industrial age, mass produced, interlocking with very similarly shaped pieces but fitting correctly only in one place. My father used to make much more artful jigsaws by hand, as his father did before him, which, apart from the border, did not interlock; in large areas of sea and sky they were cunningly ambiguous, harking back to a much older tradition, and they were double-sided; again a large variety of choices and options were tested before a correct solution was reached.

The archivist has long seen the heap of textual public records on the floor as an interlocking jigsaw with a predestined solution based on a rigid articulation derived from industrial bureaucracy. The reconstruction is satisfying: there is (or appears to be) a right answer; the "fonds" and "original order" are givens. The manuscript collection would be more like

Originally published in *Archivaria* 25 (Winter 1987–1988): 12–28. Reproduced with the kind permission of the author, *Archivaria*, and the Association of Canadian Archivists.

a hand-cut puzzle so subtly crafted that several pieces fitted correctly in different places on the pattern. The final order is liable to be more idiosyncratic, reflecting *one possible* arrangement of the collection, and perhaps a distorted arrangement at that.

The modern archivist has grown up in the industrial, technological world of the following five "transcendencies": the natural world is desacralized; only humans have spiritual qualities; what is not mind is mechanism; technology is the paramount "progressive" imperative; and nature cannot stop us overwhelming the natural processes.[1] That kind of jigsaw fits together beautifully, but like a jigsaw it is simply another artifact which scarcely corresponds to reality as we now know it to be. History is the engine which drives this machine through time, or at least a kind of history which sees time pointing like an arrow into the "future" as an extension of a "past" conceived in linear terms

I have discussed elsewhere the part played by the documentary record in cultural perceptions,[2] but however one looks at it (and I am not a technological determinist), from earliest times the media have had an impact on the way we have interpreted reality, in particular paper, the phonetic alphabet, and printing with movable type. These records have been the mainstay of our archives and libraries, and we have until recently tended to "read" other media in textual terms.

Meanwhile, it has been said that

> With the invention of atomic weapons, the world changed forever. History turned on nature and threatened to destroy it utterly. Before the bomb nature could be treated as if it were no more than the stage on which history was played. Now nature's very existence came into question . . . history has always depended on nature as its source of support.[3]

The bomb is itself pure information defining our present obsessions and modes of thinking which Einstein also warned us would have to change and change quite fast. This applies as much to archivists as anyone else. If you find this metaphor hard to take, then the exploitation, destruction, and pollution of natural resources, vast economic inequalities, and the power of transnational corporations and the military-industrial complex bear witness to the consummation of the industrial age, grossly accelerated in the electronic world of a so-called information society in its transitional stage from the old order. I make no apology for moving outside the narrow bounds of the bureaucratic office, the records centre, and the archives, because I believe that the malaise which both Terry Eastwood and Terry Cook perceive as haunting Canadian archival practice is closely bound up with the breakdown of one culture and the emergence of another which affects society as a whole.[4] We are awash in a sea of megachoice as we lay down the jigsaw puzzle and take up the transformer.

Finding a way through may be a matter of finding our way back, not to some happy simplicity of some idealized archival past, but to the nature of our humanity, who we are and what we are about, as we grapple with the extraordinary freedoms and constraints of automation and electronic communication in general.

We should realize that a sense of time does not necessarily require a sense of history. "Time is something that has been enriching in me so that time is neither something external nor something unknown . . . [so that] knowledge is fundamentally the possibility of prevision, of fore-seeing the future and thus also of mastering it."[5] This does not mean crystal-ball gazing along a path of cause and effect but, like the artist, initiating causes to produce certain calculated effects. With information moving at the speed of light, we are faced with an "implosion" which buries us in data available instantly from all directions and levels, as op-posed to the old "explosion" which moved away from the centre down fixed and dispersing chains of force or command. Our only possible re-sponse is to think mythically and in depth. "As we come back to our-selves we join again with the oldest wisdom of information processing, mythical structures of the so-called primitive."[6] We have to bring all our senses to bear—not just intellectual rationality and the old linear ap-proaches. There is emerging "a transnational theory within social sci-ence characterized by a fundamental rejection of the adequacy of a lin-guistic reconstruction of the world and our conduct in the world, but this involves a different type of knowledge and rationality."[7]

We will remain numbed and paralyzed by our merciless, automated, electronic media if we go on thinking that all we have there are bits of a jigsaw, the same old text and image moving a bit faster and taking up rather less room, to which we must make some technological adjustments to stay in business. We have to learn what is going on in a totally new en-vironment and emerging culture, which has itself helped us perceive the nature of our old environment and measure the consequences of our con-tinued self-destruction. Only the massive aggregated patterns of informa-tion revealed by the computer enable us to track the extent and damage caused, for instance, by acid rain and low-level radiation. There will still be paper and the rest, but the paper record will no longer have the impact on society that it once did. Perhaps we can be thankful for that because, properly used and understood, the electronic environment can stimulate interpersonal relations and discourse in an interactive quasi-oral mode at odds with the old analytical detachments of the age of paper, although there is, of course, a place for these.

As archivists we need, I believe, to re-examine how our present and emerging culture organizes its necessary information and wisdom at the macro level. "Encyclopaedias are mirrors of our epistemology, the way in which we seek to know."[8] When we classify knowledge, we impose a form on it and control it through the pattern of its presentation. We are "informed" and we call it "information." It is this very act of classification, essential as it has been, which in a sense diminishes knowledge, as we all know when struggling with a poor finding aid.

Paedeia was the knowledge conveyed in bringing a Greek youth to adulthood and not just a compendium of facts.[9] As with the Homeric epic, the Bible became the filing system for information and wisdom for centuries, the reflection of our ordered social hierarchy. Religion was wisdom and knowledge, but by the end of the Middle Ages, reference books, arranged alphabetically, began to "access" the Bible through loaded "key words" which broke up the totality.[10] This was a powerful instrument of retrieval but, like all indexes, the process reflected changing ideologies, and could impose them as well. Scientific reductionism, whereby investigation extended from the general to the particular through subdivided categories, was reflected in this approach.

The entries in our encyclopaedias, and archivists' inventories generally, follow this pattern today. We should not assume that it need always be so. Diderot's "circle of knowledge" was built around the stout tree of reason, with religion "out on a limb" with superstition. I do not want to argue about that. Such structures were of enormous value, but we should not take them for granted.

Today we are facing a breakup in this kind of "knowledge theory" based on the three-centuries-old ideal of the autonomy of science and "the fundamental concepts of the nature of things."[11] All the old categories are being eroded; interdisciplinary activity is the order of the day and the two meanings of "order" become significant. All this is rubbing off on the archivist precisely at a time when descriptive standards are emerging through the requirements of that same automation which is imploding information and helping to cause the above breakup. No wonder Charlie is having his problems, and no wonder he is receiving little help from his colleagues in this field of endeavour.[12] Moreover, we know that user studies have also tended to show that "cognitivism has been joined by a rival viewpoint which stresses the emotions as a more fundamental component of social interaction and of the human actor."[13] Behind every finding aid there has to be a warm body somewhere. Likewise, archivists are or will be involved at one and the same time with global, national, and local interests in history and related studies, which diverse approaches will have to be met in retrieval systems. In a similar way, this also concerns sociologists with their need "to integrate micro and macro theories in the same framework"[14] and "to revive the internal and external analyses of organisations and to integrate them with the dynamic and environmental perspective touted by the population ecologists."[15] We might do well to talk over the garden fence with sociologists about this, because increased concern with global education and awareness is now matched by an intense interest in the local scene and family roots. Archivists identify strongly with the nation, the region, the community; perhaps in addition we will have to pay more attention at whatever level we operate (and "level" is not a good word for this) to those documentary evidences which relate to the wider scene as well as to our bailiwick. This is particularly true of environmental evidence.

So what about this so-called information society? Is it a fair label? There can be no society without information, for this is the stuff of living. Daniel Bell has described us as a postindustrial society,[16] but we have seen that much still survives from the industrial era including the treatment of information as a commodity rather than a service.[17] Certainly all sectors are more information-intensive as a result of the electronic implosion with its wealth of alternative choices. William Melody writes of the mediaeval monks protecting and monopolizing access to knowledge in an age of information scarcity, and contrasts them with the new electronic monks protecting decision-makers from drowning in a surplus of information. In both cases, it is the monk who is at the information gateway. There are dangers, of course, of overzealous information professionals withholding information through their knowledge of software and databases and thereby exercising power beyond their assigned role.[18] As the control of information by senior managers decreases and the basis of their influence is thus reduced, their role will increasingly become that of coach, goal-setter, and teacher living in the future to the extent that today's events are already ancient history.

For administration as for academic research, "facts that could be established beyond all reasonable doubt remain trivial in the sense that they do not in themselves give meaning or intelligibility to the record of the past." A catalogue remains a catalogue. "Pattern recognition is the *chef-d'oeuvre* of human intelligence."[19] We have to recognize the elastic, inexact character of truth, and symbolic interpretation rather than literalism allows us to err, to change, to adapt. This will be particularly necessary if we are to realize the strength and purpose of the thesaurus, a symbolic metaphor which has its origins in the chest where treasure and ancient writings were kept as the source of power and authority. As Allen Kent reminds us, there are certain things, however, that we cannot know: as, for instance, what words will mean and how, in the future, people will view events.[20]

And so we leave the certainty of the jigsaw puzzle for the ambiguity of the transformer with its paradoxes and choices. David Gracy has nicely detailed several archival paradoxes,[21] but the ancient proverbs which stand as a timeless monument of contradictions are witnesses to the ever-present paradox which we have tended to overlook, but which the information age has once more revealed through the plethora of multifaceted information.[22] We cannot, and should not try, to resolve the paradox which adds so many dimensions to our activities; sufficient that we are seeing "the final dissolution of the big project of western civilization to arrive at the good, the true and the just by means of rationality."[23]

David Spangler has proposed four stages in the emergence of the new culture with which, as archivists, we can identify:

1. Self-discovery, challenge, investigation and exploration, pain, false starts, wrong turnings.
2. Self-development, discernment, implementation, networking.
3. Integration with history and the larger environment in a planetary sense.
4. The embodiment of new values in service, resulting from inner strength and maturity.[24]

Culture, of course, has a variety of meanings, one of which is derived from its Latin origins in the soil: agriculture and cultivation. Jacques Barzun argues for culture as cultivation and enrichment of the self through meditation on experience and discourse over against instruction and scholarship which has its place in bringing order and clarity and preparing the material for culture.[25] If we do not distinguish these two approaches, we leave the field to the "expert" with a passion for collecting and making available (in our case) archival materials, the "specialist" bent on heaping up factual knowledge through unrestrained index cards. Surely we have to move beyond this if we are to find our true role.

THE TRANSFORMATION OF RECORDS

Information has been transferred from one medium to another since the beginnings of literacy and earlier through signs and the translation of languages; the monastic scribes were constantly doing it, and their letter forms became the type fonts of the early printing presses, as manuscripts were transformed into what at first amounted to printed facsimiles. From the highly personal telegraph and telephone, the newspapers developed a wire service which transformed electric messages into a mass medium of record and exploded the information and point of view in an early form of "broadcasting" to the accompaniment of rapidly reduced costs in terms of distance; photographic images, likewise, encircled the globe through halftone and photogravure, their meanings subtly transformed by caption and context. The ephemeral nature of radio and television created a massive incentive to record and capture their sounds and images.

Thereafter, the digital technologies of automation have provided the power not only to mirror but also to enhance as they move the record onto paper, microfilm, and video disc.

Transmedia shifts provide vast stores of information resources, but the reader/audience shares in the cost of their use, which compared, for instance, with books and manuscripts, has risen sharply. Likewise, the cost of storage coupled with problems of hardware obsolescence present their own problems and together all these factors are restricting the availability of much of this new information resource to those countries and institutions that can afford to pay for it. The monks are at the gate once more; power is still the flip side of wealth. We can see that just as "stand alone" machine tools became the empowered forms of handsaws, drills, and so on that previously had to be linked to large, immobile steam engines, so the independence of the personal computer from mainframe is transforming the nature and use of information handling and retrieval, but for all their increased power and falling price they are still relatively expensive for some societies.

Meanwhile, amid all these metamorphoses, the archivist will experience increasing difficulty in securing the "original," as oral and scribal modes of input and manipulation via the terminals of microcomputers erode the sanctity of the authorized, canonical text and we return to a pre-Gutenberg environment. One should not push this probe too far because, of course, there are ways of protecting automated texts, but in our world of uncertainties, fluidity, and abandonment of fixed positions so prevalent in the age of print, maybe the "original" is not so important as it was. The lessons of structural anthropology and semiotics suggest that truth does not reside in any one statement which itself is a galaxy of symbols—whether text or image. Statements have gained their authority from being printed, published, and distributed. This authority may have little relationship with truth and authenticity.

Again, copyright did not exist in oral and scribal society, but grew out of the publication of printed books. Is an electronic text "published" or "written"? With handwriting, printing, and even the telegraph, what went "in" came "out." Electronic messages conversely approach oral communication in their capacity to constantly modify without leaving behind a clear record, as the unseen messages within the airline reservation system bear witness. "The reused floppy will be the most opaque palimpsest of all" in a constantly revolving and evolving record, and "the years between 1750 and 1950 will be seen in retrospect as the historians' centuries."[26]

Yet how important is all this? Archivists wring their hands over the loss of the automated record which is, at present and proportionately, so much higher than is the loss of paper records. Is this because we continue to value it as if it were a paper record and apply all those historical criteria which we have inherited from the age of paper? If "history" itself comes to be viewed differently, and I do not just mean the subjects that interest the historian, then we may have to radically alter our criteria for selection and appraisal. Perhaps our capacity to manipulate what we do save may compensate in some measure for the bulk of what is lost, which in paper form would have been totally unmanageable. In an oral society where the daily chatter and decision-making is without written record, the human memory preserves only that which is absolutely necessary for cultural survival. What do we really need? Perhaps we must learn to retrieve more from less. How much of the paper record stored in our archives is, or ever will be, retrievable, given the shelf life of paper and the cost of transmedia conversion which is unlikely to be cheap within the lifetime of the paper involved?[27] Perhaps we have been trapped in the illusion that more and more records represent a proportional increase in knowledge and wisdom, but there may be a law of diminishing returns operating here. "A library . . . is first of all an archive or repository in which society can find what it has already learned."[28] This is written by a librarian with, at first sight, rather a curious use of the term "archive," yet a library might be considered as a printed "archives" of countless authors recounting what they have learned, because books are "about" primary materials. Is there any more to be learned from some of the primary materials in our archives? Perhaps appraisal should embrace a wider field if we are to preserve permanently only what we need. Likewise, libraries, which also have the problem of paper deterioration, may dispose of their less valuable material based on primary sources if these sources still survive in archives. This, of course, is simply an idea which can be rejected without further consideration. You must be the judge. Appraisal cannot, in any case, avoid being subjective.

I have not discussed so far the impact of the various media of record on society and the individual, and this is not the place for discussion in detail.[29] However, I believe we should pay far more attention to the nature of these media, the way they work us over, and the way they affect our culture. Harold Innis saw them as economic staples vulnerable to monopoly and making their impact according to the ease or difficulty with which they were moved. Marshall McLuhan was more concerned with their personal impact on the senses, about which relatively little is known, and many of his assertions were little more than brilliantly perceptive "probes" and metaphors for reality. David Olson has an approach which is, I believe, of particular value to archivists as we seek a deeper understanding of the material in our care: "The key, I suggest, to linking the media of communication to the structure of the mind is through the concepts of representation and interpretation." He maintains that we must focus on the symbolic form rather than the technology and "analyze the structure of information which is explicitly represented in that medium" through the appropriate interpretive procedures, which may include semiotics.[30] Derek de Kerckhove (quoted by Olson) has said that "there is no representation without interpretation."[31] Writing does not preserve the "meaning" of the text; it has to be interpreted, and this leads to altered uses of mind and memory. Put another way, "words do not mean anything, *people* mean things by words . . . information means nothing, but *people* are informed."[32]

Eric Havelock describes the Homeric epics as a "panorama of happenings" rather than a "program of principles" in showing how oral society structures knowledge.[33] This is particularly interesting when one considers the approach to appraisal and description based on function of activity rather than on hierarchy or type of document. This surely suggests a return to conceptual orality in the wake of automation.

Information has been described above as being "represented" in the media, that is "re-presented," a meaning which takes into account transmedia shifts from speech to writing or writing to automation with its accompaniment of altered perceptions by the user in the face of new symbolic structures. If indeed ours is the age of the symbol, there is no better illustration than the television commercial:

> The meaning of an ad is created when the viewer [or reader or listener] imbues the correlatives with meanings and values, and then transfers these onto the product. Henceforth the product itself points to the same meanings and values—it *means* them now as well.[34]

Should one then spend more time considering the "meaning" of our archival materials in terms of the activities which produced them and of which they are symbols? Will this help our appraisal of them? I do not mean the minute examination or interpretation of their content (that is the role of researchers), but a more overarching consideration of the symbolism of documentary forms as an extension of diplomatic. Semiotics can help us here, but it will need careful study in terms of our needs since it "endeavours to reveal and analyze the extent to which meanings are produced out of the structural relations that exist within any sign system, and not from the external reality they seem so naturally to depict."[35]

If we take these other dimensions into account, perhaps we will end up creating "mythistories that fit experience better and allow human survival more often, sustaining in-groups in ways that are less destructive to themselves and to their neighbours than was once the case or is the case today" by "emphasizing the really important aspects of human encounters" and omitting "irrelevant background noise."[36]

An appropriate end to this section is a final word from Derek de Kerckhove:

> The [Greek] chorus is the collectivity: the actor, the single person. The collectivity contains history as lived, not history as thought, history as myth, not history as logic or patterns of knowledge.[37]

In a "postliterate" age, where we paradoxically become "literate" in all media, we may very well move again in this direction.

THE TRANSFORMATION OF THE COMPUTER

It must already be all too apparent that my neat and totally simplistic division of "transformations" is breaking down. It is impossible to separate automation from discussions of culture or the new media, and it runs as a thread through the following discussions of user studies and the archivist's role. That, of course, is what "implosion" is about: "Things fall apart, the centre cannot hold." Sharply defined centralized lines of force, command, and hierarchy tumble in on each other and I am faced with the same problem that so many others have tackled far better than I: the difficulty of writing diachronically and serially about a phenomenon which is essentially synchronic. All these transformations are in parallel and interactive, but it may be helpful to consider the engine which drives automation and its impact on the record.

The printed page has remained much the same as it was five hundred years ago and, indeed, much the same as the manuscript page long before that. The book, or for that matter a well-organized body of papers, is a remarkably effective format: a description of the ideal medium of communication beyond the voice is almost a description of the book. This is a striking way of demonstrating its properties of portability, convenience, simplicity of access, and so on; automated full texts, abstracts, tables, and spreadsheets mimic the book, and the "menu" relates directly to the culinary choice on the familiar card in a restaurant. We work from what we know; alphabetical arrangement and the extensive use of indexes came with the uniform pagination which print made possible; the device is still with us on our terminal screens. We should not, however, assume that these forms, which so admirably suited the book, will remain forever. McLuhan has often pointed out that, to begin with, the content of a new medium is usually the previously dominant medium; the computer when it first came into service was programmed to produce "books," much as the incunabula of the fifteenth century contained manuscripts. The computer first produced account books from entries on cards; the hard copies were (reasonably) user friendly and the sheets were bound into volumes. Statistics received similar treatment and as the forms multiplied, so did the paper printouts. The automated input had no status as a record; the computer was a printing machine which did clever things with the copy, and this is still one of its roles.

Setting aside for a moment the social implications of automation discussed above, what are the characteristics of the computer which boggle our poor battered minds when, as archivists, we contemplate the problem? Speed, size, cost, flexibility, issues of permanence—all these remained relatively stable factors with paper and the book. Pages are turned by hand no faster than they ever were; paper size has remained remarkably stable; costs are still relatively reasonable; a book's weight is limited by the ability to heft it; access has been at the mercy of fixed content arrangement and indexing; permanently valuable materials have to be printed or written on better paper to survive (they often are not, however).

The computer now sweeps all these comfortable familiarities away: "pages" and all they contain move (or "turn") at the speed of light; the "book" becomes a file of virtually limitless size, and whole libraries and archives can be compacted into rapidly decreasing shelf space; costs of the user remain high and hardware obsolescence is a nightmare; access depends on friendliness or "the monk at the gate"; permanence depends on rerun, enhancement, and transference, in other words, constantly moving to stay the same, with some hope of near permanence in optical technology.

Once information enters the computer via the keystroke, OCR, or Raster Scan (used for enhancement), space and time as an archivist generally understands them are demolished. The equivalent of 503 running feet of textual records collapses into one 2,400-foot reel of tape.[38] "In 1976 one megabyte of memory occupied about 512 cubic inches or roughly the size of a soccer ball. Seven years later the development of 65K chips reduced the requirements to about two cubic inches. In 1985 the 256K chip had reduced the space to one millionth of what was required in 1959."[39] Meanwhile, fibre optics has made possible a laser pulsing hundreds of millions of times a second which can be seen as the descendant within a century and a half of the Morse code and the telegraph. "Fujitsu American has announced an optical fibre transmission system that can support 12,096 voice data and video signals over a single fibre. . . . The trend towards the integration of voice data and computer technologies is now a reality" and the ability to digitize all media opens the way for the Integrated Service Digital Network (ISDN) to be reached through standard user interfaces.[40] Finally, semiconductors will continue to compact so that there may well be one million components per chip by 1990, with comparable increases in processing speeds as photography and engraving merge to achieve this photoengraved marvel.[41] Printing has moved from content to process, with the Chinese woodblock print as a distant ancestor. Already, the entire thirty volumes of the *Encyclopaedia Britannica* could be transmitted from Washington to Los Angeles in a matter of several minutes at a speed of three megabits a second.[42]

These statistics are not paraded to "wow" anyone; some may be a bit exaggerated, but there is enough here to show that the old formats may well dissolve with the new software. We talk about the sun "rising" and "setting" because the illusion has been with us for millions of years and we once thought it worked that way. We have continued to speak of the "file" long after the thread ceased to pass through the hole in the paper, and will do so long after the stiff paper covers disappear. We may have to abandon old categories and hierarchical levels in records creation; it is significant, perhaps, that the record group/record series controversy, which began to render arrangement, description, and retrieval more flexible, emerged at about the time that computers began to challenge the archivist, though there may not have been a conscious connection.[43]

Terry Cook tells us that "the era of the million dollar main frame and complicated MARC formats is over,"[44] and he may well be right. Automation is both centralizing and decentralizing, in that the early hardware required a centralized facility fed by "hard wired" terminals, with usually severe limitations on the partially decentralized archivist with regard to possible software. The rise of the microcomputer has broken this umbilical cord (which can be reattached if appropriate) and has allowed a thousand personal computers to bloom in a highly decentralized mode. What remains centralized is the consensual agreement on descriptive and other standards which is central to an effective network and ultimately to a national or international system of communication or sharing of information with the personal computer. With its marked increase in user friendliness, "the monk at the gate" may have to move over to allow end-users (as opposed to the archivists) to find their own way through the labyrinths of information retrieval.

Meanwhile, whole nebulae of databases with their complex command languages must still be served by our electronic monks, but history and archives lack "universal" on-line database coverage.[45] The available literature can be unhelpful, and user studies scarcely scratch the surface of the real problem of how much retrieved material turns out to be useful and how much is missed or irrelevant. "Recent overviews of bibliographic databases for end users concentrate more on available services than on getting the most useful information from them,"[46] which is very similar to the archivists' attitude to the user public: "To help people search effectively for themselves, we must know how they search alone."[47] Most citations to end user on-line search behaviour is within the environment of the library and not the home or workplace.[48] Fifty to 60 per cent of office workers are expected to have microcomputers by the mid-1990s, and data processors have embraced the concept of the end user; "applications programming will be done by the person who will be running the application rather than by the professional programmer" in the office and in the home.[49]

Meanwhile, on-line bibliographical searches have been a matter of trial and error, "successive iterations in modifying the search formulation until we find, finally, the one best formulation of the query."[50] Marcia Bates suggests a far better process which she calls the "barn door" approach, followed by "docking" on the precise subject required. Since a display of headings early on reduces user impatience, she favours a front-end user programme with a vast array of terms greatly in excess of the thesaurus within the database, but linked to them. This would mean that any term remotely connected would hit the barn door and produce headings from which to choose. Docking is then a method of "getting a feel for the rules and to begin [sic] interaction in some common topic area" nudging forward into a semantic funnel much as some ferries now head for a dock wide at one end and narrow at the point of tying up; spacecraft also "dock" on this principle. On-line catalogues to date have added powerful capabilities to the traditional catalogue, yet systems designs generally have still not gone beyond implementing the card catalogue in on-line form "with some established on-line search features tacked on,"[51] and hence this approach.

My account is grossly oversimplified and those who wish to explore this concept should read Bates' article. The point I wish to make is this: here is a search strategy devised in terms of automation and the computer, and not in terms of index cards. We are often told if a system works well manually it will work on the computer, which is true, but it almost suggests that the system should first be capable of manual operation when in fact we are here talking about a mental operation with perhaps no manual counterpart. Old forms and procedures will dissolve simply because they were manual in origin. The semiconductor of the 1990s with hundreds of thousands of components and interconnectors would take one person ten years to produce soldering components on printed wire boards.[52] There is a manual alternative there—just; but no one is going to try it that way round first!

THE TRANSFORMATION OF THE USER

Until quite recently, there has been a relative scarcity of archives and records. This will seem an outrageous statement to my colleagues labouring under vast backlogs and struggling to improve access to the front logs. A logjam there may still be, but the users' expectations have been quite limited and the likelihood of success very unpredictable. A researcher was content with the variable quality finding aids and idiosyncratic indexes offered by the archivist, but mostly of value to the archivist who understood the system through personal familiarity. I think we have to admit that most inventories are control documents, "snapshots" of the volumes and boxes on the shelves with a rather dreary emphasis on physical description. The user was mercifully ignorant of the backlog and was content to mine the available seams for the appropriate information. There was even a sense of great satisfaction in stumbling upon material about which the finding aids were silent, and a proprietary right, at least for a while, to this discovery; success was achieved in spite of the archivist and this was part of the fun. It was essentially a static architectural world with columns of descending subgroups and series within the inventories and whole streets and suburbs of row housing in the form of cards with subject headings as a street plan. A journey through this metropolis of information could be pleasurable or frustrating as doors opened and closed. In short, the finding aids stayed put, the user moved, and when documents were produced, they stayed put as well. There was some comfort in this. The problem was that not all the streets were marked and only the sketchiest information was available about the houses. This limited access has had, of course, a profound effect on historiography and research in general. In much the same way, "historical researchers view information files accumulated by scientists and engineers in the nineteenth and early twentieth centuries as evidence of thought processes, because the files provide a record of scientists and engineers access to information."[53] Access to the available literature can now be assumed.

The search room of the near future will house not a city of scant entries, but a blizzard of information through which the researcher must find a way. Seated at a terminal the user stays put, the information flies past and, if the records to be retrieved are automated, they will fly past as well. There is, moreover, not likely to be a records scarcity given the increasing density of automated storage. Moving successfully through such a research visit, with or without an electronic monk as guide, requires a somewhat different approach:

> In an automated environment, the user must apply two types of knowledge: knowledge of the mechanical aspects of searching (syntax and semantics of entering search terms, structuring a search and negotiating a system) and knowledge of the conceptual aspects, the 'how and why' of searching—when to use which access point, ways to narrow and broaden search results, alter-

native search paths, distinguishing between no matches due to search error and no matches because the item is not in the database, and so on.[54]

The user will have to do some technical homework, though much of this may have come gradually through the school system. "Research in psychology has shown that Boolean logic is an inherently difficult task and one that is not 'common sense'. . . on-line catalogue users tend to perform simple searches using only the basic search features."[55] Likewise, varying frequency of use presents different problems in terms of experience and, again, is the technology yet up to the intellectual search tasks and conceptual problems? "Can we distinguish between searchable and unsearchable questions?" Despite the time allotted to on-line search techniques in library schools, users feel they should be able to grasp any search system in thirty minutes, which is perhaps all the time the manual systems took to master.[56]

Increasingly, we will have to spend more time understanding the users' approach: "To state their needs, people have to describe what they do not know. In effect, people do not naturally have 'queries,' rather they have . . . 'an anomalous state of knowledge'." Matches between systematic information and queries "may be requiring a match between two fundamentally dissimilar sorts of texts."[57] Users also have problems with indexes where the uncertainty principle applies in full measure and the notion of "the perfectly objective observer is simplistic and naive." Newtonian mechanistic assumptions of an ideal indexing system are impossible.[58]

The spread of microcomputers and the increase in their capability will lead to an increase in unmediated end users who, if they are in an office complex, may be mediating for someone senior to them. The automated record with its superior retrieval characteristics is likely to be the object of extended research, even before it reaches the archives, by professional, technical, and managerial personnel, which has some implications for the archivist. Unmediated searchers also learn from their colleagues and "the major reasons for searching themselves is convenience, speed being a key facet. Performance of the system is not particularly important to them. If the on-line search does not come out well they will find an alternative."[59] This observation is within a bibliographic context, but there may be a message here too for archivists. We had better devise systems that are usable by our clients, and user oriented; otherwise, they will be back consulting us "monks at the gate" and much of the advantage of automation will be lost. We will always be available for consultation, but it should be increasingly to clarify questions rather than provide answers.

Other characteristics of the user fraternity deserve consideration. The genealogists were one of the earliest groups to set up their own networks for information exchange. There are some profoundly "tribal" attributes to genealogy which accounts for this collective approach long before the electronic "implosion," and many archives have benefitted from receiving details of family histories and pedigrees. Katherine Gavrel has reported a similar willingness among researchers of machine readable archives to share information, in that over 76 per cent said they would supply information about their files for inclusion in a union list.[60] Archivists in general may expect an increase in cooperation of this kind as, through networking among archivists and users, a more collective approach to re-search, that is the recovery of what was once known, is implemented. Learning and scholarship may well become less the isolated activities of individuals and more the collective, cooperative achievements of groups. Through automation the archives can now go to the researcher, but the nature of the medium makes for less isolation in the research community.

As expert systems, the artificial intelligence, and other front-end user programmes render the complexity and sophistication of the software more "transparent," the barriers between users' needs and their fulfilment will grow less, but there is perhaps yet another paradox here. Historians in the past fashioned what they could retrieve into narratives built upon the fragments of evidence that survived, and from this emerged the notion that meaning increased in proportion to the raw data extracted from the primary records. This pursuit is asymptotic; you never arrive at "what actually happened":

> Historiography that aspires to get closer and closer to the documents—all the documents and nothing but the documents—merely moving closer and closer to incoherence, chaos and meaninglessness. That is a dead end for sure. No society will long support a profession that produces arcane trivia and calls it truth.[61]

With the automated record so detailed and the retrieval systems so fine-tuned, the available source documents become so vast that history must begin to take on mythic proportions to avoid an electronic antiquarianism. This surely is the lesson of superabundance. Meanwhile, "as historians go through the older records they see how much has been irretrievably lost. The desire to capture the present becomes urgent."[62] They are right and there is much of contemporary value which is not automated to add to the accession lists. The rules of the game are, however, changing and with it the relationship of archivist to researcher. "The problem today is to find a system of organising knowledge that reflects a coherent and shared view of the world, something that you or I can use easily and with which we may find valid connections between things . . . in our pluralistic culture."[63] This is as true of archival retrieval systems as encyclopaedias.

Behind the information and the data lies the "act and deed." We need a new form of "social historiography" to make clear how and why records were created; this should be *the* archival task, and it may be that a typology of actions will help us see the records in new ways and respond to the "Shifting paradigm . . . in the modern research world."[64] The breakdown of knowledge theory, "which can be taken to mean that the research is connected with a basic conception of what knowledge is and how knowledge is gained, is yielding to forms of approach-based research . . . undertaken for the purpose of promoting certain considerations or reflections . . . taken to mean vaguely defined or implied interests, views and goals," such as feminism and research in technology.[65] Hence the need for the barn door and docking as discussed above, since these approaches are not based on basic interpretation patterns and formulated understanding about ethical rules and so on.

Germane to all this is the development of networks, and archivists might do well to examine some of the findings of the social scientists:

> Network research began as an empirical field and it has only gradually begun to go beyond description to acquire some generalisable theory. . . . Networks are highly empirical representations of actual human interaction . . . as it actually happens.[66]

Networks are highly charged sources of power whether they be political interest groups or human grids for information exchange; they are very much a part of, and a product of, the automated environment. We can see how approach based research is often generated in networks which challenge conventional wisdom and knowledge theory. Donna Smyth, a Professor of English, who became deeply involved in the Nova Scotia lobby against uranium mining, has declared:

> Official knowledge is not only institutionalised, it is compartmentalised and specialised. It is taken out of the citizens' sphere and placed in the hands of experts who then advise politicians who rely on the experts. In effect, we have a short circuitry of democracy whereby citizens are excluded from the decision making process.[67]

Experts just because they are specialised, can only know a part of the total scene, and it is surely part of the librarian's and archivist's roles to push for the kind of holistic access which database searchers allow to sources and documentation across departmental barriers which otherwise obscure the truth. Patterns of knowledge adopted in the *Encyclopaedia Britannica* reveal the cult of the expert which is now beginning to wane as its limitations are perceived.

THE TRANSFORMATION OF THE ARCHIVIST

In many ways we archivists resemble plumbers. Our records are like pipes through which the information flows towards the user; finding aids provide suitable taps along the way and our pipes are beautifully soldered and sealed with various branches, which makes sure that the "hot and cool" media (to use one of McLuhan's metaphors) and their sources do not get mixed up; we call this provenance. Our chief concern is that our storage tanks do not leak, our taps work, and the information comes out in a nice steady stream. Our plumbing systems are very traditional and most of us are reluctant to question principles which seem to work quite well. Most of our customers do not complain since we enjoy a monopoly of the business. There is nowhere else to go. We do not seem concerned with falling levels in the catchment areas or losses from the big conduits which lead from them, or that the purification plant may be screening out materials of value. I fear this metaphor is leading me into deep water and I will let it be!

Frank Burke in his well-known article on archival theory[68] has posed some of the larger questions which I too believe we should be addressing, and I have added a few of my own in the foregoing remarks. Cook and Eastwood are quite right in deploring the lack of general involvement of most archivists in these theoretical debates,[69] because such discourse is important to us if we are not to go on plumbing in the same old way when so much around us is changing. I have tried to say something about the nature of society in relation to its records in the "information age" and to suggest the usefulness of recovering certain insights and precepts which have become obscured and which I hope bear further examination. Gregg Kimball contends that "the level of theory that Burke advocates will not emerge from the study of archival practices and principles save in the general framework of human institutions. Theory of this sort is likely to be borrowed from one of the social sciences."[70] So be it. Defining our theories and principles solely within the terms and resources of our own discipline can be highly incestuous and suggests that records exist for their own sake and are not to be confused with the society which creates them.

In this regard, Cook asks: "Should archivists (with producers and users) not approach records description in a more global and holistic fashion?"[71] Why only description? He goes on to discuss the possibility of itinerant archivists riding their circuits like the old preachers, which is a novel and fruitful idea for North America and may well complement networks of very small archival accumulations. Such an arrangement existed for some cities and towns of West Yorkshire, England, during the 1950s when money was particularly scarce, and it worked quite well. We desperately need to think new and different thoughts, "sinful" though they may appear to the more conventional of us,[72] and we must not be afraid to be "put down" for them. Anyone working in a special interest group which does not have majority acceptance gets used to that. For instance, "relatively little has been done on written communication at the more dynamic organizational and personnel levels" in contrast to the mass media,[73] yet much of our record lies within this field. Because of his awareness of the record as a dynamic vehicle of communication with ramifications other than as an element in a static knowledge theory, Cook can say that "the older narrower, institutionally based provenance approach of archives . . . no longer suits the new producer or creator."[74]

And so we return to that mythic, dynamic quality of documents as acts and deeds.[75] Perhaps, therefore, it is not surprising that Helen Samuels and others have developed a typology of functional gerunds for the appraisal of the records of modern science: funding, planning, hypothesizing, communicating, patenting, and so on, rather than focusing on the physical format of the document. Again, Trudy Peterson stresses that "the act of fixing the information, not the type of base, nor the type of impression, nor the character of information, nor the length of time it is fixed" constitutes the record, but I cannot agree that "the format makes no difference to the fundamental nature of a document or a record."[76] The format makes a difference because the medium imposes its own meaning which cannot be separated from the document. We cannot recapture the act; all we have is the document, the residual instrument, and that is why the document *became* the act or deed,[77] limited by the symbolism of its language (itself a mass medium) and of its documentary nature. These limitations and ambiguities have sustained lawyers ever since.

It is this perception which causes David Bearman to ask "what is the purpose of archival information systems?" He replies: "to provide documentary accountability. Such accountability is important, not so much to tell us what is in the archives as to tell us how it came to be there," why it was created, and what it really did as opposed to saying it did. Access and analysis of the contents of archives are something else again. "Documentary accountability" had us looking again at our old definitions as indeed we always should.[78] Archivists must cast off the model that holds that records have only a single referent and create a system that recognizes instead that they are created and maintained as part of complex bureaucratic networks.[79]

For Peterson, "archival theory is as much a map of where archivists have been as an atlas for future travels";[80] we have forged practical experience into general operating principles. I realize that we have here no more than a metaphor, but I would suggest that maps can become dated, their information misleading and ambiguous, and that regular revisions, where necessary, are in order. We need to examine these and other assumptions of our profession to see whether they still hold up in our mythopoeic "information age."

REFLECTION, 2000

This is a large and somewhat unwieldy canvas which displays the results of my responding to the nature and context of the records and the subsequent impact on the way we archivists do our business, in a world full of paradigm shifts where change is the only constant. Of all my papers this one, together with "My Very Act and Deed" in the American Archivist, *has received the most attention, judging by the citations. Both in a way sum up what I have been about over several years, which may have been the reason. Anyway, I am glad of the interest which has been developed impressively by others, which is what I hoped would happen.*

I have to admit to operational illiteracy where computers are concerned and I never got further than pen and ink. On top of that, most of the references to automation are now seriously dated, although some general principles still survive. In the early 1960s I was excited by this new marvel as I watched a brilliant young programmer struggling to construct family trees from early parish registers in the Northumberland County Archives at a time when families were less mobile. Meanwhile, the Mormons, using their extensive microfilming programme, were preparing automated indexes of these same registers in Salt Lake City where I was later able to examine them. This was the age of mainframes, punch cards, and paper tapes making "technical adjustments" to traditional archival processes. Our grasp was well beyond our reach when it came to investigating automation of the holdings of the National Register of Archives in London, and a trial series in the Public Record Office, but the vision and exploration were there. Paradigm shifts were to come later.

I greatly appreciated Barbara Craig's generous remarks in her article that originated in a comment on my paper when it was first delivered.[81] She draws attention to the changes brought about by xerography and the photocopier, which I had taken for granted completely. She warns of the segregation of the new medium through limited understanding: "We must very soon establish links with the real managers of machine records whatever they be called. Otherwise, we run the risk of becoming a museum of communications, and not a living cultural entity."[82] She is concerned about the impact of automation on the user in the search room which will no longer be "a place of contemplation and scholarship," but "a place of diverse activities and excitement."[83] These and other considerations filled in some of the gaps which I had ignored. Written ten years ago, this essay more than any other is perhaps quite a good starting point as we constantly revise and revision the future of archives so far removed from those comfortable far off days of the 1950s when I began. But let us not be afraid of broad canvasses.

NOTES

1. Tom Berry in "History and the New Age," Canadian Broadcasting Corporation (hereafter CBC), *Ideas* programme, transcript (1984), p. 6.

2. "The Media of Record: Archives in the Wake of McLuhan," *Georgia Archive* 4 (1978): 1–10.

3. Lister Sinclair in "History and the New Age," p. 1.

4. Terry Eastwood, "Going Nowhere in Particular: The Association of Canadian Archivists Ten Years After," *Archivaria* 21 (Winter 1985–86): 186–90; Terry Cook, "Shadows in the Canadian Archival *Zeitgeist:* The Jeremiah of Terry Eastwood Considered," *Archivaria* 22 (Summer 1986): 156–62.

5. Raimundo Panikka in "History and the New Age," p. 3.

6. Derek de Kerckhove in ibid., p. 8.

7. Nils Mortensen, "Knowledge Problems in the Sociology of the 80s," *Acta Sociologica* 29 (1986): 335.

8. William Barker in "The Circle of Knowledge," CBC *Ideas* transcript (1985), p. 1.

9. Walter Ong in ibid., p. 2.

10. Barker in ibid., p. 3.

11. Mortensen, "Knowledge Problems," p. 327.

12. A fictitious character in my "From Dust to Ashes: Burnout in the Archives," to be published shortly in the *Midwestern Archivist.*

13. Randall Collins, "Is Sociology in the Doldrums?" *American Journal of Sociology* 91 (1986): 1348.

14. Ibid., p. 1349.

15. Ibid., p. 1351.

16. David Lyon, "From 'Post-industrialism' to 'Information Society': A New Social Transformation?" *Sociology* 20 (1986): 578.

17. Ibid., p. 585.

18. William H. Melody, "The Context of Change in the Information Professions," *ASLIB Proceedings* 38 (August 1986): 226.

19. William H. McNeill, "Mythistory or Truth: Myth, History and Historians," *American Historical Review* 91 (1986): 2.

20. Allen Kent, "Unsolvable Problems," *Information Science: Search for Identity,* Anthony Debons, ed., (New York, 1973), pp. 299–311.

21. David B. Gracy II, "Our Future is Now," *American Archivist* 48 (Winter 1985): 12–21.

22. Kim S. Cameron, "Effectiveness as Paradox: Consensus and Conflict in Conceptions of Organisational Effectiveness," *Management Science* 32 (May 1986), pp. 539–57.

23. Mortensen, "Knowledge Problems," p. 329.

24. David Spangler, *Emergence: The Rebirth of the Sacred* (Dell 1984), p. 91 ff.

25. Jacques Barzun, "Scholarship *versus* Culture," *The Atlantic Monthly* (November 1984): 93–104.

26. R. J. Morris, "Does Nineteenth-Century Nominal Record Linkage Have Lessons for the Machine-Readable Century?" *Journal of the Society of Archivists* 7 (October 1985): 509.

27. For a perceptive study of the problems of obsolescent hardware, see David Bearman "Optical Media: Their Implications for Archives and Museums," *Archives and Museum Informatics* (1987).

28. Abraham Kaplan, "The Age of Symbol: A Philosophy of Library Education," *Library Quarterly* 34 (1964): 297.

29. A recorded version of my course, "Society and the Documentary Record," designed to be heard and not read, consists of thirteen ninety-minute tapes and is deposited in the School of Library, Archival and Information Studies, University of British Columbia, Vancouver, and in the National Archives of Canada, Ottawa. This is as close as I will ever get to writing a book on the subject.

30. David Olson, "Mind, Media and Memory: The Archival and Epistemic Functions of Written Text," working paper 13, Ontario Institute for Studies in Education (OISE), and the McLuhan Program in Culture and Technology (1986), p. 1.

31. Ibid., pp. 1–2.

32. Kaplan, "Age of Symbol," p. 296.

33. Ibid., p. 3, quoting Havelock.

34. Marc D. Lewis, "In Sheep's Clothing: An Analysis and Discussion of the Thank You Very Much, Milk Commercial," working paper 9, OISE (1986), p. 3.

35. Tim O'Sullivan et al., *Key Concepts in Communication* (London: Methuen, 1983), p. 210.

36. McNeill, "Mythistory," p. 9.

37. Derek de Kerckhove in "History and the New Age," p. 5.

38. Harold Naugler, *The Archival Appraisal of Machine Readable Records. A RAMP Study with Guidelines,* UNESCO (1984), p. 26.

39. Charles M. Dollar, *Electronic Records Management and Archives in International Organizations. A RAMP Study with Guidelines,* UNESCO (1986).

40. Richard Dick, "Views on Telecommunications: Implications for the Future," *Journal of the American Society for Information Science* 37 (1986): 424.

41. Dollar, *Electronic Records Management,* p. 6.

42. Ibid., p. 30.

43. Peter Scott published his article "The Record Group Concept: A Case for Abandonment" in 1966. See the *American Archivist* 29, pp. 493–504.

44. Terry Cook, "The Vancouver Island Project Revisited," Chad Gaffield and Peter Baskerville, eds., *Archives, Automation and Access* (Victoria, 1986): 12.

45. Richard Janke, "Full Circle: Archival Studies On-Line: Where From Here?" *Archives, Automation and Access,* pp. 27–38.

46. Winifred Sewell and Sandra Teitelbaum, "Observations of End-User On-Line Searching Behaviour Over Eleven Years," *Journal of the American Society for Information Science* 37 (1986): 234.

47. Ibid., p. 325.

48. Ibid., p. 234.

49. Marydee Ojala, "Views on End-User Searching," *Journal of the American Society for Information Science* 37 (1986): 199.

50. Marcia J. Bates, "Subject Access in On-Line Catalogs: A Design Model," *Journal of the American Society for Information Science* 37 (1986): 357–76.

51. Ibid., p. 357.

52. Dollar, *Electronic Records Management,* p. 6.

53. Joan K. Haas, et al., *Appraising the Records of Modern Science and Technology: A Guide* (Cambridge, Mass.: Massachusetts Institute of Technology, 1985), p. 44.

54. Christine L. Borgman, "Why Are On-Line Catalogs Hard to Use? Lessons Learned from Information Retrieval Studies," *American Society for Information Science* 37 (1986): 388.

55. Ibid., p. 390.

56. Ibid., p. 396.

57. Bates, "Subject Access," p. 365.

58. Ibid., p. 360.

59. Sewell and Teitelbaum, "Observations," p. 243.

60. Katherine Gavrel, "Issues Associated with Accessing Machine Readable Records," *Archives Automation and Access*, p. 111.

61. McNeill, "Mythistory," p. 8.

62. William Barker in "The Circle of Knowledge," p. 27.

63. Ibid., p. 16.

64. Peter Baskerville and Chad Gaffield, "Shifting Paradigms and Emergent Technologies: Archives in the Modern Research World," *Archives, Automation and Access*, pp. 15–26.

65. Mortensen, "Knowledge Problems," p. 325.

66. Collins, "Is Sociology in the Doldrums?" p. 351.

67. Donna Smyth in "Finding Out: The Rise of Citizen Science," CBC *Ideas* transcript (1985), p. 14.

68. Frank Burke, "The Future Course of Archival Theory in the United States," *American Archivist* 44 (Winter 1981): 40–46.

69. Eastwood, "Going Nowhere in Particular," pp. 186–90; Cook, "Shadows in the Canadian Archival *Zeitgeist*," pp. 156–62.

70. Gregg D. Kimball, "The Burke-Cappon Debate: Some Further Criticisms and Considerations for Archival Theory," *American Archivist* 48 (Fall 1985): 371.

71. Cook, "Vancouver Island Project," p. 9.

72. Maynard J. Brichford, "Seven Sinful Thoughts," *American Archivist* 43 (Winter 1980), pp. 13–16.

73. Clark A. Elliott, "Communication and Events in History: Toward a Theory for Documenting the Past, *American Archivist* 48 (Fall 1985): 358.

74. Cook, "Vancouver Island Project," p. 8.

75. An increasing body of scholarship is now appearing which urges archivists as their central task to explore the nature and meaning of archival documents as revealed in their form, purpose, and impact on society. The following are some excellent examples that have appeared in *Archivaria*: David A. Bearman and Richard Lytle, "The Power of the Principle of Provenance," *Archivaria* 21 (Winter 1985–86): 14–27; Terry Cook, "Nailing Jelly to a Wall; Possibilities in Intellectual History," *Archivaria* 11 (Winter 1980–81): 205–18; "From Information to Knowledge: An Intellectual Paradigm for Archives, *Archivaria* 19 (Winter 1984–85): 28–49; and "Leaving Safe and Accustomed Ground: Ideas for Archivists," *Archivaria* 23 (Winter 1986–87): 123–28; Tom Nesmith, "Archives from the Bottom Up: Social History and Archival Scholarship," *Archivaria* 14 (Summer 1982): 5–26; and "Archives and the 'Circle of Knowledge,'" *Archivaria* 21 (Winter 1985–86): 10–13. In addition, the valuable "Studies in Documents" series, which began in *Archivaria* 20 (Summer

1985), examines in detail the use made by their creators, based on form and context (a modern "diplomatic") rather than content of specific archival material.

76. Trudy Huskamp Peterson, "Archival Principles and Records of the New Technology," *American Archivist* 47 (Fall 1984): 385.

77. Hugh A. Taylor, "My Very Act and Deed: The Role of Documents in Relation to Process," to be published shortly.

78. David Bearman, "Who About What or From Whence, Why and How: Intellectual Access Approaches to Archives and Their Implications for National Archival Information Systems," *Archives, Automation and Access,* p. 40.

79. Max J. Evans, "Authority Control: An Alternative to the Record Group Concept," *American Archivist* 49 (Summer 1986): 260.

80. Trudy Huskamp Peterson, "The National Archives and the Archival Theorist Revisited," *American Archivist* 49 (Spring 1986): 126.

81. Barbara Craig, "Meeting the Future by Returning to the Past: A Commentary on Hugh Taylor's Transformations," *Archivaria* 25 (Winter 1987–1988): 7–11.

82. Ibid., p. 9.

83. Ibid., p. 10.

Chapter 10

"My Very Act and Deed": Some Reflections on the Role of Textual Records in the Conduct of Affairs

ROLE OF TEXTUAL RECORDS

The intense effort by archivists across North America to redefine their role in an electronic multimedia environment is giving rise to a close look at the physical and technological nature of the record as a means of communication.[1] Meaning is no longer seen as being limited to content within the context or provenance and fonds, but must be sought also in the technology of the medium which has, since earliest times, had a profound effect on society as a whole. Writing, printing, and the television image have often been cited in this regard.[2]

Archivists reared in a largely textual environment have had a tendency to "read" all media of record literally, without realizing that all forms of communication are loaded with conventions and semiotic "signs" inherent in their respective technologies.[3] Consequently, archivists and users alike are having to employ more perceptive strategies of interpretation. This article is little more than a reflection on the physical nature and form of some textual documents in relation to the needs which gave rise to them and their subsequent impact on administrative process. The study of form and phraseology in medieval administrative instruments under the term "diplomatics" can provide a valuable precedent and starting point for a "modern diplomatics," which emphasizes not only the content but also the form of documentation over time.

Originally published in the *American Archivist* 51 (Fall 1988): 456–69. Reproduced with the kind permission of the author and the Society of American Archivists.

THE IMPACT OF THE ORAL TRADITION

A study of preliterate communication can be helpful, not because it is historically anterior to literacy, but rather because in this age of automation, we are beginning to move into a "postliterate" mode which, while not dispensing with literacy, reintroduces the immediacy of rapid interactive networking and feedback analogous to oral exchange. Our understanding is more holistic and planetary. We are becoming more conscious of ourselves as part of a natural environment threatened with destruction by exploitation, misuse, and nuclear weaponry, so that "our very idea of history as a process finding its fulfillment in the future must now give way to a reevaluation of both the past and the present."[4] If as archivists we are ceasing to see history as an arrow propelled literally from the past through the present into the future, then our approach to the evaluation of documents and the record may likewise have to undergo a change which, for instance, takes into account threats to life and environment through pollution and the disposal of waste, much of which has gone unrecorded.

Preliterate communities depended, and still depend, on memory and the spoken word accompanied by gesture and action to communicate with each other. "Primal languages are very special in that words are thought of as being sacred. The source of life is thought of as the breath which comes from the centre of one's being, from the area of the heart indeed."[5] Words are action oriented. They do not modify, analyze, or describe in dependent clauses, but speak concretely about a world of the past in the present, a mythic presentation: "Time recorded biologically without being allowed to become history," in M. Eliade's brilliant phrase.[6] All the wisdom of the old must be transmitted to the children in myth and Levi-Strauss's "science of the concrete,"[7] which observes nature meticulously in terms of use, not deduction and abstraction. The emphasis on the user in these ancient patterns of speech was also evident in mapmaking by native peoples in North America. Drawn on the ground or made with branches and twigs, they were ephemeral and dependent on memory, the remarkable preliterate data bank from which was retrieved only that which was required. D. W. Moodie has explained that "when a map was committed to media which affected its size, such as skins or bark, no attempt was made to fill in the entire space. Instead, detail was elaborated only where necessary. . . . Although Europeans frequently found these maps overly simple and often confusing, they were eminently suited to the overriding objective of most native cartography: to accentuate the environmental information salient to successful wilderness navigation."[8] Retrieval from the automated record is likewise at its most effective when only that which is required is displayed.

A great deal of work has been done, particularly during the past twenty years, mapping the effects of written communication, including the materials on which they were written. Harold Adams Innis, a Canadian economic historian, moved from studies of the social and economic impact of the fur trade and the cod fisheries as staples that totally changed the environments of those they touched, to an examination of literate communication as a staple of administration and commerce.

The ability to capture and preserve human memory through writing most profoundly differentiated preliterate societies from those called "civilized." The phonetic alphabet, with its arbitrary signs so easily learned, separated those who used it from the concrete immediacy of the natural environment from which pictograms had been drawn; thoughts became interiorized, detached, analytical, having a life of their own and yielding to reason and logic, expressed, exchanged, and preserved through text. There is evidence to suggest that writing, as developed by the Greeks from whom westerners have derived so much intellectual baggage, is what causes literate persons to think historically, rationally, in a linear manner as they follow the serial communication from one line to another. For centuries this baggage has shaped minds and attitudes; writing has filled archives and almost monopolized paper forms of communication. Like fish, the heirs of Greece and Rome have swum in this water for over three thousand years and so are scarcely aware of it.[9]

Marshall McLuhan has pointed out that new media of record absorb older ones, as writing absorbs speech; print, writing; and television, old movies.[10] The new medium is deeply distrusted until it becomes established and takes on a life of its own. Again, this is a factor in the impact of the record on process; consider, for example, legal suspicion of microfilm or the automated record as admissible evidence in courts of law.[11]

Doomsday Book marvellously exemplifies the impact of literacy on a predominantly oral society which did not even speak the same language as the Norman "public servants." The administration of William I wanted to put together a kind of land registry, a vast land title record compiled from responses to a modern-sounding questionnaire. The richly varied world of Anglo-Saxon England, however, had no Latin equivalents for many of the terms used, to the dismay of the Norman officials who somehow had to ram them into their Procrustean bureaucratic bed, matching like with like.[12] The dream of "one word one meaning" is an essentially literate one which has kept lawyers wealthy and, in this case, has provided lifetimes of study for medieval historians. M. T. Clanchy has demonstrated clearly how many in medieval England felt written charters and other documents were greatly inferior as evidence to sworn testimony by witnesses.[13]

Many charters of the early Middle Ages were seen essentially as pale copies, a photographic record if you like, of an event, which was an action involving flesh and blood people. The reality of a transfer of land might involve cutting a piece of turf and handing it from one party to the other before witnesses. The charter subsequently prepared was simply a memorandum. "Be it remembered that" or "know that" a ceremony has taken place and a transfer made, and sometimes the knife or a fragment of the sod was attached. As the literate record became established, only then did the document become the sole instrument, an act in itself, to which seals and, later, signatures were attached. Earlier in this century, it was still customary when signing a legal instrument to place a finger on the little red spot (the vestigial seal) and declare "this is my very act and deed." "Acts" and "deeds" have remained in the vocabulary of Parliament and the law, a reminder of their ancient preliterate origins and the power of new media to create new environments and new realities.

The English common law has kept alive the spirit of ancient oral custom over against written codes, and it is well to remember that the English bureaucracy grew out of the Courts of Chancery, Exchequer, Kings Bench, and the High Court of Parliament itself. These were all courts of record, where the ancient counterparts of "the people's evidences" were enrolled on parchment. These courts held the ultimate record of legal and administrative "acts," for which the copy has come to be seen as a parchment instrument secured at much cost, increased by the handwritten verbiage of common form and by delays in "moving" (affixing) the various seals. Each bureaucratic office as it was created became over time like a bee embalmed in amber and the King, when communication at a distance was required, had to devise new seals and new offices to expedite business in a process known as "going out of court." Monarchs, who could read but scorned to write, in turn devised the privy seal, the secret seal, and the signet in order to make medieval circumventions around those great monumental documents of the scribal age, the letters patent and letters close.[14] Documents designed to speed process instead led to the creation of additional process. The Tudors circumvented the ancient Exchequer by developing the Treasury, because the accounting system was totally inadequate for planning in a future-oriented renaissance world.[15] For over one hundred years, the telephone has been used to hasten process, but may have created, through lengthy follow-up memoranda, more paper than it eliminated.

PROCESS ON PAPER

In the West, the availability of paper at a cost far less than parchment, coupled with the use of the signature over the seal, again altered documentary forms and process. The courts of record continued majestically on, some increasing in irrelevance with the passage of time. Only the courts and traditional administration retained the use of parchment; elsewhere, society began the love/hate affair with the paper record which has devoured it ever since, a demon lover bent on drowning its creators. The invention of printing provided, in effect, an office copier for blank forms, with the typefaces (as in printed books) imitating the old text and set hands. Later, printed forms became more creative as the medium set its stamp on bureaucratic ingenuity and obfuscation. Meanwhile, the individualism of handwritten and signed paper documents created by an increasingly literate society rendered communication at a distance far more flexible. The newly emerging print culture—explosive, specialized, and fragmented—produced those private, wary, detached, and ruthlessly competitive public servants who gaze out of Holbein's portraits.[16] The medieval royal household built around conciliar decision making yielded to ministers with immense delegated powers heading up departments of government. Only recently has this pattern begun to reform into a renewed "household management" via inner cabinets, as information and events now move so much faster than paper.

In business, as in government, documentation on paper made the various operations increasingly specialized, from an extension of household management to the now familiar industrial bureaucracy. Chequer boards, slates, and tallies yielded to the double entry bookkeeping which became all but universal and essential for future reckoning and the deferred pleasures of Protestantism; but much of the old, more personal, less specialized approach lingered on until quite recently. As Graham Lowe explained:

> The transition from the traditional one room office of the nineteenth century to the multi-departmental bureaucracy of the twentieth century was gradual. The small, informal counting house of the nineteenth century was staffed by a craftsman-like bookkeeper, perhaps assisted by an office boy and a junior clerk. The old office was also characterized by informal social relations, unsystematic administrative procedures, and a minimal amount of records. The bookkeeper was a generalist who learned his craft by apprenticeship. He retained much of his employer's office system in his head. Overall, a rule-of-thumb approach to management matters prevailed. The smallness and modest scale of activities characteristic of firms in late nineteenth century entrepreneurial capitalism thus required little in the way of sophisticated organizational structure, records keeping, and administrative planning.[17]

Douglas McCalla has noted that in small retail businesses, there might be two partners keeping a daybook and a ledger. Single proprietors often seem to have kept very primitive accounts as a supplement to memory of payments due. For farmers and artisans, the record was of day-to-day expenses and costs, closer in nature to a diary. The costs of planting and harvesting, and receipts from yields reflect the ancient cycle of the seasons as did the old financial year.[18] As a business grew and, with it, the fragmented need for separate sets of accounts for customers, employees, suppliers, branches, partners, capital profit and loss, and bad debt, the partners became increasingly remote from middle management; in short, they had to "go out of court" to expedite business, keeping only the capital and private accounts.

It is very curious and perhaps significant that, despite all the massive corpus of writing about management and administration, so little attention has been given to the impact of the various records.[19] There has been no major study on how the nature of the printed and paper document has affected the conduct of affairs in business and the public sector, apart from those of the communications theorists. This, of course, is part of the problem of fishes and water referred to above.

Seymour Wilson asserts that decision making and the bureaucratic assumptions which underpin all policy making and administration are based on various aspects of rationality: the relation of means to ends and intentions to the effectiveness of various procedures; an objective understanding of human behaviour as a means of describing, measuring, and ultimately manipulating it; the concept of authority based on the specialized, fragmented knowledge of the expert; the matching of events to precedents through rules and regulations to be understood relatively easily and used as templates and matrices to fashion acceptable human behaviour.[20] It is this kind of rationality which lies behind Luther Gulick's PODSCORB (Planning, Organizing, Directing, Staffing, Coordinating, Reporting, and Budgeting) as applied as much to the factory floor as the office.[21] No wonder trained engineers occupied management positions and developed management systems. It is preeminently literate and, in its origin, was totally dependent on the document to capture and distribute the documentary record. Colonialism is the transnational form of bureaucratic development that often attempts to achieve the effects of private enterprise through purely bureaucratic arrangement and fiat. The old trading companies are an example of this, and indeed the East India Company stands behind the Indian Civil Service, which became the model later imported into Britain.

Before the emergence of gigantism, "the numbers game," and the massive accumulation of facts by nineteenth-century commissions, government was largely a family affair (at one point Canadians spoke of the "Family Compact") where men of influence, representing powerful interests, tried to make sense through debate and discussion and arrive at a conclusion. The emphasis was on oral exchange; clerical operations were relatively menial and ministers attended to all their own mail in person. With the growth of information flow, a theoretical, if not practical, division began to arise between those who handled, processed, and organized the enormous factual content of documented information and those who made sense of it for translation into decision making. In Britain, Lord Palmerston at the War Office was forced into this position after years of attention to minutiae,[22] and the Colonial Office was gradually transformed through what is clearly the emergence of the "mandarin" buffering the minister from a flood of conflicting detail, the generalist with a first-class humanistic background.[23] The original mandarins, those Chinese scholar officials who acted as architects, engineers, teachers, and rulers of society, "were firmly opposed to any form of specialization. There was only one profession they recognized: that of governing."[24] When the Indian Civil Service developed the principle, they were able to do so in an autocratic milieu uncomplicated by democratic government with its sharply conflicting points of view from fixed positions, which was to bring these administrators into collision at times with government and legislators in the West.

Moving from the macro cultural level to the micro operational level of business procedures and how documents are filed for the retrieval of information, the limits inherent in writing and typing on paper to some extent dictate the kind of policy which can be effectively pursued. As illustration, consider two departments of government and one trading house from Canada.

Bill Russell, author of an article on the Department of Indian Affairs (DIA) nicely titled "The White Man's Paper Burden," focused directly on documentation and process:

> It is through their musings over the problems associated with how to maintain a records system that we see DIA administrators grappling with the questions of what they *kept* and why, and to a certain extent what they *created* and why. In their discussions on how best to cope with the functions of records classification, custody, control and disposal, they provide us with something of their perceptions of the value of their records and the purpose they served.[25]

The records of DIA bear witness to a clash of those oral and literate cultures discussed above. Russell quotes A. E. St. Louis, registrar-cum-archivist, writing in 1937:

> We possess . . . in the Public Archives and in our own Department Archives an unbroken chain of chronological events relating to our Aborigines. . . . I wish to emphasize the fact that none of our papers can be classified as Indian legends or myths, but all of them bear the characteristics of historical

monuments. . . . They contain an almost continuous record of our Indian wards' progress . . . all this related chronologically by our Superintendents, Inspectors, Agents, Farmers and lastly by those worthy representatives of the Church. . . . I feel that it is incumbent on the Department to preserve from decay the remembrance of what these men have done for its wards and these records should be kept intact for historical purposes as an example to future generations.[26]

Here is the perfect expression of a value system based on the phonetic alphabet, literacy, and print.

There arose a constant tension between local offices and a highly centralized DIA, which resulted in "slow communications with the field, tardy decision making and confused lines of authority." Backlogs were finally eased towards the end of the century by a file subject index and increased staff.

What were the general implications for documents and process? Russell points out that DIA was dominated by the historical perspective both culturally, through the notion of "progress" and "civilization" for its wards, and legally because Indian claims knew no statute of limitations and the early records were vital, jealously guarded even from the Public Archives. As with many other departments, the early indexed filing systems allowed for the solution of limited, reactive problems but did not facilitate long-term planning based on coordinated information. This essentially was the principal limitation of the docket and letter book. Field office records were poorly kept; there was little bureaucratic standardization coordinated at the head office in the face of a native culture in which all this process must have seemed totally alien and irrelevant. The success of local agents was probably more the result of personal relationships with the tribes rather than paperwork.

Terry Cook, in his study of northern Canadian administrations and their records, reminds archivists that files and their titles can be deceptive. The created document's content will depend on the seniority and function of the individual creator within the process. The impact of various indexing and registry systems has to be assessed in relation to decentralization and local destruction.[27]

The heavily geographical orientation of the Department of the Interior with its jurisdiction over natural resources found a powerful tool in the patterning of information through maps and similar aids in the 1870s. Topographical registers were assembled on a geographical basis. Subject files were created which allowed for active planning compared to the passive registration of earlier times and a more reactive, laissez-faire attitude to exploration and development.[28] The records created by the department have a modern, sophisticated style appropriate to an environmental approach, albeit a rudimentary one, since its general objective was settlement and exploitation. Moreover, as new branches and departments were created around the settlement of the West, the record series became fragmented in an age of primitive copying systems. Cook warns, however, that

> Administrative policy and operational decisions were obviously not driven exclusively or even primarily by departmental records-keeping systems. In the first place, the degree to which policy is formulated at all by recourse to records can only be assumed, not yet demonstrated conclusively. As well, the role of other information sources (conversations, informal notes, senior officials' personal files) vis-a-vis the formal records-keeping system in developing policy has not been investigated. . . . Despite these qualifications, better knowledge of social bookkeeping systems in the past—their inherent biases, the characteristics of the data they collected, their shifts and changes over time—remains essential to evaluating the information contained in those systems for most research purposes.[29]

Finally, let us glance at the Hudson's Bay Company as it changed from merchant venturing activity based on the fur trade, with its officers, factors, and commissioners—generalists who had administered not only trade, but integrated a land and society. The magnificent records of the company now housed in Winnipeg bear witness to an oral, scribal subculture amongst its servants, with strong traditions of communication behaviour sharply at odds with the new retail business being developed in the 1880s and 1890s. The commissioners of that era sought to introduce printed forms in addition to the servants' contracts which had been in use since the eighteenth century.[30] The three thrusts of company business— land, fur trade, and sales shop—were strictly rationalized into departments based on function rather than geography. More and better information now arrived at headquarters in shorter time through the use of loose printed forms for standard transactions at fort, district, and departmental level. By 1900, twenty main file groups became the basis of an alphanumeric filing system. "The records system shows the need for constant communication on a wide variety of topics associated with the operation of a successful commercial enterprise. It underscores as well the relationship of this communication with an effective transportation network,"[31] explains Mark Walsh.

The company now operated not with lake boats and pack trains, but steamers and steam trains, the telegraph and the telephone, demanding much faster transmittal of information for decision making and putting a premium on facts and news rather than editorialized opinion (witness the change in appearance of newspapers, which became a simultaneous mosaic of information under a dateline). Business, likewise, required rapid transmission of facts and, like government, was set on a path of frantic speed-up: "The tendency of electric media is to create a kind of organic interdependence among all the institutions of society, emphasizing de Chardin's view that the discovery of electro-magnetism is to be regarded as 'a prodigious biological event.' "[32] This is what the old order of railway age and industrial bureaucracy had to contend with after the turn of the twentieth century, resulting in a frantic output of paper documents prior to a flip and reversal, which is beginning to take effect as computer print-out gives way to electronic mail and there is increased use of terminals to access databases without recourse to paper. Many subject filing systems contained the folder "telegrams." Perhaps there was even then an unconscious awareness that the medium was the message!

In the context of documentation, early attitudes to the typewriter are quite revealing.[33] It was, of course, a "typewriting machine," combining two media in the first word and reiterating its mechanical, industrial origin in the second. Initially, commerce regarded the handwritten letter as more effective and personal. When finally adopted, typed letters retained all the phraseology of scribalism including the ubiquitous "humble and obedient servant." In addition, the typewriter and the carbon became a powerful ditto device banishing the letter book and filling the files. Like print, the machine's output was uniform, homogenous, so that personal letters too were robbed for a while of spontaneity; type requires correct form and spelling according to the iron law of the printing press. The original "type writers" were the operators, the hundreds of thousands of women who, in G. K. Chesterton's phrase, "refused to be dictated to and went out and became stenographers."[34] They became a part of their machines as an extension of their fingers and so merged with them until "typist" was devised. By then, the habit of dictating letters, especially into dictating machines, rendered the modern letter somewhat more relaxed and verbose in style. But even these gently persuasive sentences have now become common form, as suitable paragraphs are selected from floppy discs. That flattering three-page letter from the public official in reply to a special interest protest by now should deceive no one.

The adoption of the telephone seems to have increased the work of the typist, since, contrary to conventional wisdom, the record of countless phone calls survives in public records at least through follow-up memoranda and correspondence. Those highly confidential phone calls that leave no trace upon the record probably would have once been conducted face to face behind closed doors. The loss of the record may not be all that great.

Above all, it was the telegraph and telephone that began to break down the transmission of information up and down the bureaucratic pyramid, and consequently the formal structure of documentation. The combination of the oral message amplified and speeded up by electricity, with no other authority but that of knowledge required at that moment, broke into every level of the hierarchy and hastened the "ad hoc-racy" of task forces and similar groups. The production line began to crumble, and the dots appeared on the organization chart. The retreat from the formal literate record had begun.

INFORMATION OVERLOAD AND THE RETRIEVAL OF THE ARCHIVIST

This article has been restricted to consideration of the textual record in its many forms; to stray beyond these limits would extend the discussion too far. Texts must now be pursued to the point of departure from hard copy, to suspension within the computer. The disembodied sounds and voices over the radio and the power of these vibrations to persuade are, of course, familiar, as is television with its own set of compulsions and insistent language. Automation, despite the limitations of its language, ushers its users into a world of increasing personal choice as they develop patterns of command over constantly changing configurations of data. This is very disturbing to persons brought up on assimilation processes associated with paper documents.

We archivists now grope about in the world of Sherlock Holmes's dog that didn't bark, where the comfortable old connections and relationships between sources of information no longer exist, where—like the great detective—we must rid ourselves of preconceived approaches and assumptions if we are to avoid the blindness of bureaucratic experience. As Marshall McLuhan and Barrington Nevitt have explained:

> There are, in fact, no connections in the material universe. Einstein, Heisenberg and Linus Pauling have baffled the old mechanical and visual culture of the nineteenth century by reminding scientists in general that the only physical bond in Nature is the resonating interval or 'interface.' Our language, as much as our mental set, forbids us to regard the world in this way. It is hard for the conventional and uncritical mind to grasp the fact that 'the meaning of meaning' is a *relationship*: a figure-ground *process of perpetual change*.[35]

The significance of speech changed when writing became widespread, and likewise the significance of writing changed when print dominated the scene. Now automation has changed the individual's *relationship* with writing and print. For example, a user can (or will soon) retrieve from text, not a whole book or serial, but only that portion needed. If the wheel is considered as an extension of one's feet and the pen as an extension of one's fingers, then automation, which opens up exposure to information traveling at the speed of light from all directions, almost at once becomes, as McLuhan argues, an extension of one's nervous system. No wonder people are disturbed, anxious, and uncertain. They can see the wood, and the trees, and the space between them all at the same time; this is rather frightening.

Archivists speak of machine-readable records and perhaps are comforted by that nice old word "machine." As with other media, the content is that of its predecessor. The computer starts in the guise of a rather fast mathematical engine. It replaced paper-accounting records and now absorbs vast quantities of text (much as printing absorbed manuscript books and televisions absorbed old movies) with what could become almost limitless capabilities of retrieval. A "machine" in the generally acceptable sense, the computer most certainly is not.

What are the implications for the administrator, the creator of documents? The old hierarchies are crumbling. Specialized operations are eliminated in the clerical field. Since communication through on-line, interactive transmission reintroduces old oral, preliterate patterns of communication, many familiar forms of record will go into a state of flux, and many classes of documents at the operational level will disappear altogether. There is still a vast hangover of paper, but that is a kind of supernova paper explosion before the flip into largely terminal activity—not in its sense of finality, although that is a very real danger if international fears are not overcome in other fields of automation.

The whole approach to social organization and management is taking a distinctly biological, rather than historical, turn. The continuity of man and nature is now seen more clearly. There is less inclination to desacralize nature through the concept of mankind as lords of creation. Patterns rather than causes leading to effects are sought; the constructive interval within paradox which does not necessarily have to be resolved is appreciated.[36] Flexible, "organic/adaptive" organizational structures are being built around problem solving through cooperation and consensus.[37] Involvement, participation, and autonomy are likewise stressed. The old assured recipes for a successful organization no longer hold, but are subject to circumstance as administrators learn to live with both uncertainty for want of the right data, and equivocality arising from organizational ambiguities and the failure to ask the right questions.[38] Quantum mechanics is showing that an element of uncertainty and subjectivity may be present at the heart of science and of life itself.[39]

What is the archivist's role in all this?[40] Surely, the life cycle theory of records retention and destruction is no longer appropriate in its original form.[41] Far from being a cycle (unless the paper is recycled), the progression through administrator to records manager and thence to the archivist is the old linear, fragmented, production line process. If the record is to be of maximum value to the administrator and, where appropriate, to the general public as user, then archivists must be far closer to the point of creation and original use. They must thoroughly understand the strengths of the various media as records and the needs of users. They must help to shape the forms of information capture and retrieval systems of value equally for the present as for the future. It is possible that archivists will find solutions to problems through a closer study of the way in which the information-rich, basic forms of life—the genes, chromosomes, the DNA double helix, and the organic transactions present in sustainable agriculture—retrieve what they need when they need it.[42] Is this the end of that subject/object split which literacy engendered and where "history" began? A deeper exploration of the relationship between myth and history is needed.[43] Will the postliterate, postindustrial society place the same value as archivists do on all the vast accumulation of records, most of which are already self-destructing?[44] Archivists need to wrestle with this now. A beginning has been made as we study retrieval of information in relation to the nature and purpose of the record, with less emphasis on the hierarchical level in an administrative structure and more on the process inherent in the record. Bearman and Lytle have recognized this and criticized the limitations of the record group, which "imposes the *intellectual* constraints of a *physical* shelf order system."[45] The shelf is, after all, the line, page, and book writ linear hangover from print culture. These authors' emphasis on form and function, from which content can to a large extent be inferred, is pattern recognition in the face of overwhelming information fallout rather than a hopeless concentration on subject indexing of content. Bearman and Lytle offer instead a subject inference concept, the objective of which is "to capture the full richness of provenance information—the structures, processes and activities of organizations—and to make routine the inferential process which permits one to locate information which has been or is being created by organizational activities. The power of the system will be to retrieve present as well as past information created by organizations; in fact, extrapolations to information yet to be created could be made within certain constraints."[46] Finally, Bearman and Lytle assert that "archivists hold the key to provenance information becoming a major tool for management of all resources in modern organizations."[47] This, they may agree, supports the view of an archival presence close to the point of records creation. Yet "in every field of study and research at present, the incidence of insight and new knowledge surpasses every means of systematic retrieval."[48] The gap between document creation and the information retrieval process is closing, however.

At the microcosmic level, Clark Elliott, after examining a short series of letters, has proposed consideration of inductive classifications through observed functions performed by the various letters.[49] "Archivists," he writes,"are very seldom concerned with the nature or function of individual documents."[50] In this, he is in line with Bearman and Lytle. The environment of the document is not a passive container of "content" but active processes in the manner of preliterate words, designed for action, not analysis. A final example is illustrative: persons in special interest groups send letters to their legislative representatives by way of protest or petition. Their impact is not assessed by the recipients on the basis of *content* but on the *action* of writing the letter or sending the telegram. The very act and effort of *writing a letter* indicates a body of opinion with a "bodycount" of about two hundred. Printed cards are much lower; telegrams, telephone calls, and handwritten letters are higher. Our preliterate forebears would surely understand this.

Increasingly, the act or decision which informs the conduct of affairs grows closer in time to the document that records it. The specializations of form and technology become blurred as manuscript, typescript, and letterpress now find their modern expression in a flurry of photocopies, offset printing, and desktop publishing. The concept of an "original" becomes increasingly elusive and could almost disappear. Electronic communication, especially in its interactive mode, can become a continuous discourse without trace, as both act and record occur simultaneously with little or no media delay or survival. Words once again become action oriented. Surely this requires much thought and understanding on the part of the archivist working closely with colleagues in the communication field.

This article has attempted to present the relationship of communications technology to certain classes of archives, and its impact on the user who may also be the archivist. Several disciplines have provided a range of insights in mosaic form, analogous to synchronic discussion rather than diachronic research. Statements may be more assertive than tentative, but this is intended to avoid tedious modifiers in an ambience of suspended judgement, as thoughts swarm over the subject in a nonspecialized way to let the light in and perhaps reveal some fresh approaches. This is not the path of painstaking research, which has its place, but rather of "organizing ignorance for discovery"[51] which, in a preliminary essay of this kind, may be more appropriate.

REFLECTION, 2000

The quotation which forms part of my title had been at the back of my mind for sometime since the day many years ago when an elderly relation required me to witness a signature on what I think was her will. Things had to be done right, and she directed me to place a finger tip on a little red dot while I intoned, "This is my very act and deed," as I appended my signature next to the dot. The red mark was all that is left of what was once an appliqué seal and a reminder of the long tradition of sigillography which has all but disappeared.

Here was a human decision, an "act," limited by the nature of the medium so that the medium absorbed the deed as in "title deed," to become a memory. What exactly was that decision and to what extent did the medium of record affect its meaning?

My earlier essay on administrative history was concerned more with the structure and content of public records and the importance of understanding the relationship of file series as a means of understanding the workings of bureaucracy. Then McLuhan invaded my perceptions and I felt the need to get beyond the media to the meaning and intention. I have never read much of Derrida, Foucault, et al., not because I reject the philosophy of deconstruction or postmodernism, but because McLuhan starts with the medium, in our case the archival document, which becomes the "given" to which we always return. That is our job.

Once again, I have returned to the early roots of communication which have received a great deal of attention by anthropologists. Medieval references seem to haunt my papers, but this time I was writing primarily for American archivists who also have appreciated what I had to say. Thanks to Terry Cook and many others, there has been a great deal of recent study on form and function, mind and matter over against content, especially in relation to appraisal. This paper may have helped in some way the high standard of discourse that has emerged on this subject.

NOTES

1. For example, Hugh A. Taylor, "The Media of Record: Archives in the Wake of McLuhan," *Georgia Archive* 6 (Spring 1978): 1–10, and "Transformation of the Archives: Technological Adjustment or Paradigm Shift?" *Archivaria* 25 (Winter 1987–1988): 12–28; Barrington Nevitt, "Archivist and Comprehensivist," *Argus* 10 (1981): 65–70. For a more general discussion of the Canadian discourse of technology, see Arthur Kroker, *Technology and the Canadian Mind: Innis/McLuhan/Grant* (Montreal: New World Perspective, 1985).

2. For example, M. T. Clanchy, *From Memory to Written Record: England 1066–1307* (Cambridge, Mass.: Harvard University Press, 1979); Elizabeth Eisenstein, *The Printing Press as an Agent of Change* (Cambridge: Cambridge University Press, 1979); Jack Goody and I. Watt, *The Consequences of Literacy* (Cambridge: Cambridge University Press, 1977); Eric A. Havelock, *Preface to Plato* (Cambridge, Mass.: Harvard University Press, 1963), *The Literate Revolution in Greece and its Cultural Consequences* (Princeton, N.J.: Princeton University Press, 1982); Harold A. Innis, *The Bias of Communication* (Toronto: University of Toronto Press, 1951), *Empire and Communications* (Oxford: Oxford University Press, 1950); Ernst Posner, *Archives in the Ancient World* (Cambridge, Mass.: Harvard University Press, 1972); Marshall McLuhan, *Understanding Media: The Extensions of Man* (Toronto: McGraw-Hill, 1962), *The Gutenberg Galaxy* (Toronto: University of Toronto Press, 1962); Walter J. Ong, *Orality and Literacy: The Technologizing of the Word* (London: Methuen, 1982); Brian Stock, *The Implications of Literacy* (Princeton, N.J.: Princeton

University Press, 1983); Frances Yates, *The Art of Memory* (Chicago: University of Chicago Press, 1966), "PrintCulture," *Encounter* 52 (1979): 5964; John Fiske and John Hartley, *Reading Television* (London: Methuen, 1978).

3. For a good definition of semiotics, see T. O'Sullivan, J. Hartley, D. Saunders, J. Fiske, *Key Concepts in Communication* (London: Methuen, 1983), 210–12.

4. Lister Sinclair, in *History and the New Age* (Toronto: Canadian Broadcasting Corporation, 1984), 1.

5. Joseph Brown, in *History and the New Age*, 2.

6. Quoted by David Caley, ibid.

7 Claude Levi-Strauss, *The Savage Mind* (Chicago: University of Chicago Press, 1968), 10–19.

8. D. Wayne Moodie, "Native Mapmaking," in *The Canadian Encyclopedia* (Edmonton: Hurtig, 1985), 294.

9. For a recent series of articles on this theme, see David R. Olson, ed., "Understanding Literacy: A Symposium on the Psychological, Social and Educational Dimensions of Literacy," *Interchange* 18 (1987): 1–173.

10. McLuhan, *Understanding Media*, ix.

11. Kenneth L. Chasse, "The Legal Issues Concerning the Admissibility in Court of Computer Printouts and Microfilm," *Archivaria* 18 (Summer 1984): 166–201.

12. This is an oversimplified description. For a full account, see Vyvian H. Galbraith, *The Making of Doomsday Book* (Oxford: Clarendon Press, 1961).

13. M. T. Clanchy, *From Memory to Written Record*, 208–12.

14. For a general survey of the process, see S. B. Chrimes, *An Introduction to the Administrative History of Medieval England* (Oxford: Blackwell, 1966).

15. For a full account of the changing nature of bureaucracy in an earlier paper and information explosion created by the printing press and related factors, see Geoffrey R. Elton, *The Tudor Revolution in Government* (Cambridge: Cambridge University Press, 1959).

16. In N. Machiavelli's *The Prince* (translated by W. K. Marriott with an introduction by Herbert Butterfield [London: Dent, 1958]), chapter 22 is titled "Concerning the Secretaries of Princes," which nicely delineates the ideal bureaucrat and how he should be managed. Government, in Machiavelli's eyes, was a work of art where the artist/administrator engineered certain "causes" to obtain, like brush strokes, the desired "effects" with a dedicated calculation so evident in the eyes of Holbein's sitters.

17. Graham S. Lowe, "'The Enormous File': The Evolution of the Modern Office in Early Twentieth-Century Canada," *Archivaria* 19 (Winter 1984–85): 138.

18. Douglas McCalla, "Accounting Records and Everyday Economic Life in Upper Canada, 1790–1850," *Archivaria* 21 (Winter 1985–86): 150, 153.

19. The "Studies in Documents" series in *Archivaria* 20 (Summer 1985) onwards deals with "modern diplomatics" and explores the nature of records through history, their impact on government, and the impact of the principal media of record on society and hence the user. Several articles cited are from this series. In addition, the following articles approach records in a similar manner: Tom Nesmith, "Archives from the Bottom Up: Social History and Archival Scholarship," *Archivaria* 14 (Summer 1982): 5–26; JoAnne Yates, "Internal Communications Sys-

tems in American Business Structures: A Framework to Aid Appraisal," *American Archivist* 48 (Spring 1985): 141–58; Trudy Huskamp Peterson, "Counting and Accounting: A Speculation on Change in Record Keeping Practices," *American Archivist* 45 (Spring 1982): 131–34; David Bearman and Peter Sigmond, "Explorations of Form of Material Authority Files by Dutch Archivists," *America Archivist* 50 (Spring 1987): 249–53. Also valuable are Laetitia Yeandle, "The Evolution of Handwriting in the English Speaking Colonies of America," *American Archivist* 43 (Summer 1980): 294–311; Maygene Daniels,"The Ingenious Pen: American Writing Implements from the Eighteenth Century to the Twentieth," *American Archivist* 43 (Summer 1980): 312–24. I have relied heavily on the detailed researches of others, and if I quote them generously, that is to give them their due.

20. V. Seymour Wilson, *Canadian Public Policy and Administration: Theory and Environment* (Toronto: McGraw Hill Ryerson, 1981), 8.

21. Luther Gulick, "Notes on the Theory of Organization," *Papers on the Science of Administration* (New York: Columbia University Press, 1937), 13, quoted by Wilson.

22. Henry Parris, *Constitutional Bureaucracy* (London: Alien and Unwin, 1969), 108.

23. Murray Young, *The Colonial Office in the Early Nineteenth Century*, (London: Longmans, 1961), 189–92.

24. Etienne Balazs, *Chinese Civilization and Bureaucracy* (New Haven: Yale University Press, 1966), 16–17. In contrast to the flexible use of sources in the West, Chinese historiography required quotations from documents rather than summarizing them, and this also applied to bureaucratic methodology. Copying stifles the mind, favoring the letter at the expense of the spirit. "The magic of the word (the change of intrinsic and associated meanings carried by each written character) undoubtedly has a lot to do with it. . . ." Ibid., 16–17.

25. Bill Russell, "The White Man's Paper Burden: Aspects of Record Keeping in the Department of Indian Affairs, 1860–1914," *Archivaria* 19 (Winter 1984–85): 51. I have drawn extensively on this article.

26. Ibid., 52.

27. Terry Cook, "Paper Trails: A Study of Northern Records and Northern Administration, 1898–1958" (Typescript; to be published shortly).

28. Ibid.

29. Ibid.

30. For this section, the author is indebted to Mark Walsh, "By Packtrain and Steamer: The Hudson's Bay Company's British Columbia District Manager's Correspondence, 1897–1920," *Archivaria* 20 (Summer 1985): 127–35. This is the first of a series of articles in *Archivaria* which examines the record in the context of use and impact rather than content.

31. Ibid., 132.

32. McLuhan, *Understanding Media*, 218.

33. Much of this on the typewriter and the telephone is from McLuhan, *Understanding Media*, 227–40.

34. Ibid., 228.

35. Marshall McLuhan and Barrington Nevitt, *Take Today: The Executive as Dropout* (New York: Harcourt Brace Jovanovich, 1972), 86.

36. Kim S. Cameron, "Effectiveness as Paradox: Consensus and Conflict in Conceptions of Organizational Effectiveness," *Management Science* 32 (1986): 539–53.

37. Warren G. Bennis, "Organizational Developments and the Fate of Bureaucracy," in *Perspectives on Public Bureaucracy*, ed. Fred A. Kramer (Cambridge: Wintrop, 1981). Bennis first used the term "ad hoc-racy."

38. Richard L. Daft and Robert H. Lengel, "Organizational Information Requirements, Media Richness and Structural Design," *Management Science* 32 (1986): 554–71.

39. Fred Hoyle, *The Intelligent Universe* (New York: Holt Rinehart and Winston, 1983), 201–09.

40. See also Taylor, "The Medium of Record," 1–10.

41. Jay Atherton, "From Life Cycle to Continuum: Some Thoughts on the Records Management-Archives Relationship," *Archivaria* 21 (Winter 1985–86): 43–5.

42. These ideas were suggested by the reading of Fred Hoyle's *The Intelligent Universe* cited above.

43. For further thoughts on the relationship between archivists, historians, records managers, documents, and information, see also Hugh A. Taylor, "Information Ecology and the Archives of the 1980s," *Archivaria* 18 (Summer 1984): 25–37; and a sequel (following a long published discussion by others in *Archivaria*), Hugh A. Taylor, "Through the Minefield," *Archivaria* 21 (Winter 1985–1986): 180–85. A most interesting article, William H. McNeill, "Mythistory, or Truth, Myth, History and Historians," has been published in the *American Historical Review* 91 (February 1986): 1–10; so far as I know, it is the first of its kind by a historian in a historical journal and indicates an emerging interest.

44. The terms "postliterate" and "postindustrial" have a respectable academic validity, although their meaning is open to discussion; see David Lyon, "From 'Post-Industrialism' to 'Information Society': A New Social Transformation?" *Sociology* 20 (1986): 577–88.

45. David A. Bearman and Richard Lytle, "The Power of the Principle of Provenance," *Archivaria* 21 (Winter 1985–86): 20.

46. Ibid., 25.

47. Ibid., 27.

48. McLuhan and Nevitt, *Take Today*, 105.

49. Clark A. Elliott, "Communication and Events in History: Towards a Theory for Documenting the Past," *American Archivist* 48 (Fall 1985): 357–68.

50. Ibid., 361.

51. B. Nevitt, *The Communication Ecology* (Toronto: Butterworths,1982), 149–72.

Chapter 11

Towards the New Archivist: The Integrated Professional

Last year I pictured an archival landscape in process of transformation whereby a sea change would submerge our professional insularity, but not identity, beneath the waters of holism. I would like now to present for your inspection elements of a survival kit which may help us set course as we head for the open, though possibly dangerous, waters of the 1990s.

You will recall that we took a brief look at the archivist as plumber, in which our preoccupation with technical fixes stood in contrast to the much wider questions posed by Frank Burke, Gerald Ham, Terry Cook, and others. I suggested that maps of past practice may not be reliable guides for future travels into unknown terrain.

Like all professionals we have tended to be overly conservative in our vision, preferring to be nudged and pushed by change, and content to remain safely entrenched behind our twin fortresses of *provenance* and *respect de fonds*, clad in the armour of our definition of archives in which we have finally recognized media "of every kind, nature, and description." We say with Lionel Bell that, whereas printed books and serials are *about* this and that, archives are a *part* of a record of this and that in its raw state.[1] This seems quite logical and we have often conceded to libraries the literary and scholarly manuscripts which preceded Gutenberg, and thereafter the manuscript drafts which authors prepared on the road to publication.

Unpublished manuscript of a speech delivered to the annual conference of the Association of Canadian Archivists, held in Windsor, Ontario, June 1988, and subsequently revised by the author. Reproduced with the kind permission of the author.

Confident in the governance of our territory so defined, we have cultivated our finding aids and produced a luxurious growth of hybrid
blooms which, for lack of standards, have graced our landscape with a
certain wayward charm. To our credit we are now beginning to give much
more time and effort to rendering these operations more professional and
effective, but they remain operations, techniques, means of controlling
and revealing our resources, marshalling armies of words to flush out information communicated through standard formats. First-class minds
have been engaged in this necessary work and I do not denigrate it, but
what of the larger implications of what we do? Is our territory as clearly
defined as we like to think?

I suggest that print is one of many mass media of communication and
that printed books are not necessarily separate entities *sui generis* in total
contradistinction to archives. They are forms of record which we do not
usually include in our quiver, but I would remind you that the printed
minutes of an institution signed by the chairperson can become the
archival record; official correspondence and reports are about this and
that; if photocopied they remain archival, but if printed in books they do
not, though a learned introduction may provide additional illumination.
What happens if the original drafts of printed annual reports (which librarians call government documents) are destroyed? We still do not regard these printed copies as archival. Then again, there are all those col-
orful and sign-laden brochures for which the "originals" are no more than
typescript notes and pasteups in no way resembling the finished product.
Very often these remain with the archives but we do not really regard
them as archival—or do we? Meanwhile, we have come to recognize film
and videotape as archival although they are about this and that—and often published. Strictly speaking, the archival raw material should perhaps
be limited to the documentation and outtakes which go to make a TV
news broadcast, for instance, that package being more analogous to a
published newspaper, serial, or magazine and therefore more suitable in
a library—or is it?

Similar problems arise in documentary art as to where an artist's communication, in whatever medium from correspondence to easel painting,
ceases to be archival. And so to return once more to printed books. Are
they not the final record of the author in the conduct of professional activity and duplicated for the convenience of readers? You might argue
that no, the published work is a literary widget and not archival, just as
the product of a brick business is not archival though the records of that
business are. Yes, but an author is a *communicator* as also is an artist, and
this has to be borne in mind. Drafts and sketches leading to the finished
product are approximations of the final statement, the *ordre primitif* of
which must be respected.

This final statement is in the same category as the authorised manuscript of an annual report, but here we must be careful. A strict interpretation would hold that to be archival all such material should remain part of the fonds of the originator, be it manuscript, painting, or photograph. If it is alienated then it seems two things happen: a manuscript may be transmitted in the course of public administration or private transactions within the family and still remain archival in its new fonds. If such a manuscript were to become a printed book, so this argument goes, it becomes a product designed to be broadcast, normally through purchase or gift as is an easel painting sold as a product by the artist. These products are not regarded as archival because their function alienates them from the organic archival material which gave them birth. It might be conceded by this argument that an author who, with more money than sense, had his work printed and then decided to retain all the copies for himself could still claim that such a printing was archival. The author's archives might then go to a repository, and the archivist in the course of documentary appraisal could remove these redundant printed copies and alienate them by gift, sale, or destruction without compromising the archival status of the one remaining copy, since he is not publishing copy that was printed but not published in the first place. More simply an author who inscribes in a published copy of his work "for my own use" at once rendered that copy archival if he does not alienate it, partly on the grounds of the inscription which like the label on Jenkinson's elephant becomes an integral part of the whole. Presumably even if there is no inscription, this use could be implied from a single copy in the author's files, and this particular copy has become archival. Printed books and brochures within files in the National Archives are transferred with appropriate intellectual control to the Archives Library in recognition of this dual status as printed and archival material. But wait! What about the printer or publisher who may retain a copy as evidence of the act and a record of process and style in his files. Likewise a whole library of purchased books might be said to "document" the tastes and interests of the owner as the statues of Roman emperors in the old Hanleian library provided evidence of the owner's classical turn of mind and were immortalized in the catalogue now in the British Museum. If we were to accept all this as archival, which of course no one does, the waters of holism would close over us forever and we would surely drown in our eclectic soup. I simply want to suggest that there are some fine lines here which may not be as easily determined as we think, especially when we deal with media such as television and automated records which are broadcast and are often sadly lacking in original documents as we understand them in the textual sense. As archivists we must stake out our territory quite clearly on the basis of function rather than medium of record while remaining closely attuned to other resonances in the neighbouring territory of libraries, galleries, and museums. I do not believe we have done that in the past and our insights may be the poorer for it. Are we looking here for some "meta-archival" approach which can embrace a kind of archive of created knowledge (paradocs perhaps!) which extend beyond the documents which we recognize as archival and artificial collections maintained quite properly in archives for their heritage value?

There is a sense in which the dichotomy between library and archives is an illusion fostered by the dominance of print over the past few centuries and the division of record into print and manuscript. Print is simply one of many media of communication, as we now recognize, with its own characteristics. We look after archival material as we define it and librarians take care of the books. This works very well and I am not suggesting integration with them. But are we not all keepers of the records and custodians of the knowledge they contain?

I hope you will not regard this as a digression because I believe it could become the central concern of archive/library relations to be faced in the 1990s. The dichotomy has been most valuable to culture and society in that it has enabled archivists to develop their profession and an organic approach to the record which would have been denied in a world of librarians. The division may have arisen out of too great an emphasis on the physical reality of the archival record as a unique human artifact or construct, which is what the archivists' two principles are partly about, and the separate physical entity of the book, which for the librarian has in the past transcended its contents as any standard library card bears witness. The revelation of contents by archivists and librarians alike has been comparatively primitive, partly for technological reasons.

When we begin to treat all human communication as symbolic equivalents of mental decisions, then the record becomes even broader, extending into the museums. It is time we all moved to higher ground away from the battlefields of classification and original order, catalogues, inventories and other finding aids where our professions were defined and which we must return to in the course of our work. What should we *really* be about now?

Archivists in North America have already begun to consider these matters. In 1981 Frank Burke wrote that "to date there has been no elucidation of archival theory in the United States and little, if any, in the rest of the world." By "theory" he meant "the development of universal laws, laws immutable and applicable at all times, in all places," which seems somewhat inflexible to say the least, but he is quite correct when he insists that "the theoretic assumptions should be based not on the structure but on the nature of human organizations and on humans themselves" in answer to the question "Why?" rather than "What?" or "How?" He goes on to ask whether society keeps records out of psychic compulsion or practical pragmatism? What is the relation of records to the decision-making process? What causes us to revere artifacts and is this universal?[2]

An inspection of the *American Archivist* and *Archivaria* subsequent to that date, which include the Burke-Cappon exchange and the archivist-information manager debate, is quite revealing and demonstrates directions in which some of our enquiries have moved and should be moving. The use of the case method in archival education recommended by Francis Blouin in 1978[3] certainly emphasizes the study of the "nature of human organizations" advocated by Burke in terms of decision making related to the record. Gerald Ham had also stressed the need for conceptualization in collecting strategies and the comparison of records produced, for instance, by universities, against those preserved, as a guide to possible bias by archivists.[4]

This re-examination of roles and the directions for further research has also been undertaken by librarians. Curtis Wright quotes Jesse Shera, who in 1963 declared that

> The great need of the library profession is to formulate a professional philosophy that will meet the rapidly changing needs of society for recorded knowledge. We must re-define our role in society . . . (and) make of the library the agency it should be in the total communications process. . . . We must put our intellectual house in order or we will lose control of many functions relating to the communication of the written word that are properly our own. . . . This need lies at the base of every other problem of librarianship. . . . I am deeply disturbed by the malaise that has so long gripped our profession, its shallowness, its sterility, its intellectual immaturity, and I see no remedy but to probe deeply, however great the pain.[5]

Wright then goes on to trace the twin streams of the form-philosophy (Plato) and matter-philosophy (Democritus) which have dominated the intellectual life of Western society ever since.[6] Preliterate man did not have this perception which arose from the separation of the world of ideas from that of physical realities. The Greeks still maintained the *idea* of the unity of mind and nature and that the human mind is capable of constructing a complete system of truth which remained an impossible goal. There have been reconcilers in the Socratic tradition, but "to this day philosophy has only two main problems . . . the nature of the *physical* world which includes all the phenomenal objects of scientific enquiry and *the spiritual nature* of man which constitutes the noumenal basis of humanistic study."[7]

In what has been termed the Age of the Symbol,[8] we and the librarians likewise have concentrated too much on the physical world. Librarians have wrestled quite properly with the physical and intellectual logistics of books and the printed page, but has there been too much effort on attempts to discover scientific absolutes in library practice? Degrees are granted in Library Science and we (rather less often) speak of "archival science." Curtis Wright asks whether information contained in the symbols which archivists call media of record "reduce[s] to something physical in the empirical world of matter and energy as in science? Or does it reduce to metaphysical patterns in the intellectual spirit world of ideas as in philosophy?"[9] He goes on to argue that "science analyzes the physical behaviour of symbols whereas humanism recognizes the formal meanings of symbolic referents. . . ." The progressive librarians who invariably think of themselves as "scientific" have always preferred the former to the latter; and that underscores Kaplan's point: "what is needed is a truly comprehensive theory of communication that integrates the realities at both ends of a wire connecting beings to their physical and cultural environments."[10] This endeavour should be the endeavour of archivists and librarians alike, with the help of other disciplines, including communication studies and anthropology.

Wright follows Abraham Kaplan in seeing librarianship "as an intellectual discipline based on the philosophical study of ideas, not an empirical discipline based on the scientific study of fact."[11] Do archivists see their work as essentially empirical, dealing with individual documents and series to be arranged, controlled, and retrieved as ends in themselves, or are we concerned with the recognition of forms and patterns of knowledge which may be the only way by which we will transcend the morass of information and data into which we will otherwise fall?[12] I believe we are.

It follows then that the integrated professional will not only have to study more closely the record, the symbol, and the knowledge that may be derived from them, but also the problems connected with access and destruction which we call "appraisal." Do we save that which the public wants or that which in the face of public apathy we believe will be crucial to an understanding and better management of our planetary environment? This is much more than just second-guessing fields of future research and involves a quite deep understanding of world problems of development and survival. According to Samuel De Weese, "Librarians have an obligation to educate their clients . . . they must risk unpopularity if it is necessary to serve the larger interests of society."[13] This requires a deal of wisdom if we are not to fall into the trap of a crass and arrogant subjectivity and will require a high level of self-knowledge. We will need not only integrated professionals, but thoroughly integrated and "centred" archivists who can handle the kind of tensions that will arise.

Helen Samuels recognizes the need for a more encompassing cooperative approach to appraisal when she affirms that documentation strategies require two levels of analysis: first an analysis of the history and scope of a topic so that the purpose of the strategy and the issues to be documented can be defined; and second, an analysis of the available sources of information so that an adequate record can be gathered for each issue.[14]

The broader issues that face us cannot be dealt with by isolated repositories and may well require the cooperation of libraries and even museums to identify and preserve secondary sources and artifacts. Heritage is much more than the sum of its parts.

Gerald Ham has described this new approach as the mark of our "post-custodial era." The phrase is somewhat misleading as we remain custodians and our work in this regard is intensified by a heightened awareness of conservation. However, there are signs everywhere of cooperative planning which is preparing us for a new vision of our role in relating the past to the present. At the same time, Ham warns us that

> There are many obstacles to developing needed archival research and development. We have no infrastructure to support such programs, and most of our institutions lack the resources to sponsor research. Unlike academic disciplines, we have no corps of teacher-researchers encouraged to do such work and be paid for it. The craft aspects of our work leave us preoccupied with daily practice, a preoccupation too often obscuring the need for new methods and techniques. . . . But most of all we need an institute for archival research—an institute that would not only assist us in improving our practice, but also would enable us to conduct needed theoretical studies.[15]

What kind of archival education will best equip us for this future? First, I would like to make clear that, since the archival profession is presently informed by a wide range of training and experience, we should resist for the time being an exclusive focus on Master's degrees in archival studies, important though they be. In North America, much of our corpus of knowledge was developed by the pioneers who had little or no professional background as we know it today. We have to remain sensitive to those laypersons, and to archivists less highly trained who challenge professional dogma which may blinker us against valuable insights. This may be particularly true if we are to reexamine our role in the knowledge business discussed above. "Organizing ignorance for discovery" can be very rewarding as we move into unfamiliar disciplines for solutions to both familiar and unfamiliar problems. This does not require rejection of our professional wisdom, but rather its enrichment through those new ways of thinking which Albert Einstein warned us would be necessary in the future.

However, professional schools, by their very nature, tend to be conservative and for good reason. They hand down a body of knowledge and experience won over time and they seek to maintain standards of excellence. We also know that they can be conservative in their *emphasis* which can become a distortion or aberration when seen against changing demands and environments. Some of the European archival schools showed this tendency for a while in the face of the media explosion, but many aspects of traditional training can still be used to good effect, the study of diplomatics for example. This is one of the most valuable contributions which Europe has made to understanding the nature of administrative records, and the relationship between bureaucratic process and recorded instrument. Extended from ancient to modern diplomatic and the forms of the new media, the thrust of this study can be used as a valuable probe into the meaning as opposed to the appearance of archival images in general. Apart from the limited research which the thesis allows (and this should not be discounted), extensive research and development can probably be conducted only by institutes in cooperation with archival repositories.

It has been argued that the archival discipline has too narrow a base to support a graduate degree,[16] a view quite commonly held in the United States where pragmatism has a particularly honourable place in the scheme of things, and that the academic disciplines, in particular History, with some postappointment training, furnish all that is needful for professional salvation. It is precisely this division between the material record and its intellectual exploitation emphasizing content; between matter and mind, discussed above; between archival technique and the scarcely grasped implications of the true nature of the record which diplomatics would have revealed, that ten years ago caused the SAA Committee for the 1970s to declare that archives did not provide sufficient "intellectual content" for a graduate degree (I was the only dissenter).[17] This theme is also reflected in the 1977 SAA Education Committee guidelines.[18] It is to the very great credit of the Association of Canadian Archivists and the University of British Columbia that the graduate-degree programme was established in Canada. Terry Eastwood, who has directed the course with distinction ever since, has stated what in his view are the three purposes of professional education: first, a theoretical framework of general principles constantly under critical examination, coupled with a thorough understanding of the nature, purpose, and uses of archives, a framework that is "just as demanding of students' intellect as any study they have done at university."[19] This framework and these principles will probably not have a scientific base, save in a very limited sense, since the study of archives is not a science. Increasingly it will develop into a philosophy of archives, and the time may well have come to build the groundwork on a thoroughly holistic base. This leads into Terry's second purpose: "the opportunity to acquire knowledge of a host of subjects." Initially this takes the form of courses in other disciplines, but the time will come when many archival courses will themselves have other disciplines integrated into them, as was attempted with "Society and the Documentary Record." He continues that "the third purpose and one of the most troublesome in a university setting is to build skills." Again, this age-old dichotomy between mind and hand, profession and craft, which literate civilization has perpetuated, hinders the full development of the integrated professional, though surgeons are no longer barbers, and what shall we say about a degree in music? Archival techniques (so-called) may appear deceptively simple, yet it is the constantly alert mind trained to think archivally that is sensitive to the nuances of arrangement, description, appraisal, and the like. "Universities," says Eastwood, "are places of enquiry" and enquiry brooks no bounds; it can continue to enrich the most routine tasks if a genuine mindfulness is brought to bear.

It has been a common theme of librarians for some time that archives administration is librarianship with variations, since both have the same goal. "Current library thinking," wrote Nancy Peace and Nancy Chudacoff in 1979, "focuses on organization and dissemination of information regardless of format: thus librarianship can and should encompass archives."[20] This rather suggests that "information" is simply the content of various formats, some of which happen to be archival, and are to be manipulated accordingly. If, however, we are concerned about knowledge, then the problem is a great deal more complex. Certainly there is common ground and archivists are becoming increasingly aware of this but what, I wonder, would Peace and Chudacoff say if we suggested that archives should instead encompass librarianship? Organically, as I have suggested earlier, this might be the correct approach.

Since archivists and librarians do have some common educational ground, it might be helpful to look at the views of two librarians as they peer into the future education of their profession. Michael Buckland criticizes J. C. R. Licklider's *Libraries of the Future*, written in 1966, for its overambitious claims for automation and what have since come to be known as "expert systems" to control information. What Licklider did not foresee was the vast, additional body of information and raw data which computers were to generate (material which is largely archival, though Buckland does not say so). Technology aside, Buckland sees little change in library values in terms of acquisition strategy. As for retrieval, he notes that "one might wish that the intellectual history of librarianship and library schools—the effects of different disciplines and strands of thought—had had some of the attention devoted to the institutional history (of those institutions)."[21] This is the stuff of broad cultural development which influences our perception of knowledge and its communication which so concerns Curtis Wright. "Although library schools are ordinarily viewed in relation to libraries, they need also to be viewed in their own right—as academic departments in an academic setting."²² Is this once more the problem of profession and craft which besets archival education? This may be the fault of some library schools and we should heed the warning.

Wilfrid Lancaster develops the point on which I would like to end. He believes "there is considerable support for the belief that librarianship is the most institutionalized of professions" and wonders why we do not have "librarian associations and librarian schools. . . . The librarian as provider of some form of professional service is a comparatively new phenomenon"²³ and there has been an overdependence on a physical facility. Archivists have, I believe, escaped this by the nature of their records, but we too can expect to see less dependence on our own home archives as we search the networks in response to enquiries, and this will require the development of a philosophy encompassing the nature of the recorded heritage as a whole and what it should contain. As automation reduces media transference to binary forms, there will be far more emphasis on conservation of the original coupled with a more rigorous definition of intrinsic value. Is it not time archivists, librarians, museum curators, and conservators sat around the table and did a little joint planning about the knowledge of the past that remains to us, and still communicates whether we listen or not, until it turns to dust and we are the poorer for its passing? Should we have not only an integrated profession, but also an integrated concern which spans several professions? I rather think so.

REFLECTION, 2000

I have always thought of archives in the broadest possible sense because I am something of a romantic when it comes to memory and heritage, which is what archives are about. I have therefore given a philosophical home to close relations and near neighbours of those records classically defined as archives. When you have been an archivist working in a public library in England or a provincial museum in Alberta, you cannot help but explore these relationships. The Public Archives of Nova Scotia has accumulated a charming collection of artifacts, which have arrived over the years in various fonds, and which are displayed from time to time, as well as unused sheets of early Nova Scotia postage stamps of considerable value. These are not archival, but they help to remind us that documents are also artifacts and postage stamps can be as significant as posters. We must certainly treat archives by the rules, but can we be too exclusive about what we have to offer the user? We build up reference libraries in our repositories to the extent that they relate closely to our archival holdings, and we are awash with "grey-literature" material. Perhaps this has taught us that our relationship with libraries, museums, and art galleries deserves to be a good deal closer. I have pur-

posely played around with some outrageous archival possibilities which will tease and infuriate the more traditionally minded. We should not be afraid to dance a little with the absurd from which insights may emerge.

When this paper was first written, it was still acceptable to be thoroughly conservative within the walls of our professional fiefdoms. We could at times peer over Gerald Ham's "Archival Edge"[24] and move into some unfamiliar fields of post-custodial activity so long as our basic principles remained unassailable reflections of rational positivism. Limited archival training tended to emphasize the "how to" based on these positivist principles.

Meanwhile, the Association of Canadian Archivists had been formed with an executive made of the "the young Turks" of the day, led by Gordon Dodds (yet another English expatriate) as its first President. He had envisioned a "Compleat Archivist" (with apologies to Isaac Walton) long before anyone else in Canada, who, "through a rich humanistic education and broad experience can cope in any situation. . . . The compleat archivist raids areas of knowledge and skill from beyond the traditionally allotted confines."[25] It is only necessary to glance through back issues of Archivaria and the American Archivist to map the changes that have taken place along these lines.

Over twenty years later, Jean-Pierre Wallot, shortly before his retirement as National Archivist of Canada, envisioned an even more "compleat archivist" and "integrated professional" for the second millennium.[26] Wallot is familiar with the common ground which we share with other heritage disciplines which may lead to forms of convergence after the manner of governments, businesses and, of course, diverse professions, through partnership and consortium rather than integration.[27] If we are to have arrangements of this kind, which is more than likely, then senior managers must learn to think in terms of consensus and networks rather than command-and-control mono-hierarchies, which can be very tempting to the personally ambitious.

"Compleatness" will also require an understanding of the postmodern (can no one coin a better term?) critique which casts serious doubt on the hitherto accepted meaning based on so many of those thousands of archival boxes, which contain minutiae way beyond our grasp or need. Perhaps we should set E. H. Carr against Keith Jenkins and his argument for history as fiction (which is getting close to myth in its finest form).[28] Who remembers history as we generally understand or learned it? What does the popular memory retain if not fiction and the larger mythic canvas of events? Carolyn Heald's "Is There Room for Archives in the Postmodern World?" is a question we must face and answer.

NOTES

1. Lionel Bell, "Controlled Vocabulary Subject Indexing of Archives," *Journal of the Society of Archivists* 4 (1971): 285.

2. Frank Burke, "The Future Course of Archival Theory in the United States," *American Archivist* 44 (1981): 42–44.

3. Francis X. Blouin Jr., "The Relevance of the Case Method to Archival Education and Training," *American Archivist* 41 (1978): 37–44.

4. F. Gerald Ham, "The Archival Edge," *American Archivist* 38 (1975): 12.

5. Jesse Shera, "Formulate a Professional Philosophy," *Library Journal* 88 (1963): 50.

6. H. Curtis Wright, "The Symbol and its Referent: An Issue for Library Education," *Library Trends* (Spring 1986): 730–37.

7. Ibid., p. 734.

8. Abraham Kaplan, "The Age of the Symbol: A Philosophy of Library Education," *The Intellectual Foundations of Library Education,* ed. Don R. Swanson, (Chicago 1965), pp. 7–16.

9. Wright, "The Symbol and its Referent," p. 739.

10. Ibid., pp. 739–40.

11. Ibid., p. 743.

12. Terry Cook also makes this point very well and quotes Daniel Boorstin, the former Librarian of Congress, to the effect that we should not mistake information for knowledge. Terry Cook, "From Information to Knowledge: An Intellectual Paradigm for Archives," *Archivaria* 19 (Winter 1984–85): 48. But may not some information be knowledge also? There is a danger of confusing information with raw data generated by the computer, and this is why archivists, who should be concerned with knowledge, need to be numbered among the armies of information specialists.

13. Samuel Carroll De Weese III, "A Paradigm of Commitment Toward Professional Identity," *Special Libraries* 61 (1970): 546.

14. Helen Willa Samuels, "Who Controls the Past," *American Archivist* 49 (1986): 122.

15. F. Gerald Ham, "Archival Strategies for the Post-Custodial Era," *American Archivist* 44 (1981): 214–15.

16. Robert M. Warner, "Archival Training in the United States and Canada," *American Archivist* 35 (1972): 358.

17. Philip P. Mason, "The Society of American Archivists in the Seventies: Report of the Committee for the 1970s," *American Archivist* 35 (1972): 209.

18. SAA Education and Professional Development Committee, "Guidelines for a Graduate Minor or Concentration in Archival Education," *American Archivist* 41 (1978): 105–06.

19. Terry Eastwood, "The Origin and Aims of the Master of Archival Studies Programme at the University of British Columbia," *Archivaria* 16 (1983): 40–41.

20. Nancy E. Peace and Nancy Fisher Chudacoff, "Archivists and Librarians: A Common Mission, A Common Education," *American Archivist* 42 (1979): 458.

21. Michael K. Buckland, "Education for Librarianship in the Next Century," *Library Trends* (Spring 1986): 784.

22. Ibid.

23. F. W. Lancaster, "Implications for Library and Information Science Education," *Library Trends* (Winter 1984): 337.

24. Ham, "The Archival Edge," 1975.

25. Gordon Dodds, "The Compleat Archivist," *Archivaria* 1 (Winter 1975–76): 81.

26. Jean-Pierre Wallot, "Limited Identities for a Common Identity: Archivists in the Twenty-First Century," *Archivaria* 41 (Spring 1996): 12–30.

27. Ibid., p. 12.

28. Carolyn Heald, "Is There Room for Archives in the Postmodern World?" *American Archivist* 59 (Winter 1996): 91.

Chapter 12

The Totemic Universe: Appraising the Documentary Future

This paper will not deal with the nuts and bolts of appraisal techniques and criteria, nor will there be consideration of specific media of record (such as photographs) or type of document (such as case papers). Faced with the need for reducing the bulk of an accumulation in some way, most of us have brought to bear our knowledge of the creating person or institution, the significance, as we see it, of the material in terms of the records (operational, "housekeeping," etc.) and our sense of "what is going on": is it significant or trivial? We also use such categories as "evidentiary" and "informational" and tend to give greater weight to the former as relating to the organic growth of the creating body, as opposed to incidental information on other themes. As archivists we save about 5% of the record created by governments and a great deal less from other sources unless they also are subject to records management.

There has been quite a long-standing tradition amongst our fraternity that we should try to second-guess the future needs of historians and others, and that what we retain will, in the eyes of future users, mature like good wine. There is of course merit in this and I believe we should have the freedom on occasion to save material on this basis. North Americans are, however, as David Gracy points out, more concerned with the present and their heritage reflects a pragmatic concern for the present.[1] Archives can be said to be current records of value that take a little longer; they do not suddenly change their nature and be-

Originally published in *Archival Appraisal: Theory and Practice*, Christopher Hives, ed., (Vancouver: Archives Association of British Columbia, 1990), pp. 15–29. Reproduced with the kind permission of the author and the Archives Association of British Columbia.

come archives overnight; we are dealing with a continuum. Let Gracy have the last word on this:

> Is there a future in the use of archives? Absolutely. But that future is use in the ongoing present for solving problems of the ongoing present. The greatest service of archivists is contributing to the continuity of culture by stimulating connections between the useful information from the past and the challenging needs of the present. We do not keep 'old,' meaning outdated, records. Rather we maintain records from a former present which contain vintage information, timely and exciting to the user who connects it to the present in which he or she labours. We should acknowledge the real future in the use of archives by adopting a motto such as: 'Archives: Records from the Past Working for the Present.'[2]

Beginning with the comfortably limited and valuable "left overs" from a distant past which we enthusiastically retain, we have moved with more recent records from elimination of the ephemeral to selection of the permanently valuable as being a more positive approach.[3] In this way we are being greatly aided by the insights and discipline provided by the study of diplomatics, which enables us to discover in a disciplined manner the relation between "facts" and "acts"—what in fact is going on in a group of documents as an aid to assessing their importance. It should nevertheless be remembered that the study of general and special diplomatics grew out of the study of medieval textual documents in a particular context. In Luciana Duranti's words,

> The object of diplomatics is not any written document it studies, but only the "archival document," that is, a document treated or received by a physical or juridical person in the course of a practical activity. It is true that the principles and methods of diplomatic analysis can be extended to documents expressing feelings and thoughts and created by individuals in their most private capacity. In fact, social habits and routines tend to penetrate all aspects of human life, so that love letters or diaries are likely to be very similar in their physical and intellectual form to executive letters, or ship's logs. But the inner freedom of human beings [is] such that a strict observance of rules cannot be expected in a personal context, so that a diplomatic study of forms may reveal little about the real nature of, for instance, an amateur photograph of a mother's message.[4]

The archives of public institutions are concerned primarily with the preservation of evidence for rights and freedoms and public accountability, "the peoples' evidences" which form an integral part of democratic life. These are the classic archives stretching back to the Middle Ages and beyond. The records of other corporate bodies and persons may also constitute archives, but there is much that archives administer which is not strictly archival, and it is becoming increasingly clear that we are developing a hybrid profession with elements of the museum curator and librarian which, as we shall see later, is a sign of the times. Many of our blooms are *floribunda* and exotic indeed, thanks to the new media, and changing views on heritage.

As archivists, we'd hold a near monopoly on appraisal decisions despite our committees. Most of these decisions must always have a strongly subjective element. We are all influenced by our view of the world. An informed intuition must partner rationality and link sensitivity with human maturity. Above all, we should not be captured by ideology, though this is hard to avoid and we can easily deceive ourselves.

For these reasons I would like now to move this presentation on to a much larger stage in the search for meaningful patterns of cultural need as they affect archives. We shall consider the relationships between nature (including human nature) and those technologies which create archival and bibliographical records in the communication process through time and have helped shape the way we think.[5]

It has taken around 14 billion years for the universe, the earth, and all life on the planet to reach its present state and through the human species to reflect upon itself. Three hundred years of scientific meditations (science has been described as the yoga of the West) has revealed in great detail an almost incredible universal balance maintained over time as life forms evolve and become extinct naturally. The Gaia hypothesis, which views the planet as a living organism, has a great deal going for it but even without that concept, it is becoming clear that the basic cell formation common to all life puts nature in a vast, and I believe divine, interrelationship of which we are a part. The human being is a species like any other and, as it were, a cousin of every other with the difference that we are genetically coded to reflect upon life and nature. We use the metaphor of the "code," the language of communication requiring interpretation, to describe this, and we speak of the richness of information within the genes of the DNA, an organic archive precipitating the acts and deeds of all forms of natural life.

But the human being has also been metaphorically "coded" so that we can create our own cultures in our own ways which have been developed by diverse forms of communication; we are a people surrounded by all the materials and other resources of civilization, but for the most part we have remained in conflict with the natural order of which we are a part. This has been disastrous.

I do not have to elaborate on this: David Suzuki, Ursula Franklin (in her Massey Lectures), and others, not to mention the Brundtland Report, and the recent conference on the environment in Vancouver, all bear witness. As one example of our rapacity, we are losing 20,000 species of plant and animal life a year irreversibly, which is like tearing that number of pages from the book of life. We have irretrievably lost this information which could be self-perpetuating and evolving. Is this not more valuable than some forms of information which librarians and archivists struggle to preserve? Eighty million books in the United States are "dying" from acidity on library shelves. Whether they are more important or not, they too will disappear. In addition, we have acid rain, the greenhouse effect, and the nuclear threat. In short, the influence of Western civilization, of which libraries and archives have always been a part, is destroying life on the planet. How has this come about?

Thomas Berry, a cultural historian who has long pondered the human predicament in planetary terms and likes to be known as a "geologian," details five transcendencies which have characterized the mind of Western civilization thus:

1. *A transcendent deity* in a personal covenant relationship with humankind which has often resulted (though this was not part of the covenant) in desacralizing the rest of nature and turning it over to exploitation on the way to the millennium.
2. *A transcendent spirituality* which declared that we alone are spiritual creatures.
3. *A transcendent mind* which *via* Descartes sees the natural universe as mechanistic.
4. *A transcendent technology* which has enabled humans to dominate almost all other life forms. We are a dangerous species that must become self-limiting.
5. *A transcendent goal*. We do not accept the natural world until it is used and we vent our rage against the human condition in our destruction of nature that thwarts us as in *Moby Dick*.[6]

One important element which has contributed in a profound way to this state of affairs is the technology at the heart of archives and libraries—writing, and in particular, writing with the phonetic alphabet, which provided us with an artificial memory and the capacity to conceptualize, to create forms and absolutes, to think abstractly and observe with detachment the natural world without being a part of it. Literacy made possible the covenant relationship with God and the Ten Commandments, and increased individualism, scientific reductionism, and our transcendent technology. This is a grossly generalized summary of a complex evolution, but it helps to point up the problem that our culture, our libraries, and our archives are part of the problem and to only a lesser degree part of the solution. In Berry's words, "the historical mission of the 20th Century is to reinvent the human at a species level reflectively in the community of life systems in a time/developmental context by means of a story and shared dream experience."[7]

This is a tall order to say the least, but I believe it is helpful to look at some of the characteristics of preliterate societies and in particular the characteristics of "oralism" from which our concepts of the archival record have descended and to which, through the transactional/interrogatory nature of instantaneous communication via the computer, we are in a very real sense returning.

Preliterate people lived (and still live) intimately with the earth, animal life, and the natural cycle of the seasons. Oral cultures occupy an acoustic space of sounds and voices but not linear boundaries; they do not exploit, they live lightly on the earth; their store of knowledge is specific, precise, and very rich—what Levi-Strauss has called the "science of the concrete." They do not preserve, but allow for replacement. Their libraries and archives lived undifferentiated in their heads, since appropriate acts arose out of truths within legends, myths, and stories that we in our differentiated culture would call literature. Homer was a minstrel conveying right behaviour through song;[8] the "song-lines" of the Australian aboriginals map out ancient rights for individuals laid down by their ancestors which are sung into existence again when a person goes on a "Dreaming" across hundreds of miles of territory.[9] The lyrics of rock music often have a compelling power and "We Are the World" is a mythic statement reaching across time. It is easy to dismiss this kind of thing as "hype," but its achievements in international bridge building should not easily be dismissed. Finally, behind the diplomatics of Crown land conveyancing which has its origin in the Middle Ages, there were the transfers of land before witnesses, without written record and using natural features as boundary marks. This last method of identification has produced all kinds of ambiguity in New Brunswick in the records of quite recent times. You will notice that what appears to be a wild digression may strike a chord with recorded sound archivists who must also face appraisal and selection decisions.

It is, I believe, significant that literacy may well have entered the Western tradition from Iraq through tokens, then symbols on clay, which created an archival record of commercial transactions.[10] Orality remains with us of course, but literacy became the dominant cultural engine of the West.

I would suggest that, whereas libraries became the storehouses of knowledge for arts, sciences, and religion (with the Bible as the most influential library of all, embalming *inter alia* many oral traditions), archives became the direct descendant of oral culture since they are by nature organic, not classified, forms of information, closely related to actions and decisions as the study of diplomatic so nicely reveals. It is no coincidence that the ancient and classic series of records which come down to this day relate to the courts, customary English Law, and Parliament (itself a High Court), where persuasion by oral rhetoric is still practiced. The early keepers of these records are our professional ancestors who stood in high popular esteem as the keepers of vital public evidence.[11]

During the 1960s, partly through orality in the subcultures and a kind of "orality" at a distance via electronics and automation, aptly described by McLuhan as the extension of our nervous system, we began as archivists to develop an inclusive exploration of the media of record in all its forms. This also had an impact on libraries as "nonprint" material gained more respect, but I have a feeling that archives which now began to include the entire media spectrum fall heirs to an ancient orality being reborn and stand to be the great gainers of this paradigm shift. Text is now becoming less totally dominant and our whole notion of information is fast expanding. Libraries were the first to harness automation to cataloguing and retrieval, but the automated record—its appraisal and preservation—has taxed the wits of archivists from the outset. Will the automated (and interrogated) "book" on the one hand and constantly updated archive on the other bring us closer to the memory of ancient oralism, which did not distinguish between the act generated through myth and epic and that act memorized by witnesses? *We* as literates recognize the difference, but how important will this be in a society which "seeks to reinvent the human being at the species level" in the face of a "civilized" stance which is destroying us? This is *not* to suggest a new primitivism, but rather the dedication of all our wisdom, knowledge (including scientific knowledge), and spiritual awareness to the principles of our profession.

We need to give a great deal more study to the cultural impact of our media of record on the ways in which they "work us over" as we communicate with them, and to develop a kind of metadiplomatics as we come to understand how maps, photos, film, sound recordings, and fine arts are to be "read" if they are to be interpreted accurately and their impact on us and society in general assessed. This is essential for effective appraisal, since we may have to recognize the most appropriate medium out of many to preserve an event.

I am prepared to admit that much of this material may not qualify under the classical definition of archival records (at least in the European tradition), but are they not vital cultural records serving as the people's evidences of who they are, where they came from, and where they are going? Given this somewhat broader definition of our role, there are already signs and pointers to new approaches to appraisal which deserve attention.

Hans Booms understands the need for a thorough understanding of what (in translation) he describes as "societal development":

> And herein lies the ultimate source of the difficulties encountered in the archival process. For the archivist must decide which specific events and development patterns should be preserved in documents, yet the value of such events and patterns can only be determined when the archivist has attained a comprehensive view of the total societal development process and an interpretation of the way all of society has actually developed.[12]

And he goes on to declare that

> only the society from which the material originated and for whose sake it is to be preserved can provide archivists with the necessary tools to assess the conceptions by which they bring the past into the present. In constructing the conceptual grid of history which will serve as a model for the documentary heritage, archivists must not follow the value concepts of their own time period, but rather, those of the time from which the material originated.[13]

This complements David Gracy's point with regard to useful information from the past, but it must be understood on its own terms and not ours, when used in the present. In short, how were these records viewed at the time?

Booms ends his paper with a plea for a cooperative documentary plan of appraisal and acquisition, discussed by a council of variously qualified citizens and, if possible, published so that the plan is in effect controlled by the society at large whose heritage is being decided upon.[14]

This kind of approach would seem to be more appropriate to an age which is moving away from fragmentation and reductionism through personal decisions to a more holistic and democratic involvement of the citizen in the right to know and the preservation of vital sources of information.

Helen Samuels has with others developed a documentation strategy which sets the records to be appraised within the context of other forms of information and knowledge, and the joint nature of so many institutional transactions.

> When appraising records, archivists should consider the total body of available documentation, not just the material they are appraising. Archivists should know what offices, institutions, or repositories house related material, and they should appraise in light of this larger universe of documentation. Archivists should also study the relationship among various forms of documentation. The information content of manuscript material, published records, artifacts, and other sources is often interconnected, so appraisal decisions should be made not only with an awareness of the value of each form of documentation but also with full knowledge of their relationships. A

knowledge of the available information, and their potential uses, allows the archivist to select manuscript and archival records to supplement those locating sources while avoiding duplication. While locating and studying related documentation may now be difficult, automated records of archival holdings in linked networks will facilitate this coordinated appraisal.[15]

Finally, I would like to offer some approaches in the form of questions whereby we can become more proactive in aiding that transformation of society which will be necessary for our survival, by seeking out and preserving evidence of the transformation in its early stages and providing information that will assist the process.

1. Should we reappraise what we hold already, especially in the field of government records? Is the public sector over-represented?
2. Should appraisal/acquisition be related to our capacity to retrieve more from less?
3. Can we develop internationally the material for a truly planetary experience (I do not say planetary history) transcending national boundaries which, because of the sweep of the story, will become mythic in extent?
4. How can we hold in tension the requirements of planetary and local research?
5. What do the people of a region really expect to find in an archives? Are we too elitist in our appraisal and selection, too text-oriented?
6. Can archives cooperate on a bioregional basis, which will be transnational at times?
7. How long should materials be retained in an archives? What does "permanently" mean?
8. Should more attention be paid to the retention of unstable documents and their long-term preservation, in particular transmedia transfer of information?
9. In user studies, which has a bearing not only on retrieval but also appraisal, should more attention be paid to phenomenology and hermeneutics rather than the empirical, statistical "bean counting" approach?[16]

And so my title. . . . In an article by John Honner in *Compass* which he calls "Rethinking the Universe," his last section is headed "The Totemic Universe":

Totemism is a term which attempts to describe primitive patterns of living in a particular ecology. . . . This most elementary form of religion implies that individual, clan, tribe and environment are connected. A spirit that is literally Aboriginal hovers over the present and makes it one with the past. . . . We have gotten used to the ideal of ourselves as isolated objects living in the absolute space and time of ideal histories. We have developed one outlook towards the material universe and another towards the spiritual. . . . If modern physics continues along its present course, in many ways it will teach us once again to live totemically, connected with one another, connected with our past and futures, and with a healthy skepticism about material objects as ultimate models of what is real.[17]

This is the universe which we are beginning to inhabit again, although it has always been there. Ten years from now the world should begin to look different, with profoundly different society configurations and expectations which we archivists must try and prepare for. It is a daunting task, but an exciting one.

REFLECTION, 2000

For most of us in North America, until quite recently, appraisal meant "Schellenberg," with his evidential and information values assigned to accumulated file series for the most part to determine their archival retention or destruction, with "housekeeping" records happily and correctly rejected. Terry Cook and others have challenged this doctrine with a new top-down functional approach. Material from the private sector presents less of a problem in most cases, given the usual heavy losses from attrition and neglect. Appraisal can also mean selective acquisition of whole fonds.

Are we appraising and then accessioning the right stuff? Probably yes, since we preserve what our culture at this point in time considers worth accessioning. Perhaps now and again, however, we should stand back from government department, databanks, and the records of prominent dead citizens and institutions to re-examine our priorities.

Some may argue that I've stood back too far on this occasion and toppled over into outer space, but I was trying to view our planet as a whole and briefly review the steady destruction of our heritage in libraries, museums, and art galleries, which are our nearest neighbours to the archives. Does our present mind-set allow us to embrace what is essential to the survival of our memory spanning the past and the needs of the present? To what extent do we cooperate with our archivist neighbours, who can be worldwide?

Luciana Duranti, who shared the platform with me, delivered a paper[18] which provides a highly disciplined and logical framework which seeks to identify authenticity and a sound relationship between the creators of records and the records themselves. I certainly agree with her that "Society preserves what it must for our survival and growth within, rather than independently of, the complex of political, cultural, economical and moral factors which make up the society that created the documentation through an ideological process."[19]

Duranti first makes clear that the act of appraisal is antiarchival since all documents are related to each other in an undisturbed, complete fonds, antihistorical since the documentary record is not made up of "facts," and antijuridical since some records may be relevant to a case in law but not sufficiently significant to be retained at the time of appraisal. The act of appraisal, then, is a cultural phenomenon limiting totality in the interests of comprehension.

What I have attempted to do is to draw attention to records which may be overlooked or dismissed by our overriding corporate culture which fails to grasp the importance of evidence related to our planetary survival. Granted that this too is an ideology that I am suggesting should be represented in current appraisal, which to be effective reflects a web of often conflicting ideologies which in a democratic society "preserved what it must for survival and growth," but also records of activities which provide evidence of ongoing environmental destruction, for instance.

I am particularly concerned that the archival profession should not be polarized between positivism and postmodern deconstruction at the other extreme. Both approaches help to reveal meaning through discourse and dialogue, albeit acrimonious at times. There is no perfect appraisal, least of all this "appraisal" of appraisal!

NOTES

1. David B. Gracy II, "Is There a Future in the Use of Archives?" *Archivaria* 24 (Summer 1987): 4.

2. Ibid., p. 9.

3. Hans Booms, "Society and the Formation of a Documentary Heritage: Issues and the Appraisal of Archival Sources." *Archivaria* 24 (Summer 1987): 76.

4. Luciana Duranti, "Diplomatics: New Uses for an Old Science." *Archivaria* 28 (Summer 1989): 15. This is the first of a series of articles by Professor Duranti to be published in *Archivaria*.

5. The study of communications history and theory can be helpful to archivists when considering media of record within their cultural setting. For James W. Carey, "communication is a symbolic process whereby reality is produced, maintained, repaired and transformed." "A Cultural Approach to Communication," in his *Communication and Culture: Essays on Media and Society* (Boston: Unwin Hyman, 1989), p. 23. The same could be said of archives.

6. I am indebted to Thomas Berry, *The Dream of the Earth*, San Francisco, Sierra Club, 1988, for the above and for his views on the cultural transformation of the human species through the spontaneities of our genetic coding.

7. Thomas Berry, "The Human Presence within the Earth Community" (Sonoma, CA, Global Perspectives, 1988), Audiotape 2, side 1.

8. There is now a considerable body of writing on the relation of literacy to orality and its impact on Western culture. For an excellent overview, see CBC (Canadian Broadcasting Corporation) *Ideas* Programme, "Literacy: The Medium and the Message," 1988.

9. Bruce Chatwin, *The Songlines* (Penguin Books, 1988). For a similar theme in a northeastern B.C. Native community, see Hugh Brody, *Maps and Dreams* Penguin Books, 1981.

10. Denise Schmandt-Bessarat, "Tokens: Facts and Interpretation," *Visible Language*, vol. xx, no. 3 (Summer 1986): 250–72.

11. For an excellent survey of record-keeping practices from earliest times, see Luciana Duranti, "The Odyssey of Records Managers," *ARMA Quarterly* (July 1989): 3–11 and (October 1989): 3–11.

12. Booms, op. cit., p. 103.

13. Ibid., p. 104.

14. Ibid.

15. Helen Samuels, et al., "The MIT Appraisal Project and its Broader Applications." (unpublished) MS, p. 2.

16. Daniel Benediktsson, "Hermeneutics: Dimensions Toward LIS (Library and Information Science) Thinking," *Library and Information Science Research* 11 (1989): 201–234

17. John Honner, "Rethinking the Universe," *Compass*, vol. 8, no. 1 (March 1990): 14.

18. Luciana Duranti, "So What Else Is New?: The Ideology of Appraisal, Yesterday and Today," in Christopher Hives, ed., *Archival Appraisal: Theory and Practice* (Vancouver: Archives Association of British Columbia, 1990), pp. 1–14.

19. Ibid., p. 4.

Chapter 13

Chip Monks at the Gate: The Impact of Technology on Archives, Libraries, and the User

The "monk at the gate" has for some time symbolized the manner in which the monasteries of the early Middle Ages preserved wisdom and knowledge within their walls and, at the same time, through the great ecclesiastical bureaucracies which fed the state administrations of Europe, stood guard over their monopoly of literacy and used it to their advantage in an age of scarce literacy. By contrast, the secular "chip monks" of today control and manipulate the nature and flow of patterned knowledge as a protection against information overload in an age of abundance. But where, then, in this context, does technology make its impact?

The structure of this paper is based on experimental physicist Ursula Franklin's 1989 Massey Lectures, *The Real World of Technology*, which extend the field of inquiry far beyond the crafts and machinery of material culture to the systems which are developed to render them viable and productive. In short, technology involves "organization, procedures, symbols, new words, equations, and a mindset."[1] For the theologian Matthew Fox, wisdom is dying as a consequence of technological systems.

> The Enlightenment produced so much knowledge and information that we have found it necessary to invent a multi-billion dollar industry to store it all and retrieve it all on command. Computers are the libraries of such a civilization. But what would it take to store all the wisdom we have accumulated these past three centuries? Where is the wisdom? . . . Wisdom is of Mother

Originally published in *Archivaria* 33 (Winter 1991–1992): 173–80. Reproduced with the kind permission of the author, *Archivaria*, and the Association of Canadian Archivists. An earlier version of this paper was read at the annual conference of the Archival Association of British Columbia, 25–27 April 1991.

Earth, for nature contains the oldest wisdom in the universe. Wisdom requires the right brain as well as the left, for it is berthed by both analysis and
synthesis.[2]

Fox further believes that to speak of wisdom in a university today is a bit
like talking of chastity in a brothel.[3]

This point is also taken up by the cultural historian William Irwin
Thompson[4] and Professor Franklin herself,[5] who both maintain that the
requirements of technological systems impose the utilitarian curricula
which are in tune with the job market. In the university we should experience our place in the universe.[6] In the ways in which we structure our
information in archives and libraries, are we playing along with this technological imperative? Technology can be used for good or ill. It is the systems we build around it which determine this.

Arthur Kroker, in his *Technology and the Canadian Mind*, examines the
writings of Marshall McLuhan, Harold Adams Innis, and George Grant.[7]
Kroker sees Canada as lying culturally between Europe with its ancient
continuities from guild and craft over and against the U.S.A. with its drive
for transcendent technology as the spearhead of modernity. In his view,
Grant saw a lack of morality and vision in this technological dynamo,
which also includes technocratic bureaucracies. Innis, on the other hand,
saw Canada representing a balance between civilization and power.
McLuhan was concerned with the impact of technological media, which
include the media of record, on the user: this in the archival context, has
been discussed at length elsewhere.[8] What impact does technology, using
Franklin's definition, have on the archivist and librarian?

Since most of us ply our trade within some form of bureaucracy, and
since we are all limited by the literate mindset and the tools of literacy
which make such structures possible, it is not surprising that we are di-
minished in our potential by these technologies. Jeffrey Katzer,[9] editor of
Library/Information Science Review, deplores "too little research in our writings and too low quality in our research." What about the role of the
American Library Association? There are those who would argue "that
ALA is simply an organization of practitioners," in other words they are
trapped in the daily operation of the library machine. Howard Zinn, in a
lively address to the Society of American Archivists some years ago[10]
(which the very conservative editor of the *American Archivist* would not
publish), pointed out that professionalism is a powerful form of social
control resulting in almost total immersion in one's craft. Knowledge for
Zinn has a social origin and a social use and reflects the bias of a particular social order (the Marxist position): hence, until recently, a neglect of
the records of fringe movements making their way towards the centre.
Assuming that libraries and archives are technologies based largely on

printing and text in one form or another, how neutral and impartial are we? Are we as "user-friendly" as we think?

The impact of technological systems on libraries and librarianship can inhibit personal communication with users. As Beverley Lynch points out:

> Professionals tend to chafe under perceived bureaucratic constraints and strive for greater participation in library affairs. . . . In many libraries the decision to change classification schemes was made on the grounds of greater efficiency, as managers sought ways to reduce the costs in technical service operations. . . . Rarely was the decision based on extensive analysis of classification schemes or on an assessment of how the particular library's clientele need the old scheme to find needed materials and information.[11]

But professionals, through their training and administration and management, buy into the bureaucratic system and become managers themselves.

Archivists, for their part, often rely too heavily on finding aids designed more for their own use than for the client's research tools which mirror the bureaucratic structures which created the records in the first place, and neglect communication skills which would elicit what the user is really seeking. Whereas librarians have carried out a whole range of user surveys (though with limited success), archivists have been slow to respond; some introductory studies have nevertheless appeared. Linda Long has shown[12] how the techniques used in counselling, such as active listening, feedback, and self-disclosure, can be of considerable assistance. Our profession is not exactly overwhelmed with technological systems, but it is still locked into an approach which is not always as user-oriented as it should be.

So much for mindsets. As Franklin points out, however, technology also restructures social relations,[13] and the anthropologist Jack Goody has shown how writing was essential to the evolution of the bureaucratic state. I believe that *The Logic of Writing and the Organization of Society* should be on the bookshelves of all of us.[14] His comparison of the ancient world and medieval society, in terms of their record-keeping, with the oral cultures of Africa is most revealing, especially in light of Ursula Franklin's discussion of what she terms holistic and prescriptive technologies—which is central to her thesis.[15]

"Holistic technologies (HT) are normally associated with the notion of craft," where the artisans control the entire process of their work and enjoy the fullest possible freedom of decision. Prescriptive technologies (PT), on the other hand, require discipline, planning, organization, and a command structure with very little latitude for personal decision-making by the operative. The work is fragmented, sequential, and monotonous; it is designed for compliance (as is much preparatory education).

Allied with these technologies, Franklin identifies the growth model (GM) where "the features of growth, the very process and cycles of growing, the diversity of the components of each growing organism, all have resonated through the historical written record. . . . In any given environment, the growing organism develops at its own rate."[16] With the production model (PM) "all essential parameters will become controllable" and there is a noticeable disregard for context and natural surroundings.

Let us consider these typologies in relation to archives and libraries, where there is a striking contrast. Archives could be said to employ a holistic technology in that, wherever possible, the archivist is involved in all the operations of acquisition, arrangement, description, and public service, and resists division by function among specialists. Archives also exhibit a growth model in accordance with their organic nature, although bureaucratic imperatives increasingly focus on production. Libraries, on the other hand, have long exhibited a prescriptive technology:

> Much of the work performed in libraries is divided into specialized tasks and is conducted outside the framework of the client relationship. Rarely does a librarian participate in all the tasks required.[17]

Librarians in consequence often chafe at the limitation of their freedom, as noted above. The circulation of published material through loan and reference also tends towards a production model as the yardstick of effectiveness.

This is not to argue that in each case one is good and the other bad—a mix of holistic and prescriptive is probably essential when economics of scale are considered, which should take into account the human environmental context. The danger is that PT and PM will dominate to the detriment of archivists, librarians, and their users.

Insofar as archivists and librarians are communicators in the full sense of that meaning, communication studies can be helpful. James Carey makes a similar distinction to Franklin between the *transmission view* involving the passage of information by technology, largely in a serial manner, where various textual references lead to the required work, followed by its receipt and return, as "the extension of messages across geography for the purpose of control"—Franklin's PT—and the *ritual view*, her HT, through sharing, participation, association, fellowship, that typify the oral elements in communications, which means "living with the contradictions and ambiguities of our culture as exemplified in the New England Town Meeting."[18] Prescriptive technology sees people as the source of problems; machines and devices as the source of solutions. Machines are so much more reliable, but what becomes of the human beings?

Another consequence of the technological orientation is the downgrading of experience and the glorification of expertise[19] and the expert. One problem that leads to this reliance on "the expert" is that tools redefine the problem. This is particularly true of the "Arms Race"; it is equally true of word processing (WP). For Michael Heim, "the word processor is the calculator of the humanist" (which includes the archivist and librarian). He asks, "Will literature be eroded?" Does it crank out fastfood prose?[20] His critique is that WP eliminates handwriting, which is "a sign and signature of the self, the linkage of hand and thought through gesture." The typewriter was originally a person operating the "typewriting machine." The elimination of the person, as the machine takes over, is also true of the telephone.

Meanwhile, we struggle to make words become units in the technology of cataloguing and retrieval through one word, one meaning. This is perhaps a chimera, for, in J. C. R. Licklider's words, "No one seems likely to design or invent a formal system of automating sophisticated language behaviour. The best approach, therefore, seems to us to be somewhere between the extremes—to call for a formal base plus an overlay of experience gained in interaction with the cooperative verbal community."[21] Allen Kent lists the following unsolvable problems with information systems: (1) What society will be like; (2) What words will mean; (3) How people will act; (4) How people will view events.[22]

Diane Beattie's user study on sources for women's history[23] illustrates some of these points quite well as they affect archival perceptions and discusses the way in which archivists in the past were victims of a social mindset and approach to history which virtually ignored women and ethnic minorities. Likewise, we do not know what society will be like in the future or how people will view events, and our information systems may be seriously flawed if we rely too heavily on technology. The archivist and librarian must provide "the overlay of experience" as they interact with the "verbal community."

One historian describes "a new seam of history," which

> describes the reality of people's lives in addition to the image they would have liked us to see or . . . the way we would like to seem to them. In other words, the new history has unmasked heritage history . . . and moves on from people's individuality into an attempt to describe the culture within which and through which they express themselves. Perhaps the simplest word to use here is *lifestyle*.[24]

How will our various research tools deal with this kind of approach?

Words do not always provide absolutes, and we are all in danger of diminishing both ourselves and the user in a lonely deadlock if our technologies become inappropriate and lacking a human context. Abraham

Kaplan's article, "Age of the Symbol: A Philosophy of Library Education," though written in 1964, is still full of wisdom of which we archivists should also take note:

> Everything in the library must ultimately be related to its uses, and these uses must ultimately depend upon the users. Words do not mean anything. *People* mean things by words. Information means nothing, but *people* are informed and then take action or make informed decisions. . . . A library then is first of all an archive, a repository in which society can find what it has already learned.[25]

It is this edifice at the gate of which, as monks, we serve those who seek to enter.

I have no doubt that the world of librarians is divided over the extent to which the scientific method should rule. With us archivists, librarians share the multimedia corpus of recorded information, and it is tempting to speak of library science and archival science, where it would be more accurate to speak of two technologies and their systems in Ursula Franklin's real world. However, the root of *scientia* is knowledge, not just science, from which should come *sapientia*, wisdom; but we have tended more and more to equate knowledge with scientific knowledge, to the exclusion of knowledge built upon information as ideas. Curtis Wright, in an extended investigation into the philosophy of librarians, notes that "Kaplan has consistently argued that librarianship is an intellectual discipline based on the philosophical study of ideas, not an empirical discipline based on the scientific study of facts."[26] This to a lesser extent applies also to archival science, concerned as it is with the relation between acts and facts in the real world of transactions between parties. It is significant that archival studies of appraisal and description are increasingly focusing on the purpose of the record, on the activity, rather than on being lost in the serbonian bog of content. Likewise, Curtis Wright asserts that "if librarians go for content, . . . they must either become encyclopedists, who go for all of it, or specialists who go for some of it."[27] Kaplan maintains that the first is no longer possible and the second would fail dismally to perform the broad knowledge functions of librarianship. Archivists and librarians alike are swimming for their lives in a sea of symbols, and technology is only of limited help. We must design our own rafts from the riches of humanism and a new cosmology which, for Matthew Fox, consists of "a scientific story, our psychic response to the universe, and art which translates science and mysticism into images."[28] What will archives and libraries be like then, I wonder? Whatever happens, the monk must never be sacrificed to the chip.

To return to Franklin again, as she discusses the elimination of the human element from "successful" automatic and automated processes:

Once the development and the social integration of the technology has been accomplished to the satisfaction of its promoters, once the infrastructure of needs had been eliminated, the technology began to remove the human links.[29]

She then cites the virtual disappearance of the telephone operator, whose mediation rendered the telephone "user-friendly" in the first instance, adding that, "As the technologies matured and took command, women were left with fragmented and increasingly meaningless work."[30] Let this serve as a warning to us all, especially in the context of David Bearman's announcement of the imminence of the wrist phone and data tablet on the lap (shades of the ancient world!), receiving satellite transmissions and storing them so that the "individuation of information resources" will be greatly enhanced.

> Individuals will increasingly carry their knowledge and the means to access
> new information in any format from any place around with them—which for
> archivists is a prospect greeted with some foreboding.[31]

This surely is a neo-oral culture in which we carry our knowledge around in an extension of our brains.

In the light of all this, Eric Ketelaar wonders whether researchers, who will be able to process so much automated information for their own purposes relatively easily, will accept the information available in archival finding aids which served their purpose one hundred years ago. "Can, in future, someone who has consulted a data bank be expected to turn over pages and find nothing?"[32] Will this lead to "fastfood research," to adapt Heim's expression?

Meanwhile, electronic technology is beginning to change the nature of recorded information in other ways which should also alarm the archivist. Ronald Weissman in a recent paper warns us that in the world of "hard copy," during which the archival profession came of age, "documents existed in clearly defined and separate classes of things."[33] Archivists of various media of record have developed their own disciplines and expertise "but, for an increasing number of document related types of work, the old world in which different types of information required the skills of different kinds of document specialists is rapidly disappearing."[34]

Compound records composed of text, graphics, tables, sound, and images, for all their complex nature, "stand alone" and can be isolated, separated, and preserved if necessary.[35] In contrast, the hypermedia database is a much freer form, controlled by navigational and data-oriented links by which

> the content of one document can be embedded in another, so that, as changes
> occur in a table, corresponding changes in the underlying data in a spreadsheet
> or data base are automatically reflected in updated charts in word-processed

reports. In a system employing 'hot links,' changes in one document are reflected automatically in every document that 'subscribes' to that source document's content. In a system employing 'warm links,' users are given the option
of updating documents as source documents change.[36]

Weissman points out that this powerful flexibility is also a source of weak-
ness, since there are "neither rules nor formalism."[37] In this kind of environment, documents as we know them will lose their separate formal identity and dissolve into a fluid mass of "tagged" content and information all
too easily detachable from the initial documentary act, in the manner of Al-
ice's Cheshire cat of which only the smile remained. Modern diplomatics
will have a hard time with all this. The virtual (original) document will become increasingly elusive and fragile as it is plundered by data bank users
transmogrifying sources through a multitude of links and object-oriented
software "in a content mark-up architecture."[38] We may need to rethink
some aspects of archival methodology if we are to deal with this babble of
electronic discourse. What is information in the *archival* context? Will the
monk standing bravely at the gate be swept away in a flood of content without form? On the other hand, perhaps we attach too much importance to
originals in this environment of neo-orality, echoing the impermanence of
speech in contrast to the persistence of cultural memory.

   A clue may be found in the archival administration of written records
created by or for aboriginal peoples to preserve tribal history and traditions. For instance, the Maori approach to this knowledge is one of reverence and love within a cosmology alien to the *pakeha* (white) archivists,
which demands an appropriate ritual whenever such records are used
and, in particular, their location close to the tribe and the land. "There are
spiritual connotations surrounding Maori manuscripts which contain traditional knowledge,"[39] which require accommodation. Perhaps, if we are
not to drown, we too need to let go of our concern for the material minutiae of documentation grounded in scientific reductionism, and give
thought to Matthew Fox's new cosmology referred to earlier. Let Curtis
Wright have the last word:

> Does information reduce to something physical in the empirical world of
> matter and energy as in science? Or does it reduce to metaphysical patterns
> in the intellectual spirit world of ideas as in philosophy? Is information the
> machinery of communication? Or is it distinct from communicative machin-
> ery? . . . Scientific theories of the physical are paralleled today by humanistic
> theories of the symbolic referent.[40]

Our world of symbols surely requires human mediation to reveal their
changing meanings, as we search for knowledge and hope to acquire
wisdom.

REFLECTION, 2000

Ursula Franklin's Massey Lectures revealed an aspect of our society which had not struck me before, but it seemed a warning which we should take seriously when we are obliged to utilize all manner of "high tech" devices. Once again we are faced with the possibility of dehumanising our operational needs.

As archivist of Leeds Public Libraries in Leeds, Yorkshire (my first job), I developed a very close relationship with the printed word which continued when I moved to Liverpool Public Libraries. In terms of public service, archivists and librarians are much more closely related than we care to believe when it comes to our heritage on paper. Our roles back then were quite distinct, but our common interest lay (and still does) with the users who moved quite comfortably between us. Admittedly these were relatively small archives but it was the user who constantly reminded us that, when it came to sources of information and knowledge, they saw no distinction between us and librarians because we were human beings first, a characteristic we shared with our public. We often had to interpret the nature of the record or help them towards a satisfactory visit, and in so doing we became part of a human relationship which in a small way gave meaning to their day—and ours. Do we, through this exchange, generate a little wisdom? If nature contains the oldest wisdom, this is also our origin and through our skill with personality we can contribute our share to this tradition.

In the 1950s we were not much subject to the "technological imperative." We—the archivists—were the finding aids. This was a remarkably satisfying symbiosis within the old-style archives where the archivist searched the stacks, bringing out material which in turn would be searched by the user, a direct relationship with originals which bore the mark of time. The memory was there in all its richness, grounded in the original record—save for a limited amount of microfilm. Many small, community archivists continue in this manner. I do not want to idealize this model, but the steady growth of a technological forest can alienate us and our users from each other. Highly sophisticated retrieval systems remote from the records themselves discourage or render impossible the old tradition of manual browsing by the archivist within the stacks, very different from surfing the Internet where direct contact with authenticity is severely reduced.

In our desperate attempts to keep alive materials that are self-destructing, we are doing so at enormous cost, often in isolated chambers of microclimate tended by experts in conservation in a building which may be at a considerable distance from archivist and user. There may be good reasons for this as a stopgap solution, but, over time, materials, archivists, and the public should be brought together again with the aid of good public transport.

We like to speak of "archival science" as a body of knowledge in its own right, but I believe there is an element of the craft in what we do and we should not lose that distinction in the fragmentation of tasks or veneration of technology.

NOTES

1. Ursula Franklin, *The Real World of Technology* (Toronto, 1990), p. 12.

2. Matthew Fox, *The Coming of the Cosmic Christ* (New York, 1988), p. 21.

3. Ibid., p. 22.

4. William Irwin Thompson, Chapter 2, "Walking out on the University," *Passages About Earth* (New York, 1973).

5. Franklin, *Real World*, p. 28.

6. Fox, *Coming*, p. 22.

7. Arthur Kroker, *Technology and the Canadian Mind: Innis/McLuhan/Grant* (Montreal, 1984).

8. Hugh A. Taylor, "The Media of Record: Archives in the Wake of McLuhan," *Georgia Archive* 6 (1978): 1–10.

9. Jeffrey Katzer, "ALA and the Status of Research in Library/Information Science," *Library and Information Science Review* 11 (1989): 83–87.

10. Howard Zinn, "Secrecy, Archives and the Public Researcher," *Boston University Journal* 19, (Fall 1931): 37–44.

11. Beverley P. Lynch, "Libraries as Bureaucracies," *Library Trends* (Winter 1978): 262.

12. Linda J. Long, "Question Negotiation in the Archival Setting: The Use of Interpersonal Communications Techniques in the Reference Interview," *American Archivist* 52, no. 1 (1989): 40–51.

13. Franklin, *Real World*, p. 13.

14. Jack Goody, *The Logic of Writing and the Organization of Society* (Cambridge, 1986).

15. Franklin, *Real World*, pp. 18–24.

16. Ibid., p. 27.

17. Long, "Libraries and Bureaucracies," p. 264.

18. James W. Carey, *Communications as Culture: Essays on Media and Society* (Boston, 1989), pp. 15–18.

19. Franklin, *Real World*, p. 40.

20. Michael Heim, *Electric Language: A Philosophical Study of Word Processing* (New Haven, 1987), pp. 1–4.

21. J. C. R. Licklider, *Libraries of the Future* (Cambridge, 1965), p. 204.

22. Allen Kent, "Unsolvable Problems," in Anthony Debous, ed., *Information Science: Search for Identity* (New York, 1973), pp. 299–311.

23. Diane L. Beattie, "An Archival User Study: Researchers in the Field of Women's History," *Archivaria* 29 (Winter 1989–1990): 33–50.

24. Michael Honeybone, "The Nature of History and the National Curriculum," *Teaching History*, no. 60 (July 1990): 9.

25. Abraham Kaplan, "The Age of the Symbol: A Philosophy of Library Education," *Library Quarterly* 34 (1964): 296–97.

26. Curtis Wright, "The Symbol and its Referent," *Library Trends* 34, no. 4 (Spring 1986): 743.

27. Ibid., p. 745.

28. Fox, *Coming*, p. 1, note.

29. Franklin, *Real World*, p. 107.

30. Ibid., p. 110.

31. David Bearman, "Communications in the '90s," *Archives and Museums Informatics* 4, no. 3 (Fall 1991): 1.

32. Eric Ketelaar, "Exploration of New Archival Materials," *Archivum* 35 (1989): 172, quoting P. René-Bazin, "Vers une informatique archivistique," *Gazette des archives* (1985): 114–115.

33. Ronald E. F. Weissman, "Virtual Documents on an Electronic Desktop: Hypermedia, Emerging Computer Environments and the Future of Information Management," in Cynthia Durance, ed., *Management of Recorded Information: Converging Disciplines* (Munchen, 1990), pp. 37–60.

34. Ibid., p. 38.

35. Ibid., p. 41.

36. Ibid., p. 42.

37. Ibid., p. 42.

38. Ibid., p. 47.

39. Jane McRae, "Translating the Grey Maori Manuscripts for the Public," *Archifacts: Bulletin of the Archives and Records Association of New Zealand* (June 1985): 52.

40. Wright, "Symbol and Referent," p. 739.

Chapter 14

Opening Address to the "Documents That Move and Speak" Symposium

Since archival documents are the recorded product of action-oriented communication, the impact of the "media of record" on the individual and society should be understood by archivists as an element of archival significance. As we move from a society based on Western literacy to the new "orality" of the electronic age, archives must account for growing numbers of documents that move and speak within traditional, textually oriented structures. The rapid rate of technological change, space limitations, and high preservation costs demand clearer definitions and stricter selection criteria for audiovisual documents in the future. This paper addresses some of the major themes of this symposium.

DEFINITIONS AND CHARACTERISTICS

I would first like to congratulate Sam Kula on the title of this symposium. It suggests an active rather than a passive approach; it is about doing rather than describing, which is the distinguishing characteristic of archives defined as documents created as part of the conduct of affairs of any kind. Archives are not about an activity, they are an integral part of the activity itself. The media with which archives are created should also be considered as elements in the documentary act.

Originally published in *Documents That Move and Speak: Audiovisual Archives in the New Information Age. Proceedings of a Symposium Organized for the International Council of Archives by the National Archives of Canada* (K. G. Saur: Munchen et al., 1992), pp. 18–29. Reproduced with the kind permission of the author and K. G. Saur.

The way in which I am behaving at this moment helps to emphasize the limitations and strengths of the "media of record" as we call them. I move and speak, but I am also reading from a text, not because I prefer it that way but because my memory prevents me from making all the points that I would wish to make, as well as for other reasons. I would prefer to enter into a discourse with you in the oral mode, and your responses would help trigger in me the development of my theme; there will, of course, be time for this later. Meanwhile, we are used to orderly presentations for the very good reason that we have grown up with literacy and texts. I am locked into what I am saying, and you are locked into what I have to say whether you like it or not! The medium, then, has a powerful influence on my act of communication with you which is as yet not true communication but a one-way stream of information which you then process. If I go on using these long words and measured phrases, you will quite rightly wish that I would simply hand out a copy of my paper for you to read, a paper which can now be "faxed" across the world in minutes. An unlikely situation, but it illustrates the strength of yet another (electronic) medium working with paper to produce a hybrid product of great power.

However, the whole richness of the oral discourse and exchange, whereby meanings are groped for and arrived at, is lost. In short, I may be speaking to you but this is not "orality." The record and source is this piece of paper and any other record which might be made, be it a sound tape recording or a "talking head" on video, would lose much of the original act in the process of recording. In keeping with the spirit of this symposium, my text will be as informal and oral as possible, but my point is that archives are a subset of the whole communication process and the media we use affect our individual perceptions and impact on society as a whole. As archivists we could have become aware of this since the 1960s through the works of Marshall McLuhan, Harold Innis, Walter Ong, and many others, but we have been slow to recognize this aspect in our search for meaning and value. We were all reared for the most part on the heavy gruel of text. But those in the so-called new media have taught us much already as custodians, through technology, of the oldest communication of all: movement and speech. Archives have come down to us as the direct heirs of communication within preliterate societies (a horrid term rather like "nonbook material" as librarians call audiovisual documents). Their thoughts and words from the archive of the mind were (and are) closely bound to their acts and movements; theirs is the "science of the concrete" as Levi-Strauss has described it. This is in direct contradistinction to libraries which are filled for the most part with the detached thoughts and conclusions of the literate mind about various subjects. It is no coincidence that the classic archives, public records, and "people's evidences" are of those institutions where oral discourse plays a large part;

the courts and parliament, where for the latter we now have in addition documents that move and speak.

What are archives kept for? This is a crucial question which is not asked as often as it should be. The quick answer from textual archivists would perhaps be "for research," principally historical research. A large part of textual archives consist of the people's evidence of their rights, freedoms, public accountability, and, through genealogy, who we are and where we come from. Frank Burke of the National Archives of the United States notes that "it gives one pause to realize that of the 200,000 research visits to the nation's largest archives, where the material is so unique it is not duplicated by any other institution in the world—a national magnet for serious researchers—70 to 80 percent of these researchers are genealogists."[1]

Documents that move and speak, it seems to me, march to a different drum. They may provide evidence for the above categories, but their contribution enriches what I would call the nonliterate part of our lives. They communicate with us as we respond with our critical attention. As Jack Goody, the anthropologist, has pointed out, "Systems of communication are clearly related to what man can make of his world both internally in terms of thought and externally in terms of his social and cultural organization."[2] As persons involved in these media, you are deeply concerned with what people can make of their worlds in a way which cannot be expressed in text, and I would like to deal with this when I come to consider the user. Of course, we cannot and should not deny or reject our textual literacy, but we must resist reading the "new" media in a literal, textual manner and begin to learn unfamiliar grammar, syntax, and semiotics, and then to teach our users to do the same. We must now consider to what extent the specific materials that move and speak are strictly speaking archival.

I think all would agree that the textual documentation in support of film, television, and sound productions are part of the process and therefore qualify as archives; likewise the outtakes and all those stages which go toward the completion of the finished product up to and including the master composition. Of course, because something is archival, we are not bound to keep it. Copies made beyond and from the master, since they are not part of the process of production, cannot be considered archival, but rather as a kind of limited publication after the manner of a book and should, therefore, be part of a library operation. On the other hand, the kinescope made as a record of early television would be archival, as being a record of the performance on which future decisions might be based. A library of documents that move and speak, insofar as they are copies of masters and not archival, should certainly be part of all such archives, much as copies are held on microfilm in a textual archives. In this manner, the provenance of the original materials will help the assurance of authenticity and integrity. Prints in circulation are subject to all manner of editing and censorship, as anyone who has seen *Cinema Paradisio* would know, and, of course, many of you would know already.

I realize that moving image archives are full of rare and unique old film production prints and other copies which enrich our knowledge and enjoyment, much as other archives are full of rare and valuable printed ephemera and pamphlets often surviving as one of a kind which, strictly speaking, are not always archival. It seems to me that this distinction is not serious in custodial terms, provided it is clearly recognized in the management process and intellectual control.

It must be remembered that archives and archival theory are the product of literacy and texts and it is maintained by many in the profession that archival principles hold good for all media of record (which may be so, but we should be vigilant about this). However, just because archives are about actions, and so are documents that move and speak, I believe archivists and those with a thorough archival understanding may be the best people to handle all such materials whether they are strictly archival or not. A study of archives has taught us the value of context and documentary relationships with which librarians are less concerned; the very word "text" is related to "texture" and so to the characteristics of the medium which is so essential to take into account. The "people's evidences," as the record of a people's culture in terms of those communication systems which define them, now extend far beyond text and for the nonliterate exclude text altogether. Let us examine this a little closer, because it has everything to do with the archives of the new media.

For well over 2,000 years literacy has been the norm for societies educated in the Western tradition, arising out of the Greek experience. It has played a major part in our achievements and, as we are now realizing, in our attitude towards nature which, through our detachment and imperative to exploit, could well destroy life on earth as we know it. Our religions have been textually based, and our hierarchies and bureaucracies have a largely religious and textual origin. Literacy is also bound up with colonialism. This is saying far too much in far too short compass, but I believe that with the onset of automation in all its manifestations in science and the humanities and the nature of the information it is providing, our worldview is rapidly changing. Our perceptions are no longer so linear and logical, and we are recovering a sense of the acoustic space of preliterate societies which may be our salvation. If, as McLuhan suggests, automation is metaphorically an extension of our central nervous system,[3] then in this unified field of a wired and dangerous world we are coming to search for and rely far more on the mythic truths of who we are and where we are going—and many of these truths are being revealed to us in ways other than text. I am not suggesting that some kind of millennium is in sight; far from it. The extraordinary insights which can be derived from the new media about ourselves are capable of an infinite manipulation by those concerned that we do not make such discoveries, but remain in a comfortable state of complacent narcosis.

I believe that literacy and text are losing their centrality in the popular mind and, while the need to be literate still remains for a number of reasons, the lack of it is no longer regarded by a number of scholars as a shocking aberration.[4] What is advocated is rather the development of our oral sensibilities and all the self-fulfilment that goes with it. We must remain literate, but we will regain the values of oral tradition at the centre of which will be the documents that move and speak. Today we speak of visual aids to texts; perhaps this secondary role will one day be reversed. I am sufficiently convinced that audiovisual archives are about to move towards centre stage. History based on text has largely become a closed circuit in which historians write for each other and popular historians are rather suspect. Louis R. Harlan, President of the American Historical Association, quotes the veteran historian, Theodore S. Hamerow, when he says, "The methodology of historical scholarship appears inadequate for an understanding of the world in which we live." Historians of different specialties do not talk to each other, and Harlan asserts, "the unity of history, the synoptic view of human experience, has been sacrificed to specialties!" He then goes on to say, "The adult American public has, over the past decade or so, shown increased interest in history being offered . . . through various public media. The public cannot get enough of the historical documentaries shown on television."[5]

Meanwhile, the new media are contributing to the changing fabric of social organization; the impact of television on Eastern Europe, Pakistan, and China cannot be underestimated; rigid bureaucracies are being eroded by desktop computers. Catherine Covert, writing on the impact of radio in 1924, declared: "Here were the ambiguities: the sense that one was participating yet alone; in command [of the dial] yet swept blindly along on the wave of sound." Radio was an intrusion, an alienation from social and personal relationships. For the listener it was a crazy quilt of reception, and Covert quotes E. D. Lindeman, "Ye may hear too much for our capacities for experience." In Johan Huizinga's words, "Radio excludes reflective assimilation." Traditional mediators of knowledge [such as parents] were circumvented, but freedom could lead to loneliness.[6] The same could be said today of television simply because it is a new medium. Print had the same explosive effect when introduced in the 15th and 16th centuries. The public, which is watching history in the making on TV, is at the same time making history. Surely they will demand that archives keep these people's evidences.

I do not wish to overstate the case; an adequate record must span all media, appropriate emphasis is a matter of appraisal. Nor am I making a case in this context for media archives and the fracturing of the total body of a person's or an institution's created record—the *fonds d'archives*. What then are the choices facing archives in a video age?

THE ORGANIZATIONAL CHOICES FACING ARCHIVES

The options which will be considered here will be those which revolve around the kind of archives administration and management that are appropriate for the new media in the context of all other media of record in a repository. The traditional approach was to consider the new media as decidedly "odd-ball," the exception, almost an aberration within a deposit of predominantly textual material. In such cases it was quite common to put audiotapes or a reel of film in a separate box, but to include these items in the general inventory of the deposit. The microclimate was probably not ideal and film and tapes just had to take their chances with the rest. I am sure this is still the practice in small archives, but it has one important advantage: the fonds continues to be respected, the totality of the deposit remains unbroken, and the material is easy to retrieve in the context of the whole deposit.

In many national archives with very extensive accessions of new media, specialization becomes the norm. The National Archives of Canada, Moving Image and Sound Archives (MISA), was created with a much more clumsy title in 1973 and joined seven other media divisions. (Public records and private manuscripts were under separate management, though not strictly different media.) I believed at the time this solution was correct and fully justified, but detaching material from a deposit on the basis of medium led to a dispersal which could be very inconvenient for the user. At the same time it emphasized that media were very different *sui generis*; each required a different custodial pattern, different archival techniques, and each required interpretation in quite a different way. Up until the 1970s, the textual approach was largely dominant in the way the media were used. Photographs were seen largely as an illustrative aid to textual documents and were a section in the Picture Division, i.e., documentary art. MISA likewise began in this stable, and it was absolutely essential at that time that archivists of each medium should have the mental and physical space to work out their own appropriate disciplines and establish themselves, free from the domination of the more traditional forms. It was, of course, mandatory that intellectual control on paper should be maintained over the multimedia deposits, but this did not always happen once dispersed.[7] Compromises were, however, worked out. Quite early on it was agreed that movie "stills" should stay with MISA, as did the considerable resource of printed material. Since then, some media divisions have been combined once more, but they are now, I hope, secure in their discipline and approach. Is it possible to avoid division by media in a large archives and, if not, is it possible to hold the fonds together in one division where one media is predominant? There is no immediate answer to this so far as I know, but it is certainly worth exploring.

The National Archives of Canada has been described as a "total archives" accepting not only government records but also documents from the private sector. Some countries follow the models of Great Britain and the U.S.A. which rely on the British Library and the Library of Congress respectively to receive accessions from the private sector and this has been a long tradition in both cases. It is interesting that here we have the administration of archives in a library, which can work well and is often the situation in universities, but the problem here lies with the overriding authority of the Chief Librarian in terms of budget priorities and sometimes the failure of management to appreciate archival requirements and methods.

There has also been a long tradition with moving image archives to be housed in a library or cinémathèque where the imperative to acquire has been based on the artistic and cultural merits of the exhibited film, with little consideration given to the archival components generated in the making of the film, which were probably still in the hands of the producers, if they survived at all. This is not to criticize the heroic efforts which were made by the great collectors to establish film as an art form, but simply to point out certain drawbacks from an archival point of view. Ideally the film companies should have their own archives professionally run but, as I understand it, the industry is no longer in the hands of a few giants.

The British Broadcasting Corporation has three media divisions: sound, film/videotape, and textual archives. The National Sound Archives, as a department of the British Library, handles mainly broadcast music. The BBC's program is firmly in the hands of archivists,[8] but it is not a public archives.

To sum up, it would seem essential that a film and sound archives should have a library component built into it when a fair proportion of the holdings is of a nonarchival nature, although cataloguing and retrieval systems may be very similar in both components.

A word needs to be said about oral history, which has no easy resting place. In Ottawa, along with film, oral history recordings were originally housed in the old Picture Division of the National Archives and were considered, I suppose, as sound without the pictures. In a sense, oral history sits comfortably in a textual division, since it is, strictly speaking, neither oral nor history, but a report or discourse in words, sometimes transcribed. The problem here is that the technology and custodial functions are different, with different skills and discipline more akin to sound, film, and videotape.[9] Although archivists should only rarely become interviewers, I cannot accept the notion that they would be generating a record which is somehow invalid because of their personal involvement. It is really no different from an exchange of written correspondence seeking information. Oral history seems to find its most congenial setting in a department of folklore, if only because custodians and users alike are absolutely comfortable with the patterns and dynamics of speech. The National Archives solution, followed by many other repositories, seems a reasonable compromise, in its treatment of oral history, as it were, as broadcast radio without the broadcast.

THE RELATION BETWEEN TEXTUAL RECORDS AND THOSE THAT MOVE AND SPEAK, IN TERMS OF HOLDINGS

In the summary of this session in the symposium's program, the question is posed: "Should archives keep the same cross-section of audio-visual records as they do for textual?" which suggests that the textual record is a kind of norm to be perhaps enriched by sound and images. There is, of course, some merit in this when one thinks of Hansard's conventional cries of "oh!" when politicians vilify each other in a parliamentary uproar. Oral history can fill out gaps in the textual record; body language and inflection can certainly help towards the meaning of utterance on paper. All this, however, is a secondary support role which, as I have said, may one day be reversed, though it does help the evidence in one medium to complement, and perhaps remove some of the limitations in another.

By far the most important role of audiovisual documents is in the field of broadcasting as the people's evidences of their culture, taste, and, more specifically, the information communicated to them that helped shape public opinion and the lives of citizens. There is, of course, a symbiotic element here whereby broadcasting supplies the programs that listeners prefer, in particular what Fiske and Hartley have called "bardic television,"[10] which essentially reinforces prevailing norms. Examples of the continuum of programs and commercials should also be preserved through an occasional 24 hours in the life of the viewer.

Feature films should also be selected together with actualities for the same reason, but neither are likely to be archival outside of the producer's custody as discussed above.

Nothing illustrates the shift in the centrality of text and print more than the immense and influential output of broadcasting in the lives of the taxpayers who, if asked, may give much of the traditional record short shrift. Writing was in origin an aid to oral administration, not the engine of bureaucracy: will the broadcast and other audiovisual documents become, through technology, the central record of a new oral tradition, with text in support?

THE MOVING IMAGES THAT BEST REPRESENT
THE SOCIETY THAT PRODUCES THEM

Apart from documents useful for genealogy, textual archives are of value principally to elite groups of scholars both amateur and professional who may or may not transmute their studies into forms of history for a wider but still limited public. Exhibitions of textual material, unless filled out with other images, receive little attention; moving images are quite otherwise.

Film and television features may be preserved if they have been seen by a very large public as one of the criteria for appraisal and may have high research value on account of this. The myths by which we live (and I do not use the term pejoratively) are often buried in the popular movies and sitcoms which may mirror us more accurately than textual records, and their evidence may be increasingly acceptable to viewers as they become image "literate." (See how we are tied to text?)

There will, of course, be films and videos preserved quite rightly for other reasons such as unique content, presentation, or high artistic quality which reflect significant minorities. Feature films, serials, talk shows, commercials, of course sports and news broadcasts, and even some home movies,[11] all these and more have to be preserved systematically by way of archival appraisal. Much of this may originate in countries other than that in which it is viewed, and the need for the networking of accessions is essential to avoid too much duplication internationally. Many of the popular programs come from the United States and are seen worldwide, with or without subtitles, and therefore have a planetary validity whether we like it or not.

A study by Elihu Katz and Tamar Liebes shows that overseas viewers carry on long discussions of the television series *Dallas* and "use this program as a 'forum' to reflect their identities." They become involved morally, playfully (in role play), ideologically, and aesthetically which helps them to define themselves. The authors cite three reasons why so little is known about the "phenomenology of viewing programs." First, funds are usually only available for the study of institutions and audience ratings; secondly, the division of labour in communication research; and thirdly, there is no "adequate theory of the nature of viewer involvement." Viewing *Dallas* and the "soaps" may be much more of a communal and interactive experience with a wide interest in decoding, as viewers liberate themselves from the "texts" of the programs.[12]

Likewise, news programs have also attracted a lot of similar attention and analysis. According to Katz and Liebes:

> Viewers are surprisingly good at making critical statements about television. This phenomenon not only speaks to the several competing theories of the television experience, but also to the likelihood that viewers' abilities are seriously underestimated by producers, critics and academics.[13]

"ONLY THE GUESTS CAN APPRECIATE THE QUALITY OF THE FEAST"[14]

Before considering the subject of appraisal, a word should be said about the user of archives,[15] because in future we will be a great deal more "user driven" than in the past. There is a sense in which the users define the archives through activating them. User studies in archives were, until very recently, almost nonexistent and limited to statistics with little attempt at phenomenology—how users behaved and how successful were their searches. Disillusioned by consultations with historians who were liable to say "keep everything" because it might all be useful one day, archivists have tended to "go it alone" and make their own decisions as best they can. This will still be our lonely and unenviable task, but it may be that the pubic that views and hears the media may be able to offer insights which those trained as academics might miss,[16] especially in the field of popular culture. We have to guard against too much emphasis on contemporary relevance, fads, and trendiness in our selection, but I have a feeling that there are far more textual records in our archives than will ever be used, and some reappraisal will certainly be in order as we learn from our mistakes. With audiovisual materials we will not be able to afford the luxury of this kind of error in future, given the cost of their maintenance and processing for use.

Frank Burke makes the point that

> Instead of studying how much and what kind of documentation should be saved, perhaps archivists should study what research methodology is being employed, what the historians are doing for sources, and then whether it is appropriate in spite of their methods to continue to retain or search out certain documentation.[17]

The other key issue for users is access, about which much more will be heard in the course of this symposium, which includes not only retrieval from the available, but freeing restrictions on what is unavailable. A record which is inaccessible is, to all intents and purposes, nonexistent to the user. Howard Zinn has stressed the need for archivists to be active in securing the release of material where possible and not to be blind to the records of protest and the counterculture.[18] Paolo Cherchi Usai, in discussing the new demands being made on the world's film archives, has remarked that: "For several years the only list of holdings in FIAF archives—better known as *Embryo*—was considered strictly confidential (as the list of silent feature films still is)" and goes on to say that

> Researchers do have some power over film archives. They can influence institutional policies of acquisition and preservation: which images should be preserved, restored and shown, and how these images should be made available to the public.[19]

THE APPRAISAL OF DOCUMENTS THAT MOVE AND SPEAK

You will not expect me to descend like Moses from the mountain with the Ten Commandments (that most pervasive of all textual archives); Sam Kula in his more tentative "Conclusions and Guidelines"[20] has racked up fourteen, upon which I certainly cannot improve. "The Final Edit" session which follows will deal with the subject far better than I can.

Rosemary Bergeron, in her admirable article on the appraisal of television productions, rightly emphasizes the technological problems of preservation and the difference between the requirements of archives and the in-house preservation of production resources by the broadcasting industry. We are also reminded that selection by archives is usually based on historical, artistic, and sociological values,[21] but it may become increasingly difficult to maintain this conceptual separation on a kind of "divide and conquer" principle. Appraisal involves division into logical categories, but we should be cautious about taking this too far. Malarmé's dictum "To define is to kill: to suggest is to create" will serve us well in this as in much else archival.

Suffice it to say that audiovisual documents can be appraised systematically and not collected at random. Records management practices and studies in appraisal and sampling have demonstrated this, if only to indicate the possibility of success. We should, however, remember that in the heat of the battle to preserve the media, we may not have the time or opportunity to adhere to the strict logic of principles, and a well developed intuitive sense should not be discounted in the final decision.[22]

Can we afford the cost of preservation and archival process given the obsolescence of formats and the frightening escalation of technological change? The old cliché is unavoidable: We cannot afford not to. If the most appropriate record and not the cheapest is to be retained, humanity must reflect on its most deeply valued mythic experiences, many of which will be apparent in audiovisual documents. Because of this cost we may have to do more with less record than in the past. Historical minutiae requiring an infinity of evidence may yield to a much deeper study of archetypal forms for which the intensive examination of limited materials may be mandatory. In short, what do we need for our cultural survival on this planet? It may be less than we think. I am sure all of you hope so.

REFLECTION, 2000

Confrontation with moving images and recorded sound provided a wholly different experience for an archivist like myself, brought up on the traditional public records and private manuscripts with a smattering of maps, photographs, and documentary art. In the steps of such masters as Muller, Feith, Fruin, Jenkinson, and Schellenberg, we felt reasonably secure and comfortable, but here with moving images and recorded sound were media which did not fit easily into the familiar processes of arrangement, description, and use. In fact they challenged a wide range of assumptions about the administration of archives. To what extent were they archival at all in the accepted sense?

The Public Archives of Canada established the National Film Archives, as it was first called, under my jurisdiction, as a Division in the Archives Branch, later titled the Moving Image and Sound Archives and later yet merged into various "media" administrative configurations. Needless to say, the seven other divisions raised multiple eyebrows, especially when they saw the size of the NFA budget that was required to make it viable.

My enthusiasm for the arrival of yet other media of record was in direct proportion to my ignorance, which probably caused some alarm. However, we secured Sam Kula to head up the new Division who brought with him a wealth of experience and was given more or less a free hand. He managed very well in very difficult circumstances, which included lodging in a largely unsatisfactory old office building with wild changes in temperature and humidity which had to be checked to some extent. The result was a learning experience for all of us, as we sought to define "recordness"—to use a term not then in use—for these newer media. This gave us a much broader understanding of our role as archivists and keepers of a memory now rich with images and the dreams that went with them.

Appraisers of these "new" media had to give consideration to the cultural value recognized by the citizen in addition to the functional value of operational records. It soon became apparent that a film library had a very close relationship with the archival material, as did the ephemera of posters and publicity information generally. The print of a film is, in a sense, a published document. Does that make it unarchival? Are we too rigid in our definitions of archival material?

Should not an archives be more than its current (and often narrow) professional definitions, when instead it is conceived in terms of societal memory? How then do we relate to libraries, museums, and art galleries given our expanded role?

The immediate task for us was to understand something of the meaning of all media entrusted to us, so that each Division in the (then) Public Archives of Canada would come to respect the others' perceptions of a body of records with origins rooted in the first human sounds.

NOTES

1. Frank G. Burke, "Commentary," *American Archivist* 51 (Winter and Spring 1988): 47.

2. Jack Goody, *The Interface Between the Written and the Oral* (Cambridge: Cambridge University Press, 1987), p. 3. See also Jack Goody, *The Logic of Writing and the Organisation of Society* (Cambridge: Cambridge University Press, 1988).

3. Marshall McLuhan, *Understanding Media* (New York: The New American Library, 1964), p. 302.

4. David Olsen maintains that "the most important aspects of social organisation and thought are tied to speech, not writing." CBC (Canadian Broadcasting Corporation) *Ideas Programme*, "Literacy: The Medium and the Message," 1988.

5. Louis R. Harlan, "The Future of the American Historical Association," *American Historical Review* 95 (February 1990): 2.

6. Catherine L. Covert, "We may hear too much: American Sensibility and Response to Radio, 1919–1924," in C. L. Covert and John D. Stevens, eds., *Mass Media Between the Wars: Perceptions of Cultural Tension, 1919–1941* (Syracuse: Syracuse University Press, 1984), pp. 199–220.

7. For a discussion of this policy see Terry Cook, "The Tyranny of the Medium: A Comment on 'Total Archives,'" *Archivaria* 9 (Winter 1979–80): 141–49; and Andrew Birrell, "The Tyranny of Tradition," *Archivaria* 10 (Summer 1980): 249–52.

8. Ernest J. Dick, "Lessons from the BBC on CBC Archival Practices," *ACA Bulletin* 14 (March 1990): 1–4.

9. For a recent discussion, see Dale Treleven, "Oral History and the Archival Community: Common Concerns About Documenting Twentieth-Century Life," *International Journal of Oral History* 10 (February 1989): 50–58. For a further discussion on archival permanence in the same issue of *IJOH*, see David H. Mould, "Digital Archive Storage of Oral History," pp. 59–63.

10. John Fiske and John Hartley, *Reading Television* (London: Methuen, 1978). For a similar kind of analysis see Paul Rutherford, "Researching Television's History: Prime-Time Canada 1952–1962," *Archivaria* 20 (Summer 1985): 79–93.

11. Richard Chalfen, "Home Movies as Cultural Documents," in Sari Thomas ed., *Film/Culture: Explorations of Cinema in its Social Context*, (Metuchen, New Jersey: Scarecrow Press, 1982).

12. Elihu Katz and Tamar Liebes, "Interacting with 'Dallas': Cross-Cultural Readings on American TV," *Canadian Journal of Communication* 15 (February 1990): 45–60.

13. Ibid., p. 57.

14. J. J. Rousseau, quoted by Therése Paquet-Sévigny in the 1989 Southam Lecture, "World Information and Its Impact on Society," *Canadian Journal of Communication* 15 (February 1990): 97. This article gives an excellent overview of the present global nature of broadcasting. The implications of this for archivists are worth pondering.

15. For a fuller theoretical discussion see Hugh A. Taylor, *Archival Services and the Concept of the User: A RAMP Study* (Paris: ICA, 1984); and the keynote paper by Eric Ketelaar on the new media and the user, 111th International Congress on Archives, *Archivum* XXXV (1989): 189–99.

16. Hans Booms, "Society and the Formation of a Documentary Heritage: Issues in the Appraisal of Archival Sources," *Archivaria* 24 (Summer 1987): 104.

17. Burke, op. cit., p. 48.

18. Howard Zinn, "Secrecy, Archives and the Public Interest," *Boston University Journal* 19 (1971): 37–44.

19. Paolo Cherchi Usai, "Archive of Babel," *Sight and Sound: International Film Quarterly* (Winter 1989–90): 48–50.

20. Sam Kula, *The Archival Appraisal of Moving Images: A RAMP Study with Guidelines* (Paris: ICA, 1983): 92–98.

21. Rosemary Bergeron, "The Selection of Television Productions for Archival Preservation," *Archivaria* 23 (Winter 1986/1987): 41–53.

22. For a fuller discussion of appraisal in general, see Hugh A. Taylor, "The Totemic Universe: Appraising the Documentary Future," a manuscript to be published by the Association of British Columbia Archivists as part of the proceedings of a joint meeting with the North West Archivists (USA) in Vancouver, April 1990.

Chapter 15

Recycling the Past:
The Archivist in the
Age of Ecology

I am writing this in a very personal way as a poor substitute for what would be my contributions to invigorating discourse with friends and colleagues, who would have contributed so much more, and because what I have to say is very tentative in its application to archives. I strongly believe that the present times demand a major shift in our way of thinking, and I have developed this theme at some length in recent articles. I should like now to outline and comment on some further ways in which archivists and others may be pointing us in the right direction, that is to say, in the right-brain direction!

Ralph Metzner, in summarizing the characteristics of the age, asserts that "a growing chorus of voices is pointing out that the roots of the environmental disaster lie in the attitudes, values, perception, and basic worldview that we humans of the industrial, technological global society have come to hold."[1] He believes, as I do, that we are in a transitional stage on the way to an ecological age, "the outlines of which are being articulated in the natural sciences, the social sciences, and in philosophy and religious thought." He further believes that the so-called information age is more of the same mindset, since the approach is fundamentally mechanistic, as in the previous industrial era, characterized by continuing mass production, narrow economic models of efficiency, and unbridled competition, and "does not represent a real shift in values such as the ecology and the environmental crisis demand." I do not entirely agree with this, since computers are not engines and machinery in

Originally published in *Archivaria* 35 (Spring 1993): 203–13. Reproduced with the kind permission of the author, *Archivaria*, and the Association of Canadian Archivists.

the old sense and are already changing the way in which we regard information and knowledge. Thanks to our mechanistic culture, we still treat automation like Babbage's computing "engine" and still speak of "machine-readable archives," which simply present us with data a little smarter and a little faster.[2]

Whereas others write and speak of a postmodern age of "deconstructionist relativism," following a rationalistic and positivist era, Metzner can already discern aspects of a consistent worldview emerging from the separate disciplines. There is cultural historian and "geologian" Thomas Berry's evolutionary time covering more scale than 65,000,000 years from mammals to the emerging ecozoic era, "in which humans take their rightful place as members of the integral, interdependent community of all life"; there is the Gaia hypothesis, which sees the planet as a vast evolutionary organism; there are the profound uncertainties of quantum physics; there is chaos theory. The old atomistic view of ultimate reality is, in Metzner's eyes, giving way to

> a holarchy (nested hierarchy) of systems with complex multi-level interactions of phenomena from sub-atomic particles and atoms to galactic clusters and [the] universe. . . . In the post-modern philosophy of science, the reductionist orientation is complemented by integrative systemic perspectives including the possibility of divine causation 'from above.'

This is, I believe, reflected in our attitude to archival materials, where the "bottom up" and "top down" approaches are now in a kind of healthy tension, which perhaps makes Metzner's "nested hierarchies" an analogy worth pursuing.[3]

I should like now to take a closer look at some positions assumed by Thomas Berry and Matthew Fox, to whom I have referred before[4] and who currently hold a central place in my thoughts on archives and their relationship to culture and religion. For Berry we must now, in a sense, reinvent the human as species within the community of life species. Our sense of reality and of value must consciously shift from an anthropocentric to a biocentric norm of reference. We think of ourselves as ethnic, cultural, language, or economic groups. We seldom consider ourselves as species among species,[5] except perhaps in biology. We are above all members of nations and other human allegiances; all our records reflect the implications of this. Records bearing witness to the equal validity and legal right of survival of the natural world are very limited by comparison. Prior to the modern period, liturgies celebrated the cycle through the seasons and from birth to death. "There was no functional awareness of an irreversible unfolding universe within developmental historical time,"[6] which has made cosmology impossible and has resulted in Berry's five ways in which civilizations transcended nature—which I have discussed elsewhere.[7] Consequently, in Berry's opinion, "[t]here is need for a *functional cosmology* . . . once we consider that the universe, the earth, the sequence of living forms and the human mode of consciousness have from the beginning had a psychic-spiritual as well as a physical-material aspect"[8]—which should induce a sense of reverence transcending institutional religion.

I believe that a new cosmology will emerge along the lines suggested by Berry, which will not require us to commit intellectual suicide, but rather result in a holistic, planetary renaissance built upon "our experience in a dominant time-developmental mode of consciousness and with our empirical instruments of understanding,"[9] in order to enrich rather than dominate our approach to the rest of nature.

Berry makes a clear distinction between genetic coding, which links us to the mystery of creation, and cultural coding, transmitted from one generation to another as a result of "special educational processes."[10] These must undergo significant changes, with which archives will be involved together with the whole range of current heritage information and artifacts, if the paradigm shift discussed above is to occur.

This brings me to theologian Matthew Fox and his definition of the new cosmology, which is generally similar but more specific:

> By the term 'cosmology' I mean three things: a scientific story about the origins of our universe; mysticism, which is a psychic response to our being in the universe; and art, which translates science and mysticism into images that awaken body, soul and society. A cosmology needs all three elements to come alive: it is our joyful response (mysticism) to the awesome fact of our being in the universe (science) and our expression of that response by the art of our lives and citizenship (art).[11]

It is the last element which concerns us most as archivists and citizens.

It may be argued that I have strayed a long way from my theme, but this has been necessary in order to provide the basis for those societal changes over the next century (quite a short archival time), which will reintroduce humanity to the world of nature.[12] In this context, I do not believe that theology along the lines indicated is an optional addition.

We are already becoming less anthropocentric as we begin to recognize intrinsic values in other living systems and societies, and cease to treat them as irrelevant or simply as resources for exploitation. For instance, property and ownership, the hallmarks of civilization and the subject of the earliest textual records, is a concept which still divides Aboriginal peoples from immigrants, and many of the assumptions about possession are being called into question. National archives are the product or aspiration of nation states with political and economic systems now under severe stress, if not actually breaking down. As massive changes in central- ized power structures are revealed, what will be the future of these archives? Metzner argues that all our long-held assumptions are social values, many of which are now coming under fire, "are cultural and not biological" (which is in line with Berry's "cultural coding"): "the alterna- tive attitudes and values now being advocated in many circles are uncon- ventional but not unnatural." I hope that the same also goes for my own observations about archives in this context.

What signs are there within our own profession that we are reacting in a sensitive way to these early beginnings of change? The examples which I shall choose in no sense constitute a definitive overview. Many are taken at random from recent articles in *Archivaria* and the *American Archivist*.

At the head of all these must stand Frank Burke's galaxy of right ques- tions which he asked of a largely unresponsive audience in 1981. Very lit- tle has been done to answer them, yet we should strive to find answers if we are to make our way in an age where many of the old landmarks may be gone: "What is it within the nature of society that makes it create the records that it does?" asks Burke.[13] What records will be created and needed when the nature of society changes, as change it will? We would do well to study this relationship if we are to be responsive to changing needs; this is not the same as being user-driven, which is more reactive than proactive and far too specific and uncoordinated.

Arising out of Burke's article, the vigorous discussion on the relation of theory to archival practice has been quite fruitful and many helpful in- sights are to be derived from it. It may be that he placed too much faith in theories derived from the scientific method and its objectivity. For John Roberts, archival theory overcomplicates and oversimplifies by turns; ba- sic procedures do not need a complex philosophical component, and the complex relationships involved in the analysis and appraisal of records, for instance, defy any theory which attempts to allow for all circum- stances.[14] This is a warning which should be heeded, as we so easily fall into the trap of a scientific reductionism and technological structures in- appropriate to archives. We are not arm's-length observers testing hy- potheses because, although we can control the physical form of docu- ments, their content and meaning become a part of our own subjectivity and make general application particularly elusive. The word "theory" has its roots in the Greek *theoros*, spectator; we do not experience that kind of detachment any more than the historians. We can and must think at times in terms of ideas, abstractions, metaphors, paradoxes, hypotheses, and the like, as one means of sharpening our perceptions. "Information is of course an 'idea'—in its broadest sense as the representation of the intel- lect,"[15] and must in turn be subjected to rigorous scrutiny. I am reluctant to attach the term "theorist" to those who in effect think as all archivists

should, nor do I favour the term "archival science" unless used in its literal sense as *scientia*, or knowledge. However, I strongly disagree with
Roberts when he claims that archival work is "intrinsically, inescapably
ad hoc," that archivists are reactive and dependent, that we are trapped in
our social and intellectual milieu, and "cannot set about filling gaps until
somebody recognizes they exist."[16] It is our responsibility to move beyond
conventional wisdom and away from that passive response to the status
quo which Howard Zinn deplored in an article which the *American
Archivist* would not publish at the time.[17] We have to play our part in recognizing changes in outlook at an early stage.

Frederick Stielow's response to Roberts is based on a definition of theory as "systematically organized knowledge applicable in a relatively
wide variety of circumstances,"[18] the result of hypotheses and empirical
testing; he quotes Henry James that theories are instruments, not answers.
This embraces much of the work done in the development of descriptive
standards, which is essential if we are to have a common language of automated identification. For Stielow the study of archives is above all a
metadiscipline,[19] and this is precisely its strength in the context of the ecological age. The fact that archivists cannot be labelled or defined is perhaps a source of hope rather than despair, and will encourage multidisciplined generalists in place of the "specialist" of whatever stripe; therein
lies the paradoxical rigour of our professional education, which the requirements for the new graduate degrees and other related programmes
are now recognizing.

Especially at the present time, there is a close relationship between
archival theory, however defined, and the technology of automation. Real
dangers exist of diminishing the archivist as the human component of research which the data bank cannot replace.[20] The challenge which faces
us, in particular our embrace of a new cosmology such as Matthew Fox
proposes, and the difficulty which we have in making the effort, quickly
reveal our heavy dependence on "left brain" thinking, which stresses the
logical, mathematical, linear, detailed, sequential, analytical, and intellectual approaches so prominent in our culture. Often they are at the expense
of lost contributions from our holistic, artistic, symbolic, intuitive, emotional "right brain." Recalling that we drew before we could read and
write, I enrolled in a drawing course along the lines of Betty Edwards's
Drawing from the Right Side of the Brain, which has—I believe—some relevance to our profession.[21]

When, as adults with no formal training, we sit down to draw a human
figure, the result is quite literally childish and we decide that art is not for
us. We look at the subject, but our left brain knows what an eye or an arm
or a hand should look like on paper and down goes a stock symbol reminiscent of childhood. Young children who have not yet come under the

spell of Berry's "cultural coding" have an instinct for emphasizing ...essentials of what they want to express through the consistent use of their own pictorial conventions, in effect their own pictograms for heads and bodies and so on. As time goes by, literacy has them striving for likeness, accuracy, and realism—which defeats them. Their spontaneity disappears and their cramped and wooden images are frozen in the left brain. In the course we were taught to follow the contours of our model with our charcoal sticks, looking far more at the model than the paper. This helps us to eliminate left brain's memory of familiar objects and requires a fresh and sensitive line, while we try to forget that the subject is a body. The cumulative effect, after a few hours of this exercise, has been astonishing. The left brain becomes impatient with all this observation of detail, the old symbols fade away, and we begin to learn to draw.

Pattern recognition is a powerful answer to information overload. Do we search for the pattern with our left or right brain? Is there too much fragmented analysis confused by an overlay of stereotypes from our left brain, or do we bring to bear right-brain holism and intuition in order to help trace accurately the total parameters of the overload? We can then use our left brain not to say, "I know what a data bank on the theme of X more or less contains," but for the subsequent record and analysis of what is significant.[22]

Relationships too have an artistic counterpart called "negative space," such as between the girders of a bridge, and one exercise is to draw the negative spaces of a chair to produce the "positive" chair. When we as archivists appraise, do we wish to see the pattern of content while ignoring contextual relationships which may have a profound bearing on our decision, including absent information? Edwards calls these techniques "information processing,"[23] which has a familiar ring.

Extending this idea and assuming a vastly increased element of pictorial symbols and systems for the conveyance of information through virtual reality, virtual documents, and the mixed media of hypertext, over and above automated archives as we currently know them, would it be possible to design profiles of the documentary flow and information capture in an institution, along with diagrammatic relationships (after the manner of a web-chart) for all documentary material in a department or institution? Could the relative importance of the material be made visible in its totality for both hemispheres of the brain to work upon and, if necessary, set alongside of the records of another agency for comparison and contextual understanding, all the time avoiding too much detail?

R. S. Wurman's "information anxiety" from overload can often be resolved by maps rather than by tabulation.[24] The age of ecology may see us mapping our information with the double helix and other natural data banks as model or metaphor. J. B. Harley believes that we still have too narrow a view of what mapping is: "In our western culture, at least since the Enlightenment, cartography has been defined as a factual science. The premise is that a map should offer a transparent window on the world,"[25] accurate and without bias—which of course is an illusion. Harley maintains that maps can be discussed as text rather than as a mirror of nature, regarding maps as "texts" in the same sense as other nonverbal sign systems.[26] Maps of archival and information patterns could therefore be conceived of as textual description, without the linear characteristics of prose leading to left-brain dominance and analytical fragmentation at the outset.[27]

David Bearman has given us what would seem to be a remarkably prophetic work, entitled all too prosaically *Archival Methods*.[28] He deliberately offers no new theory or technology, but suggests new approaches which are more in tune with the times. Appraisal and acquisition based on the preservation of a representational record of human culture are abandoned as considerations of value are substituted for risk management: What can we not afford to destroy?[29] To my mind, archives, along with other heritage institutions, have in a sense been marginalized by a technological society which sees them as the source of a harmless leisure activity in pursuit of history and "culture" generally.[30] At the same time, archives have been given an almost unlimited licence to acquire, provided the exercise does not cost too much, and our success is often measured in the linear metres of full shelves. Bearman, on the other hand, argues that those government records retained should be records which we need for our identity and protection as citizens and for the conduct of our lives; that, conversely, records which cease to have continuing value should be destroyed through retrospective reappraisal:

> We tell ourselves that society values our efforts for their balanced contribution to posterity, but I will argue that our role is more closely akin to that of the storyteller remaking the past in a fashion relevant to our time. . . . Our value rests with the contribution we make to the continuity of culture by connecting the present with the recent past, not by passively conserving the evidence of a distant past for the unmeasurable benefit of some equally remote future.[31]

This recycling of the past for the sake of the present places the record at the centre of our lives and not detached in some genteel academic ghetto of the mind.[32] Let the future understand our world on the basis of what we need, just as we have come to understand the Middle Ages through the skills of the historian working on the great series of vital government records as the essential basis of that society. What, then, of the private sector? I am not sure that this approach is quite so applicable, but we can still be more selective than we are now, gathering material in the context of documentation strategies based on present societal needs,[33] not just those of Ph.D. candidates. As it is, the evidence of the more distant past is terminally wasting away as a result of age, pollution, and obsolete technology. Let us use it while it is still "alive." In any case, however, our selection was never neutral or objective but, like the writing of our users, the historians, reflective of the myths which are part of our culture.[34] In failing to recognize this fact, archival repositories may become a "museum of communications and not a living cultural entity,"[35] especially if we neglect essential networking with records managers, "where numerous, small data archives in an organization are like isolated gene pools, inbred, narrow and lacking the strength which comes from cross fertilization"[36] (shades of Thomas Berry!). Through all of this the presence of the archivist is vital, since "in manual retrieval systems the human mind makes leaps across categories which are not supported by existing mechanisms in automated systems."[37] Citing M. T. Clanchy on the emergence of the written record in England, Bearman portentously asks whether there will be a divergence away from the textual record as it loses its credibility as evidence in the face of slippery electronic software.

I have left mentioning until last an article clearly grounded in the age of ecology. Many others discussed above deal with more effective ways of conducting archival business, but these could have been put in place within a continuation of our present assumptions; not so Candace Loewen's article on the appraisal of environmental records.[38] She covers some familiar ground on the consequences of the Enlightenment and its antecedents, but many of her sources and insights are fresh to me, especially those on environmental history written by women and including the ecology of the Ancient World. Loewen emphasizes the dominance of patriarchy through the centuries—it is still with us and accounts for many of our problems—and the role of gender in this context.[39] Using all this as a background, she then deals specifically with issues relating to the records of the Atomic Energy Control Board. The extent to which records have a bearing on the natural world should be one of the first considerations in archival appraisal. Sensitive recognition of the implications of our present dilemma will be hard-won nevertheless, since we are children of the industrial age and our parentage will continue to show for some time.

What will be archivists' professional environment in the Age of Ecology? The world around us will certainly not be an ideal Arcadian utopia, as Berry warns us. Growth and change often produce hardship, stress, privation, and violence.[40] The failure of the present global economic system to encourage social justice and a developing sustainability of natural resources may end in turmoil and collapse, which would greatly weaken the structures of centralized government. Out of this could emerge in time a network of bioregions and "soft energy paths," relatively self-supporting.

In the aftermath of a consumer society, the necessities of life may become more expensive as the social costs are built in, but they will be simple, of good quality, and designed to last. Reliance on fossil fuels will be drastically cut; citizens will increasingly gain satisfaction from the qualities of their own region. In contrast to the trends towards simplifying lifestyles, information in all its forms will be global in outreach, easily and cheaply available. Government at all levels will be decentralized, "smaller," more responsive to citizens, and more diverse, few reminders surviving of the old industrial bureaucracies largely built upon the paper record in a mass society. The gleaming technoculture of the future, residing in vast cities surrounded by sanitized greenery, is a projection of our industrial mindsets and the centralized corporate ideal of the multinationals, which remains a real threat to ecological solutions. This is not the place in which to rehearse detailed scenarios, but we should nevertheless try from time to time to envision generations beyond our own, the better to prepare for them. Serious futurologists such as Hazel Henderson[41] can be of help and so can the more literary science fiction.

In my view, there is likely to be a demand for a kind of integrated history which might well encompass the whole planet, indicating trends in the lives of humans and other species in a symbiotic relationship which will require vast areas of automated compatibility in order to detect significant patterns. Displayed on such a broad canvas, the result will be mythic in extent. The bioregions will receive similar attention, but one wonders whether the byzantine affairs of the old national governments will ever again engage the creative imaginations of future writers once they pass from the scene. Departments of the environment may likewise have disappeared, as both public and private sectors will be deeply involved in the natural world at all levels as part of the art of living.

Unlike today, it will be increasingly difficult to single out "cultural activities" as being "over and against" the rest of life. The dichotomies inherent in "work" and "play" will likely be resolved as work becomes more playful and play is recognized as something which we need to work at as part of human nature. Generations to come will value documentary evidence which reflects the public temper of the age, and in particular the heroic efforts made to reverse the rush to disaster: pioneer work done by individuals and organizations which has always preceded commitment by governments. The danger is that the records of the old discredited industrial age will be neglected by the politically correct, as were those of the Dark and Middle Ages by the Enlightenment.

Although their roles will remain distinct in many ways, libraries, archives, art galleries, museums, and theatres will work far more closely together as they all celebrate the richness of past and present life on earth. The possibilities of virtual reality and virtual documents are enormous as a means of re-creating past and present environments not otherwise accessible. Family histories will increase in popularity as families become grounded in their bioregions and become more conscious of their place in nature. Automation will allow families to secure and disseminate their archives around their homes and through time, so that each generation will be able to enter into and assume as a mask the lives of their ancestors.[42]

While the nineteenth century rediscovered history as we have come to know it and the old record-keepers provided the major source materials, the twentieth century rediscovered the complexity of information,[43] and modern archives are now in danger of falling into the clutches of information scientists. We archivists must nevertheless follow our own path, where the verifiable record remains central to our concerns. We should be wary of hypertext's siren song luring us onto the reefs of lost provenance. At the same time, we shall join with other heritage professionals in order to make leaps of the imagination from documents to the artifacts of "material culture," to art and (why not?) to literature and theatre, always bearing in mind that the origin and context of human heritage lies in life-forms which antedate and still surround us. The new age will see a conceptual fusion of these phenomena as we strive to live in the shadow of our ancestors and their fellow creatures as parts of the whole.[44]

I suspect that I could be accused of advocating politically correct attitudes under the cover of professionalism. Others will see these impressions as hopelessly idealistic; the wholesale destruction of life on this planet through neglect or violence may proceed beyond the point of no return. That might well happen, in which case the documentary heritage could disappear as well, and a break in cultural continuity would pose communication riddles for some phoenix intelligence rising from the ashes.[45] I prefer to believe that this agenda will not proceed—at least not to the very point of extinction—because behind our speck in the universe is a caring God delighting in creation, a mystery beyond description and anthropomorphism. The glass remains very dark, but a pattern of living has been revealed to us if we shall but accept it.[46]

REFLECTION, 2000

By now you must be tired of my plugging away with the deteriorating environment and a lack of ecological awareness. This will be the last time I will keep harping because I believe it is necessary to develop an attitude and a mindset which sharpens our awareness of what we have gotten ourselves into and hence to value those sources which are seeking either to record past disasters as a cause of future comparisons, or, through scientific research, to help us towards the way out through a greater understanding of the breadth of natural complexity. I have been musing in a philosophical way about this subject for some time, and I am anxious that more archivists join in the debate now that I am laying down my pen.

Candace Loewen's article is still the only one (at the time of writing) to take a concrete example of a federal agency, the Atomic Energy Control Board, and ensure the preservation of individual dossiers of the staff in the event of subsequent medical consequences due to radiation. This appraisal decision is set within an excellent review of environmental literature from sources quite other than mine.

A good place for further Canadian examples would be the "Studies in Documents" section of Archivaria, *and I make bold to suggest four major sources: public records, since so many agencies have an impact on the natural world, which should certainly include municipalities and their policies in dealing with local environmental problems; the observations and diaries of those who are deeply observant of their communities; the records of environmental activists who seek to change the attitudes of government and the general public; and business archives which reveal "greening" strategies. These are of course interrelated, since letters of discourse and protest are to be found in public records, and the microcosmic records of the informed observer may provide valuable practical insights which escape the more general and theoretical approaches of the scientists formed by their discipline and specialization.*

Almost all of us will have useful environmental information in our repositories which should be identified in the way that the existence of women on record was finally recognized. This would form useful groundwork for acquisition in the private sector as archivists become familiar with the field and develop a real interest. A useful ally in all this could be the local historian. John Sheail of the Institute of Terrestrial Ecology in England has used the City of Norwich as an example to show the interrelationship between urban and rural developments which is quite revealing when set in this context of environmental studies.[47] The editor of the journal Local Historian *has challenged community historians to break away from endless narrative history to address these wider issues. Sheail writes, "The increasing concern shown by contemporary opinion for environmental issues has yet to make its mark on the historian's craft. If true it might be argued that the most effective way of arousing interest would be to identify the rewards for the historians themselves."[48]*

Shortly after World War II, a few professional historians in Britain began to take local history seriously with some outstanding results and an increased interest by schools in research by students. This of course dealt with people and institutions in the context of town and country. This is surely only a step away from exploring the natural world in the context of people, institutions, the business world, and sustainability.

I have spent some time as volunteer archivist of the Sierra Club of British Columbia which has grown mightily since the 1970s when the environmental move-

ment began to take off in North America in a big way, thanks to some outstanding pioneers. Records of this kind deserve much more attention from established archives than they are receiving.

NOTES

1. Ralph Metzner, "Age of Ecology," *Resurgence* No. 149 (Nov./Dec. 1991): 4–7.

2. Automation is a challenging mix of the logical lineality of software design, the traditional mechanism which operates the "drives," and the holistic impact of automated communication systems. Terry Cook has recognized a move away from the first generation of computers, based on content, to a second generation based on "context, relationships and functionality" where automated records cease to be "machine readable" and become "electronic." See his review article, "Easy to Byte, Harder to Chew: The Second Generation of Electronic Records Archives," *Archivaria* 33 (Winter 1991–92): 202–16.

3. This healthy tension is apparent in Richard Brown, "Records Acquisition Strategy and Its Theoretical Foundation: The Case for a Concept of Archival Hermeneutics," *Archivaria* 33 (Winter 1991–92): 34–56; Terry Cook, *The Archival Appraisal of Records Containing Personal Information: A RAMP Study with Guidelines* (Paris, 1991); Terry Cook, *An Appraisal Methodology: Guidelines for Performing Archival Appraisal* (Ottawa, 1992).

4. Hugh Taylor, "The Totemic Universe: Appraising the Documentary Future," in Christopher Hives, ed., *Archival Appraisal: Theory and Practice* (British Columbia, 1990), pp. 15–29.

5. Thomas Berry, *The Dream of the Earth* (San Francisco, 1988), p. 21.

6. Ibid., p. 27.

7. Taylor, "The Totemic Universe."

8. Berry, *The Dream of the Earth*, p. 66.

9. Ibid., p. 21.

10. Ibid., pp. 92–93.

11. Matthew Fox, *The Coming of the Cosmic Christ* (San Francisco, 1988), p. 1, note.

12. Stephen Toulmin, *The Return to Cosmology: Post-Modern Science and the Theology of Nature* (Berkeley, 1982), p. 256. The scientist, says Toulmin, is no longer the spectator (Greek, *theoros*) but must work inside nature: "We need to discover in what respects and on what conditions the world of nature can continue to provide a home for humanity," p. 265.

13. Frank G. Burke, "The Future Course of Archival Theory in the United States," *American Archivist* 44 (Winter 1981): 42.

14. John W. Roberts, "Archival Theory: Myth or Banality?" *American Archivist* 53 (Winter 1990): 111.

15. Terry Cook, "Leaving Safe and Accustomed Ground: Ideas for Archivists," *Archivaria* 23 (Winter 1986–87): 124.

16. Roberts, "Archival Theory," p. 116.

17. Howard Zinn, "Secrecy, Archives and the Public Interest," *Boston University Journal* 19 (Fall 1971): 37–44.

18. Frederick J. Stielow, "Archival Theory Redux and Redeemed: Definition and Context Toward a General Theory," *American Archivist* 54 (Winter 1991): 17.

19. Stielow, "Archival Theory," p. 21; see also Terry Eastwood, "Nurturing Archival Education in the University," *American Archivist* 51 (Summer 1988): 229–52.

20. Hugh Taylor, "Chip Monks at the Gate: The Impact of Technology on Archives, Libraries and the User," *Archivaria* 33 (Winter 1991–92): 173–80; Terry Cook, "Viewing the World Upside Down: Reflections on the Underpinnings of Archival Public Programming," *Archivaria* 31 (Winter 1990–91): 123–34.

21. Betty Edwards, *Drawing from the Right Side of the Brain* (Los Angeles, 1979). Terry Cook has reminded me that when pictograms came to be used in the ancient world as a rather primitive alphabet, textual richness and context were increasingly lost because of this very left-brain-influenced representation. I am also grateful to Robin Wall, artist and teacher, for his help in this connection.

22. Edwards, "Crossing Over: Experiencing the Shift from Left to Right," in *Drawing*, pp. 46–59. Archivists of documentary art and photography will be particularly familiar with this phenomenon.

23. Ibid., p. 35.

24. R. S. Wurman, *Information Anxiety* (New York, 1989), pp. 260–90.

25. J. B. Harley, "Text and Contexts in the Interpretation of Early Maps," in D. Buisseret, ed., *From Sea Charts to Satellite Images: Interpreting North American History through Maps* (Chicago, 1990), p. 4.

26. Ibid.

27. For a more philosophical approach to maps as text, see J. H. Andrews, "Maps and Language: A Metaphor Extended," *Cartographica* 27 (Spring 1990): 1–19. I am indebted to Ed Dahl of the National Archives for drawing my attention to this paper and that by J. B. Harley above.

28. David Bearman, *Archival Methods*, Archives & Museum Informatics Technical Report 3 (Spring 1989).

29. Ibid., p. 16.

30. Hugh Taylor, "Information Ecology and the Archives of the 1980s," *Archivaria* 18 (Summer 1984): 25–37.

31. Bearman, *Archival Methods*, p. 59.

32. All the more reason for us to be sensitive to our cultural blindspots and therefore be better able to minimize them. Bearman warns us nevertheless that "cultural blindness and sudden cultural insights are both equally culture bound." Ibid., p. 62.

33. Helen W. Samuels, "Improving our Disposition: Documentation Strategy," *Archivaria* 33 (Winter 1991–92): 125–40.

34. "Myth" in the technical sense is open to many definitions, and in a way defies definition. Joseph Campbell in *The Power of Myth* (New York, 1988) is evasive of abstract formulations, because that is exactly what myths are not about. Bill Moyers, who interviewed Campbell, summarizes his views thus: "Myths are stories of our search through the ages for truth, for meaning, for significance. We all need to tell our story and to understand our story. . . . We need for life to signify,

to touch the eternal, to understand the mysterious, to find out who we are," *The Power of Myth*, p. 4. For Campbell today, there are no boundaries. The only mythology which is valid today is the mythology of the planet—and we do not yet have such a mythology (Ibid., p. 28). This echoes to some extent Fox's new cosmology, discussed above.

35. Barbara L. Craig, "Meeting the Future by Returning to the Past: A Commentary on Hugh Taylor's Transformations," *Archivaria* 25 (Winter 1987–88): 9.

36. Ibid., p. 9.

37. Bearman, *Archival Methods*, p. 51.

38. Candace Loewen, "From Human Neglect to Planetary Survival: New Approaches to the Appraisal of Environmental Records," *Archivaria* 33 (Winter 1991–92): 87–103.

The first section of the article seeks to explain how our long-standing neglect of the consideration of the whole, or context, has led to the deplorable state of the environment—and of archives, "especially with regards to appraisal." Section two emphasizes that "nature is a perception dependent on the perceived world view," and that archivists should be aware of this. The third section discusses "survival" values in the appraisal of environmental records, using the Atomic Energy Control Board as an example.

On a quick perusal, this article would seem to be no more than an archival recognition of the records of the environment appropriate to this age of ecology and comparable to the emphasis in the 1970s on quantitative sources, such as parish registers and case files, which reflected the emergence of a new sense of "people power"—in other words, more traditional, value-laden appraisal reflecting sensitivity to current issues. In fact, the article takes a position outside the bureaucracy, which is highly contextual and critical of the bureaucratic mindset that also afflicts us as archivists. This is Terry Cook's reading, and mine also. Loewen is concerned about records which have a bearing on our planetary and cultural survival, not simply a new research field stimulated by social change.

39. For a similar view see also Berry, "Patriarchy: A New Interpretation of History," *Dream*, pp. 138–62; and Fox, *Coming*, Part 1, pp. 12–34.

40. Berry, *Dream*, p. 216.

41. See for instance Hazel Henderson, "From Economism to Systems Theory and New Indicators of Development," *Technological Forecasting and Social Change* 37 (1990): 213–33.

42. There is now an extensive literature on every aspect of planetary transformation. The critical bibliography compiled by Thomas Berry in *Dream* (pp. 224–40) is excellent; to it should be added Murray Bookchin, *Toward an Ecological Society* (Montreal, 1980).

43. Stielow, "Archival Theory," p. 20.

44. This from Madeleine L'Engle, *A Stone for a Pillow* (Wheaton, Ill., 1986), p. 42: "In a recent article on astrophysics, I came across the beautiful and imaginative concept known as the 'butterfly effect.' If a butterfly . . . should be hurt, the effects would be felt in galaxies thousands of light years away. The interrelationship of all Creation is sensitive in a way we are just beginning to understand."

45. On the theme of cultural continuity see Kenneth E. Foote, "To Remember and Forget: Archives, Memory and Culture," *American Archivist* 53 (Summer

1990): 378–92; in science fiction, moreover, Walter M. Miller, *Canticle for Liebowitz* (New York, 1959), and David Macaulay, *Motel of the Mysteries* (Boston, 1979). Both deal with strange attributions given to artifacts when there is a total cultural breakdown.

46. Finally, I should like to acknowledge the especially helpful comments, suggestions, and citations provided by Terry Cook of the National Archives of Canada, which deserve far more than a note. His colleague, Candace Loewen, moreover, has gently and quite rightly taken me to task for not drawing attention in this paper to the contribution made by women to the environmental discourse. She has already filled the gap most admirably in her own article (*supra*, note 38), and I shall not repeat her sources here.

47. John Sheail, "Environmental History: A Challenge for the Local Historian," *Archives* 22 (1997): 157–69.

48. Ibid., p. 168.

Chapter 16

A Life in Archives:
Retrospect and Prospect

Most of us have come to a career in archives apparently by chance, as the doors of opportunity have opened. Popularly seen as a very esoteric pursuit, far from the easily defined "Army, Navy, Church, or Stage" of earlier generations, archives beckon to us as a voyage of discovery into the unusual. Once chosen and found to match our gifts, reflection may reveal an accumulation of influences which stretch back in time long before university graduation.[1]

My mother and her sister chose the stage, and I suppose that it is fair to say that dramatic art re-creates the printed record of speech and song. Mother chose a career in Edwardian musical comedy; my aunt became a Shakespearean actress and manager, with her husband, of her own company. She lived in Bath, England, where circumstances took me in 1927 at the age of seven. The city then as now evoked the extraordinary grace, symmetry, and order of the eighteenth century and continued to be the home for a mix of genteel folk, and those who served them, in the years following World War I. My aunt had a prodigious memory for "lines"; for her all of life was a drama, and in the lead role relative to me she demanded (and got) absolute obedience. She taught me how to speak before an audience, and I have always tried to re-create the record, whether printed or archival, by enveloping it with a kind of dramatic enthusiasm. Of course, I never read history then or much later, but Bath was an endless backdrop of elegance and famous lives, commemorated on plaques beside Georgian front doors, which worked upon me symbiotically. For

Originally published in *Archives and Manuscripts* 21 (November 1993): 222–36. Reproduced with the kind permission of the author, and the Australian Society of Archivists, Inc.

me the record of the past was to be projected and re-created with excitement or not at all. This was the least we could do for it.

During the Great Depression of the 1930s, Father returned from building bridges in Africa, our secure world collapsed, and we returned to his birthplace on the rugged, windswept, northeast coast, to a world of total and at times exhilarating contrast and a family more attuned to sport than the arts. Then came World War II.

Looking back now, I realize that six years as a wireless operator introduced me to an electric language upon which our lives in the air at times depended, a medium utterly different from speech, printing, or writing, a prophetic experience which depended entirely on the interval, and the binary opening and closing of a circuit. At the time, of course, I was just a humble "key basher" who was fortunate enough to be involved in momentous historical events and to survive them, thanks to a very experienced Australian pilot from Townsville. By the end of the war, all I wanted to do was read history at Oxford and have a career in something less destructive than previously. I got my wish.

The tale now becomes more focused. Our parish decided to celebrate the tercentenary of its church in 1947. This took me into the vestry safe and a close encounter with the first churchwarden's minutes and accounts written in the unfamiliar "secretary hand" of the period, a "code" which cried out to be "broken." The volume became the centrepiece of a documentary exhibit. From then on, no matter what direction exploration in archival studies was to take me, the original document with all its contextual implications, evidential power, and legal sanctity was to remain central as the point of return.

On returning to Oxford I took the chance of a "dry run" to see if the life of an archivist would really be the answer. I went to work for the Northamptonshire Record Society, a quintessential English institution presided over by Joan Wake, a woman of awesome drive, energy, and enthusiasm who learnt to be an archivist at the feet of Hubert Hall of the Public Record Office. As a member of the local gentry, she bullied and cajoled all and sundry to deposit their papers at the headquarters of the Society in a wing of Lamport Hall, a magnificent Palladian mansion. The juxtaposition of splendid architecture and eight hundred years of accumulated record made up for a desperate minimum of funding, whereby the first thing you learnt to do was fill the document boxes in such a way that they could be stacked five high without collapsing (there being almost no shelving). For those who have never worked as archivists in England, it is hard to imagine the variety of surprises buried in those hundreds of years of uncatalogued material which could be unearthed almost daily. It was the intensity of enthusiasm at Lamport Hall which overcame mundane shortages. My immediate superior, Pat King, remained on to become the first County Archivist of Northamptonshire until his retirement. I have deep admiration for those who devote their whole career to one community; their immense local knowledge is not readily available in any other way save through themselves. No software technology will ever match them. My own fate was to be a moving generalist, but there will, I hope, always be room for both kinds in the profession, with other mixes in between.

Three months later I was at Liverpool University taking the Archives Diploma under Geoffrey Barraclough, where the centrality of the original document was further emphasized, given the nature of what had to be mastered. Over half our time was taken up with palaeography, diplomatics, and, of course, Jenkinson and the three Dutchmen.[2] My only practicum was "slave labour" sorting a few wills; there was little else on archives administration available in English—Schellenberg was not recommended; the *American Archivist* was never mentioned. There was little chance of our whoring after strange gods! However, the course was excellent for its day; the rest, without making grievous mistakes, we would learn by experience.

As archivist of two large public libraries in Leeds and Liverpool successively, I learnt very early on the value of a good local collection of printed material close at hand which had been built up long before the archives were started.[3] During the 1950s there was a good deal of feuding and misunderstanding between archivists and librarians which still survives in some quarters. We were "the new kids on the block" and particularly vulnerable. The Society of Local Archivists had only recently dropped the "Local" and there was a polite standoff with the staff of the Public Record Office who, at that time, felt themselves to be the real professionals who dealt only with public records. The Historical Manuscripts Commission, especially under Roger Ellis, was much more considerate. These attitudes were quite understandable because the new record offices set up by the local authorities of counties and cities acquired material from both the public and private sectors, and the public records were very different from those of HM Government. Because much of the early record in England was in Latin and required a knowledge of palaeography to understand it, there were fewer very small archives than in Canada and, I imagine, Australia. There is always a tendency for the large to look down on the small and I think this is most unfortunate because their roles can be very different.

We in local archives were all fervent evangelists at a time when all England was becoming aware of an enormous documentary heritage. Our first priority was to the Clerk's records of our local authority, unless we were in libraries, but an invaluable network was spreading into the countryside supported by the National Register of Archives (NRA) under the

Historical Manuscripts Commission. Archivists received small expenses for listing archival material in private hands, the resulting inventory being sent to the Registrar in Chancery Lane, London. This was both a service to owners, valuable information for the local archives, and a means whereby various fonds would be placed in an archives for safekeeping. After a while these inventories would be duplicated by the NRA and placed in local libraries. Such networks of information could be seen as the forerunners of their automated counterparts.[4] At Leeds we were able to organize an itinerant archivist supported by local authorities unable to engage one full time. While it is perfectly true that the core of our work lies in the disciplined appraisal and processing of our holdings for convenient use, the smaller archives in particular must, in addition, try to offer a range of services within what American archivists call "Public Programs." They are essential for their survival and continuous funding. Such archives are deeply integrated into the heritage nucleus of small communities who see them, for all their limited resources, as essential to their sense of continuity both for the "old timers" and new residents. To some extent they fill the role of village churchyards in an age of cremation and private cemeteries, and we should never belittle them. Unfortunately, there is a tendency in hard times for the national and state repositories to limit external commitment, refuse collections from the private sector, and so place a heavy burden on the smaller repositories which have limited space.[5]

On moving to Liverpool in 1954, the Local Collection was in the Archives under my charge but unlike my predecessor I did not meddle with it and left my librarian in peace to look after it. Here I had custody of a splendid collection of documentary art relating to the city[6] and a massive collection of old "lantern slides" which resulted in early examples of audiovisual presentations when linked with the early reel-to-reel tape recorders. These were all very crude experiments by present standards, but they were quite effective in telling the story of the city.[7] Most archives contain a great deal which is not strictly archival, but archivists, who are generalists at heart, at one time or another take everything from medals to ephemeral "grey" literature under their wing, because no one else will. Much of this is very evocative to the general public for whom too many documents are tedious to view. Here I learnt for the first time to defend my department against the incursions of a somewhat predatory City Librarian who scented an anomaly within his bibliographic universe. George Chandler later became National Librarian of Australia. We did not see eye to eye on many things, but he had an extraordinary talent for prising funds out of a tough socialist City Council for which he must be given credit. He told me I would be most effective once I left England. In that he was right.

And so back to Northumberland to start up the last County Archives in England on my home ground—an archivist's dream. Its history spanned the Roman occupation, Anglo Saxons and Danes, mediaeval settlements, the coal trade, the wool trade, and the agricultural and industrial revolutions. The early years of a new repository are most exhilarating as fonds after fonds are acquired from the private sector over and above the early administrative and court records of the county. There was not much difficulty in following Jenkinson's dictum that an archivist should not be a historian—there was no time![8] The rich complexity of the surviving record over hundreds of years provided all the stimulation we needed to stick to our post and not allow the discipline of history to dictate our agenda or warp our methodology.

In addition to the usual extension activities,[9] we founded local historical societies and brought local history, through documentary evidence in the audiovisual mode, to those interested, under the aegis of the quaintly named Workers' Education Association, which harked back to its blue-collar origins. Then we would pile our audience onto buses and take them out into the country to tramp the ground and view ancient architecture and terrain. By the 1960s local history had been liberated from picturesque stories and became a "respectable" branch of study for the past twenty years, but there was still the need for popular approaches which mediated the work of the academic historian and archaeologist. I believe this is still the role of an archives which feels the need to establish a rapport with its constituency particularly in the early stages. I realize that this had nothing to do with archive administration per se, but is complementary to it.

Overwhelmed by the older records and seduced by their multifaceted richness, we were caught up in a hundred-year-old "historical shunt" in which we worked closely with the historians, the results of which we can be justly proud. At the same time, however, we neglected the more mundane and recent departmental records of our authorities, which should have been our concern as the descendants of the old record keepers—records management was in its infancy.[10] Moreover, with only two small land registries in England, we became bogged down cataloguing "muniments of title" extending over centuries. The life of an English archivist at that time was very rich in a documentary sense, but otherwise we lived for the most part in genteel poverty enjoying an occasional dinner with the aristocracy and gentry whose interests we courted in their castles, mansions, and other stately homes. But it was all great fun. At an annual conference of the Society of Archivists in Newcastle-upon-Tyne, the local arrangements committee varied the usual routine by taking their colleagues down a working coal mine to get a feel of the world which lay behind the business archives of the colliery companies. At the same conference we visited one of the first major national government departments to be automated and presented a conceptual scheme to automate the National Register of Archives. In the age of punch cards, paper tape, and key punching, this project was about twenty-five years ahead of the appropriate technology! I believe, however, this kind of exposure, seeing records in the context of the creators or exploring heuristically the potential of archival activity, is stimulating even when the ideas are rather wild. In those days archivists tended to be conservative in their ways and in the "small-c" conservative material they accessioned. Minorities and the counterculture for the most part passed us by. Have we changed that much? Yes, to some extent.[11]

In 1965 the Taylors, with their three small girls, immigrated to Canada. Starting up and running a provincial archives promised new experiences and a new vision.[12] From now on, there may be much that will run parallel to the Australian experience whereby Europeans settled in an ancient land peopled by its aboriginals. Alberta had imported the Torrens system of land registration from Australia, so there were no old title deeds to worry about. The old trackways were overlaid by grids. There was no ancient network of surviving records. We began to acquire material from the 1900s when most English archivists were thinking of giving up as being too modern to process immediately. The founding documents of settlement being thin on the ground, we were able to give much more attention to early governmental accumulations prior to records management.

Since the archives was set up as a department of the Provincial Museum, I began to take the artifactual base of records less for granted. They could be seen as a part of our material culture over against the constant presence of native peoples with an oral tradition which predated us by thousands of years. This presence and their survival, in spite of all we had done, became haunting, disturbing, and inspiring. My portfolio of experience with media of record was expanding with the custody of photographs by the great pioneer cameramen of the Plains, whose evidence is central to our understanding, as they well knew. Oral history also played a part, capturing styles of expression and emphasis that marked those interviewed in a unique way.[13] Since the archives took care of the Museum library, a great deal of local ephemera was received along with standard works.[14] When I had to give a recorded commentary on Blackfoot transferral ceremonies in a teepee, when medicine bundles were sold to the museum, I felt I had reached the ultimate edge of an archivist's work!

Two years later found me setting up the Provincial Archives of New Brunswick in Fredericton on the other side of Canada. With records dating back to the 1780s piled three feet deep in the attic of the Legislative Assembly, this seemed like England all over again, in the land of the United Empire Loyalists who left the United States after the War of Independence. For a brief moment in time, I had the archives, records management, forms management and analysis, and the Legislative Library[15] under my care, which was a sizeable information empire, but Fredericton was memorable for something else. Tutoring in history at the University of New Brunswick to help pay the mortgage, I ran into Marshall McLuhan's *Gutenberg Galaxy* and *Understanding Media* and began to grasp their relevance for archivists. If we were to administer the whole spectrum of ancient and modern media of record, we had better understand their impact on society in general and us as individuals, as we refined our appraisal decisions and gave assistance and guidance to users. The media of parchment, paper, and automation, together with text, maps, and paintings, are not just carrier pigeons of information but change agents in the way we perceive meaning.[16] This led me to pursue as a layman the whole subject of communication theory, starting as we did with orality (and, through the medium of the computer, regaining a kind of neo-orality after five centuries of textual dominance).

As a member of the SAA President's Committee of the Seventies, I was very disappointed with the majority report on archival education which held that short institutes, sessional courses, and some on-the-job training was all that was required for a good history graduate to be an archivist.[17] Edwin Welch and I spent several years trying to have guidelines for postgraduate training approved by the Association of Canadian Archivists become the common standard for North America, without success.[18] The "total archives" approach, embracing the parent institutional records, records management, and archives from the private sector in all media of record, requires archivists to be at arm's length from historians in their methodology. This is not to deny the value of historical training (though other disciplines are also appropriate), but we now see ourselves as part of a very distinct profession continuing a very old tradition as "keepers of the evidence."[19] The SAA has been so impressed with the guidelines as recently revised by the ACA that they are now using them as a basis for their own.

I became the Director of the Historical Branch of the Public Archives of Canada in 1971, surrounded by division chiefs who had grown grey in an institution dominated by the manuscript tradition. In the next few years four new divisions were created, pointedly oriented by media. I was convinced that these new divisions needed their autonomy to develop their several disciplines and methodologies within overarching archival principles. This arrangement stirred some controversy at the time,[20] and there have been amalgamations since, but I still believe it was necessary for achieving maturity and self-confidence. After six years with what became the Archives Branch on my request (and the Historical Resources Branch when I left!), I returned to the provincial scene in Nova Scotia satisfied I had accomplished what I had set out to do.[21] I realized I was a regional person at heart; a national archives is a difficult geographical expression to accept beyond the federal records mandate, because collections "of national importance" in the private sector are often in conflict with the provinces. The National Archives of Canada has a good reputation and has handled the problem well, so that now it is recognized that collections of this nature can properly be housed in the region where they were created.[22] I believe archivists may well be national or regional by temperament and background, but crossovers do occur from time to time.

I have continued to ponder the relationship between oral and literate traditions as they affect archives and the powerful analogies which the postliterate age of automation present to us.[23] What then of the archivist in the age of ecology, which is already witnessing the erosion of centralized bureaucratic structures, the proliferation of networks, and the multimedia world of communication, the nucleus of which will be archival within an emerging strategy for planetary survival? We have to become biocentric rather than anthropocentric for, as Chief Seattle warned us, "Everything is connected," and a great river of genetic information flows through all life. In addition to our genetic coding, we are also coded culturally, a code transmitted from one generation to another. Archives are a part of this transmission process, and we will become increasingly linked to all sources of information which work for our cultural survival. I believe archivists are inherently comprehensivists and generalists, given the span of the documentary record, who will have a powerful role to play as one of the principal mediators in transferring information into structured knowledge which Saul Wurman sees as a major problem in the future.

In this very superficial account which links my writings together, I have tried to show the evolution of one archivist over the past forty years through experiences with which others can identify and share. Only by exploring and extending our professional reach to the limit of our integrity, as I have tried to do, will we escape that backwater which, though apparently calm and comfortable, may also be stagnant with the signs of approaching irrelevance.

REFLECTION, 2000

As this essay is itself a recent reflection on my career, it seems superfluous to comment on it further, especially in light of the new essay that concludes this book and reflects for a final time on my work. That essay may be seen as an expansion of the themes from this Australian piece.

While part of the context of this paper is set forth in note 1 below, this piece was submitted to the journal in response to "the Editor's request for something to remind us of the author's visit to Australia in 1992," as was explained in an editorial forward. I then told the editor in a personal letter that I rejected the use of "My . . ." for the opening title: "I wanted to suggest that this profession can be exciting, varied, and challenging in any generation; it may help those seeking a career in our field; it may resonate with the experiences of some readers." I added that "it may be helpful for people to know where ideas and perspectives come from and in what experience they are rooted. This provides a human context and context is what archives are about. Papers do not always have to be disembodied intellectual products!"

NOTES

1. In September 1992 the New South Wales Branch of the Australian Society of Archivists invited me to tour Australia with my wife, Daphne. I gave a series of lectures on the theme "Information as Memory" and two seminars with the title" Recycling the Past: Cultural Heritage in the Age of Ecology." For the former I drew together material mostly from three published articles (those cited in note 23), and for the latter I made use of an unpublished paper. This was submitted later to *Archivaria* since it rounded off a series devoted to archives in the widest possible context that has appeared in North American archival journals.

I was asked to submit a paper for *Archives and Manuscripts* which would cover what I had to say on my tour for those who were able (and unable) to attend. Rather than warm over what has already been published and is quite readily available, I decided on this autobiographical venture to give a context to what I have written, including what appears to have influenced me in the direction my career has taken. I have also taken the liberty of filling out details and ideas in the notes for those who might be interested, together with citations of articles which develop these ideas further. I have left all evaluation to others and have generally avoided covering the same ground as James K. Burrows and Mary Ann Pylypchuk in "The Writings of Hugh Taylor—A Bibliographic Review," in Barbara L. Craig, ed., *The Archival Imagination: Essays in Honour of Hugh A. Taylor* (Ottawa, 1992), pp. 244–54, which is followed by a complete bibliography to 1991.

This paper is not intended as an exercise in self-promotion, but rather as a way of suggesting facets of experience out of which ideas have come, which others may identify with and find useful.

2. Hilary Jenkinson, *A Manual of Archive Administration*, 2nd ed. (London, 1937); Samuel Muller, J. A. Feith, and R. Fruin, *Manual for the Arrangement and Description of Archives*, trans. Arthur H. Leavitt (New York, 1940). Student archivists were able also to make use of some excellent administrative histories of the major English institutions which were a great help in arrangement. This resource was lacking in Canada. See Hugh Taylor, "Administrative History: An Archivist's Need," *The Canadian Archivist/L'Archiviste canadien* 2.1 (1970): 4–9.

3. Hugh Taylor, "The Collective Memory: Archives and Libraries as Heritage," *Archivaria* 15 (Winter 1982–83): 118–30, derives from experience of archives in libraries. The vast information resource in manuscript and print is the invisible underpinning for all that is popularly known as "heritage" and is often taken for

granted, especially in North America. There are now some signs of convergence of the two disciplines while still retaining their separate identities. See Cynthia J. Durance and Hugh A. Taylor, "Wisdom, Knowledge, Information and Data: Transformation of Archives and Libraries of the Western World," *Alexandria* 4.1 (1992): 37–61.

4. Because these were early days for the Northumberland Record Office, a brief guide to the holdings in local archival repositories was compiled as a starting point for researchers seeking an overall view of what was available in the area. In contrast to guides to individual repositories, this was the first of its kind and much appreciated. See Hugh Taylor, *Northumberland History. A Brief Guide to the Records and Aids in Newcastle-upon-Tyne* (Newcastle-upon-Tyne, Northumberland County Council, 1963).

5. It could be argued that small local archives have a radically different role in society than their larger counterparts. Situated in the visible and felt neighbourhood that created the record, they are a locus for local heritage material in association with the local museum. Although the collections are small and disparate with a preponderance of photographs, they help to define the community for residents and visitors alike, much as the parish church, parish records, and tombstones did in earlier times. Few such repositories are prepared to deal with large and complex fonds which were best accommodated in the regional archives with adequate resources to deal with them. The future may well see the expansion of local repositories, given the increasing effectiveness of modern communication networks.

6. Hugh Taylor, "Documentary Art and the Role of the Archivist," *The American Archivist* 42 (October 1979): 417–28, discusses in archival terms the value and limitations of such material as a source of historical information and to what extent it can be regarded as archival. The article draws on English and Canadian experience which began in Liverpool.

7. Hugh Taylor, "Local History: An Experiment with Slides and Tapes," *Archives* 5, no. 27, (1962): 142–44.

8. As archivists we published articles on local history from time to time, often to highlight the value of records in our care. Jenkinson meant that we should not see ourselves as historians, but keepers of the historical record and in this he was quite right. I was once interviewed by him for a job and my interest in "outreach" did not go down too well! But then the Public Record Office did not have to beat the bushes for archival material in the private sector as we in the counties did!

9. English archives have had, since World War II, a close relationship with history teachers in schools to the extent that a written local history project could be submitted as part of the examination for the General Certificate of Education. See Hugh Taylor, "Clio in the Raw: Archival Materials and the Teaching of History," *American Archivist* 35 (July–October 1972): 317–30, which is largely the result of working with schools in England. Canada and, as far as I know, the U.S. had not yet developed this kind of service at the local level to the same extent.

10. This theme was developed later in Hugh Taylor, "Information Ecology and the Archives of the 1980s," *Archivaria* 18 (Summer 1984): 25–37. The metaphor "Information Ecology" comes from the work of Wes Jackson, founder of the Land Institute, Salma, Kansas, a specialist in sustainable agriculture whom I met briefly

and who speaks of the "information rich" resource of diversified crops planted together and interactive, as opposed to the "information poor" resources of crops resulting from monoculture and soil deterioration.

11. This point was to be developed further in Gerald Ham, "The Archival Edge," *American Archivist* 38 (January 1975): 5–13; and Howard Zinn, "Secrecy, Archives and the Public Interest," *Boston University Journal* 19 (Fall 1971): 37–44.

12. Hugh Taylor, "Archives in Britain and Canada: Impressions of an Immigrant," *The Canadian Archivist/L'Archiviste canadien* 1.7 (1969): 22–33; and Hugh Taylor, "The Archival Experience in England and Canada," *Midwestern Archivist* 4.1 (1979): 53–56.

13. Hugh Taylor, "Oral History and Archives," *Canadian Oral History Journal*, 2 (1976–77): 1–5. The involvement of archivists in oral history is controversial. Many of the interviews are light on solid information, and the experience of "oldtimers," proving up and maintaining quarter sections in the settlement of the Canadian West, can be repetitive. On a more fundamental level we have been accused of "creating the record," as being none of our business. I maintain that something like this record is already in the mind of the interviewee. It must be admitted, however, that we control the record through the questions we ask. In the 1960s archivists conducted interviews, but wherever possible had others trained for this work of supplementing the written record when necessary.

14. I have always had a strong feeling about the value of printed ephemera as cultural symbols, in addition to the information they contain. Such material is not archival, but is often closely associated with archives. Many interesting items appear in fonds of all kinds, but this is a "grey area" we share with libraries. At a personal level, the Taylors have collected ephemera directly connected with activities involving the family to enrich our photographs and papers. The Taylor Family Archives are now in the Provincial Archives in Nova Scotia in Halifax.

15. As in Northumberland I found myself compiling a checklist of sources (this time secondary) in local libraries and archives to provide a starting point for researchers while material in the new Provincial Archives was being made available.

16. This is discussed in Hugh Taylor, "The Media of Record: Archives in the Wake of McLuhan," *Georgia Archive* 6 (Spring 1978), pp. 1–10. Archivists are better equipped than their classifying colleagues, the librarians, to practice "pattern recognition" as we struggle with "information fall-out" through archival arrangement. Communication processes in relation to the use of the media of record are also reviewed in Hugh Taylor, *Archival Services and the Concept of the User: A RAMP Study* (Paris: ICA, 1984).

17. My unofficial "minority report" was published as "Information Retrieval and the Training of Archivists," *Canadian Archivist/L'Archiviste canadien*. 2.3 (1972), pp. 30–35. Also on this theme see Hugh Taylor, "The Discipline of History and the Education of the Archivist," *American Archivist* 40 (October 1977), pp. 395–402.

18. In 1976 Edwin Welch and I prepared guidelines for a graduate program in archival education which, suitably amended, we hoped would be adopted for all North America. These guidelines became the basis for the Master of Archival Studies at the University of British Columbia five years later and were, later again, published as "Association of Canadian Archivists: Guidelines Towards a Curricu-

lum for Graduate Archival Training Leading to a Master's Degree in Archival Science, 1976," *Archivaria* 16 (Summer 1983): 44–51. It amazed me that in the United States with ten times our population the Society of American Archivists would not at that time move in the same direction.

19. As Chair of a Committee of the Future I was determined that the archivists should make a clean break with the Canadian Historical Association, should have an English-language association parallel to L'Association des archivistes du Québec, and should be run by "young Turks" and not the "old guard." All this came to pass, and with it *Archivaria* replacing *The Canadian Archivist*. A bureau links the two associations for joint consultations.

20. See Terry Cook, "The Tyranny of the Medium: A Comment on 'Total Archives,'" *Archivaria* 9 (Winter 1979–1980): 141–50; and "Media Myopia," *Archivaria* 12 (Summer 1981): 146–57.

21. Before departing I was granted three months' leave to prepare what ended up as *The Arrangement and Description of Archival Materials*, International Council on Archives Handbook Series (Munich, 1980). I was asked to undertake this assignment and gave it my best shot. All media of record had to be covered in a very small space, and the deadline was short. The result was a brief overview which assumed the possibility of some guidance from an experienced archivist and access to earlier manuals and articles for study in depth. Reviews in England and Canada quite properly panned it, though without knowing the limitations imposed on me. At least I discovered I was not a writer of manuals!

22. Nova Scotia boasts the oldest Public Archives in Canada, dating from 1857, and the first provincial archives to have its own repository, specially built for that purpose, in 1931. It was my great privilege to see a new building to completion, designing it with the architect Keith Graham. He, quite rightly, demanded to have particulars of every operation to the last detail and delivered a magnificent structure opened in 1980 on the brink of an economic depression which would likely have killed it. I became increasingly interested in the concept of regional archives, based on geography rather than political boundaries, which had captured my attention in Ottawa some years earlier with an abortive scheme to describe the evolution of South Western Ontario through extensive use of quantitative history from series such as census returns, taxation records, etc., together with fonds from the private sector. See Hugh Taylor, "Archives for Regional History," *Annual Report: University of Western Ontario Landon Project* 2 (1978): 295–317. At the same time I tried to encourage the assembly of family archives in a province deeply conscious of its roots and genealogies, using our own family as an example. See Hugh Taylor, "Family History: Some New Directions and Their Implications for the Archivist," *Archivaria* 11 (Winter 1980–81): 228–31.

23. Following on early retirement in 1982, I became a consultant. Contracts included teaching a course titled "Society and the Documentary Record" for the MAS program at the University of British Columbia. This has been recorded which is as close as it will ever get to being published! More time was now available for writing, which resulted in the following that deal with themes touched on at this point in my paper: "Transformation in the Archives: Technological Adjustment or Paradigm Shift," *Archivaria* 25 (Winter 1987–88): 12–28; "My Very Act and Deed: Some Reflections on the Role of Textual Records in the Conduct of Affairs,"

American Archivist 51 (Fall 1988): 456–69; "The Totemic Universe: Appraising the Documentary Future," in Christopher Hives, ed., *Archival Appraisal: Theory and Practice*, Archives Association of British Columbia (Vancouver, 1990), pp. 15–29; "Recycling the Past: The Archivist in the Age of Ecology," to be published, probably in *Archivaria* 36 [actually 35], in 1993; and "20/20 Vision," concluding paper in a series under this title, Society of American Archivists' annual conference, Montreal 1992, to be published 1993 [actually *American Archivist* 57 (Winter 1994)].

Once I became an independent archivist, I became more involved with Daphne in the peace movement and concern for the environment. This has undoubtedly influenced my views and shaped my experience since 1982, in particular the immense contribution of women and the native peoples of both genders. As an Anglican, I have become particularly interested in the increasing relationship between spirituality and science as expressed in, for example, Brian Swimme, *The Universe Is a Green Dragon: A Cosmic Creation Story* (Santa Fe, 1985), which is dedicated to Thomas Berry, whom I have mentioned several times in my articles. The former is a physicist specializing in gravitation; the latter is a "geologian" in the Teillard de Chardin tradition. See Thomas Berry, *The Dream of the Earth* (San Francisco, 1988).

Chapter 17

The Archivist, the Letter, and the Spirit

So that you know where I am coming from, I am a Christian and an Anglican; but this will certainly not be a sermon despite the barely concealed text in the title, "The letter killeth, but the spirit giveth life," from the King James version of the Bible.[1] Closely related to this aphorism is the dictum of Stéphane Malarmé: "To define is to kill, to suggest is to create." My theme is to suggest that we may be able to deal with the "technological imperative" more effectively through the insights of a spiritual approach, whatever the tradition, as we seek a reality beyond the material "real."

From the beginnings of literate society to the present, the technology of utterance upon the ancient media of record up to, and including, paper has cast the archivist in the role of keeper and remembrancer, controlling the record for the security of content in the context of creation. In more recent times, we have helped to decide what shall survive out of what has survived by means of piecemeal appraisal based on an arbitrary evaluation drawn from our own limited reason. This reason has in turn responded to the tenets of scientific reductionism and includes a rather narrow view of what constitutes the needs of historians, and those of a general public bent on supporting, for the most part, a triumphalist view of progress at both national and local levels, from sources clearly defined within a hierarchy of relationships which we call "provenance."

There was something very reassuring about ranges of shelving filled with the records of government, and other institutions approved or at least tolerated by society, together with individuals who have made their

Originally published in *Archivaria* 43 (Spring 1997): 1–16. Reproduced with the kind permission of the author, *Archivaria*, and the Association of Canadian Archivists.

mark in a generally acceptable manner. Here, so we believed, was solid material evidence of "acts and deeds" under our control at the service of the user, albeit through our idiosyncratic retrieval systems, our limited concept of description, and our insatiable, joyful thirst for acquisition. We were mostly "establishment" people with a conservative cast of mind, in more senses than one, when it came to deciding what constituted our documentary heritage.

Given the accepted norms of the recent past we have not done too badly; at least we have clearly exemplified these norms in the records which surround us as the evidence believed to be important in our time. How will posterity view these accumulations and what of the future? Prior to the emergence of the historian writing from the archival record in the early nineteenth century, the old keepers kept in reasonably good order what was necessary for daily business—the rest was left to the mercy of a not very enlightened neglect.[2]

As we know, all this is now changing rapidly. In 1992, the International Council of Archives meeting in Montreal attracted associations of archivists from across North America. The Society of American Archivists assembled a number of experts charged with the task of mapping trends over the next thirty years, under the clever and ironical title of "20/20 Vision." However, insights into what lies that far ahead may lack clarity. According to Ronald Weissman, "The fundamental task of the archivist is to manage meaning rich information, not simply to store or classify raw bits of data."[3] Luciana Duranti quite correctly countered by stressing our role as keepers of impartial evidence, not just information.[4] At the same time, meaning cannot be left entirely to the historians; in our role as appraisers, we must try to understand the role of the documents in terms of their purpose and impact on the users (which include us) as we strive, in Weissman's words, "to uncover patterns and to wrestle creatively with ambiguity,"[5] which matches McLuhan's remarks about perceiving patterns in information fallout.

The emerging documentary database model offers essentially "views" as opposed to file systems: "As a data object is changed all views based on those data change to maintain currency across data and documents."[6] Without safeguards which formerly resided in a concrete sheet of paper, impartial evidence will be at risk. Massive additions to our comfortable rows of boxed accessions will be coming to an end as we face information overload with its characteristic ambiguity and incompleteness. The more we know and have on record, the more we will worry about what is missing, unless we control destruction as Duranti insists,[7] rather than resorting to record compression, which for the user puts the "over" into "overload" and renders the sum total incomprehensible. In the context of the documentary inheritance, arrival at the truth will remain, as always, asymptotic, just beyond our grasp, whatever the quantity of information.

Over all this broods Heisenburg's uncertainty principle, as when the archivist responds to the need for the appraisal of records, as Terry Eastwood proposes,

> on the basis of an analysis of the use to which they are put by the society that created them all along the continuum of their existence—an existence, after all, determined, continued and terminated on the basis of usefulness . . . appraisal must be undertaken with closest attention to the immediate social context of creation.[8]

Eastwood goes on to say that "appraisal calls forth one's knowledge of the world."[9] This is nicely expanded upon by Ramon Gutiérrez in his "20/20 Vision" paper in which he shows how the physical appearance of human beings was once seen in "immutable" rational categories and how science has helped deconstruct such attitudes into "culturally constructed systems of signs, symbols and meanings."[10] As archivists, do we not have other blind spots now that Afro-Americans and women have been removed? Can we recognize significance through signs, systems, and meanings in our documents? A study of diplomatics certainly helps us to recognize executive process within social systems which are more technological than we imagined.[11]

Thanks to Ursula Franklin[12] and others, we now have a concept of technology which stretches far beyond the mechanical. Peter Lyman includes not only "rule governed social forms such as bureaucracies and corporations" but also "the scholarly and scientific disciplines themselves . . . They are tools for the organisation of knowledge workers, their thought and the information they produce."[13]

Examples from "20/20 Vision" were chosen in part because the authors included many who were not archivists, but were prepared to explore with us the extraordinary complexity of future information and knowledge. Many of our professional colleagues, especially in Canada, the U.S., and Australia, have also in their various approaches provided valuable and practical insights into this complexity and our role in dealing with the problems as we struggle to recognize almost limitless interrelations between our archival sources.

This new expansion may have grown out of, or revisioned, the debate in which we sought to identify our roles as "hyphenated archivists" groping for a less narrow definition of our profession.[14] Terry Cook and Tom Nesmith, meanwhile, had begun to lead us out of our "taxonomic thinking," to use Cook's phrase. Nesmith asked, "Can we not also begin to provide insights into the evolution of society throughout the study of communication? Why are records like they are?"[15] The task of bringing all these professional strands together points to a more holistic, multidisciplined, and, above all, uncertain future.

At a slightly later date, David Bearman, who, significantly, was not an archivist by profession, and could therefore appraise us from the outside, wrote: "Occasionally a major technological revolution introduces new forms of communication, and with them new cultural definitions of the information content they convey."[16] Recognizing new "cultural definitions" takes us far beyond the evidential and information values of Schellenberg and those happy taxonomic days of the 1950s, though these values should not be entirely ignored. Margaret Hedstrom saw the 1990s as a time for "reinvented archives" as institutions whereby "electronic records can be a vehicle for archives to move from rowing to steering, towards more enterprising and customer driven approaches to service delivery and towards empowering others to take action in a decentralised records management environment."[17] Empowerment is a term which grew out of the women's movement and has more to do with the heart than the head, and as such is another sign of a new approach. Terry Cook points out that there is no such thing as neutral data. The mind and the ego are always present as we seek to probe the collective minds behind the records. Appraisal should, therefore, be inviting "spirit and nature, mind and matter."[18]

We have to stretch the mind to its limit as we stumble over separate linear categories to achieve cultural understanding across society as a whole. Attention, rather than mental dexterity, is required for this. Brien Brothman asks us to reflect on how our culture affects archival practice, which likewise is not neutral.[19] Richard Brown asserts that our preconceived notions of structural functionalism as applied to the public archives has given it a false sense of order and enduring knowledge which "block and filter out the elements of complication, discordance, chaos, disruption and disorder" requiring a new hermeneutic approach.[20] So much in our archives is people-centred that Candace Loewen has declared that we need to search not only for records of value to humans, but also to the planet as a whole.[21] If all this was not enough, Joan Schwartz relates "visual literacy" to the study of diplomatics and implies that every medium of record contains signs which must first be understood before the context comes fully into focus.[22]

These examples from current archival wisdom in the postmodern mode require of the mind a discipline and imagination which challenges both hemispheres of the brain. The use of pure mind will not be enough without a spiritual awareness which stems from the ground of our being in all of us. Through religious faith and/or sheer intellectual endeavour coupled with a sensitive understanding of fellow human beings, some of the authors quoted above may make their way to a threshold beyond classical humanism in preparation for the "ecozoic" age which is presently emerging, and which Thomas Berry and Brian Swimme have so eloquently celebrated in the context of the universe story.[23]

I hope that the preceding observations have shown that many of the old archival certainties, norms, and values have now been replaced by uncertainty and ambiguity. This, along with deconstructed technologies and prejudices embracing social organization have resulted in a vaguely felt "fuzzy logic" whereby patterns emerge, as it were, out of chaos theory in the manner of Mandelbrot's fractals. Meanwhile we continue to arrange and describe the ship's logs on the *Titanic* while others rearrange the deck chairs.

Is there another approach, less dependent on the mental conflicts and paradoxes which assault us daily, which will help us find our way through change, while at the same time mastering the discipline required by digital processes without becoming a slave to them? Arthur Kroker offers us hope when he asserts that "At work in the Canadian mind is, in fact, a great and dynamic polarity between technology and culture, between economy and landscape."[24] For Canadians,

> technological society jeopardises at a fundamental level the received traditions of western culture. . . . The Canadian discourse is, then, a way of seeking to recover a voice by which to articulate a different historical possibility against the present closure of the technological order.[25]

This understanding is in contrast to the United States, which Kroker sees as the "spearhead of modernity" and the technological imperative with all its implications.

As archivists, we are coming to understand more fully the meaning of documentary relationships in all their richness. If we take the universe and its Creator, or the scientific concept of the "Big Bang" theory as the beginning of cosmic evolution, then cosmogenesis, the creation moment, becomes the ultimate context of all matter as it moves down through the galaxies, nebulae, planets, and stars to life in all its forms on our own planet; all creation is connected in various ways in a marvelous spatial balance. Out of the formation of new entities has emerged information resulting in communication and memory.

Communication is offered both by way of genetic coding through the evolution of all life-forms and the cultural coding of self-reflective human beings through experience and education in its broadest sense. This brings us to memory, which works across all life. There is a sense in which a tree must remember to balance its member branches to survive during growth. Brian Swimme, a scientist specializing in mathematical cosmology, uses a Socratic format to explain in nontechnical terms how, in the context of the cosmos, the specialized hoof of the mountain goat evolved over millennia: "the hoof is the memory of the ancestral tree. It didn't show up accidentally; it was shaped by the experience of millions of goats. The point is, matter remembers the elegant hoof."[26]

And so on to memory in the formation of humans via information as evidence of experience and action in genetic coding, modified in the course of time by the cultural coding of the hunters and gatherers. The distinction between the codes becomes clearer over the millennia, and for memory we come to rely on the written and printed word: "Archives are the only evidential window we have on the action oriented past in relation to one another and the events in the world,"[27] writes Eastwood. He goes on to remind us that

> we remember in order to survive because all present actions are shot through with the process of making sense of past experience, which is the only guide we have to future action for controlling events and making things in our environment somewhat predictable.[28]

This in effect is what Swimme is saying about "the elegant hoof" and genetic coding.

With this kind of background, the great body of preliterate, aboriginal wisdom everywhere, which recognizes a creator, a Great Spirit, takes shape and meaning for us through the oral myths and tales as interpreted by the elders. Truth is conveyed through myth as it was in the Homeric epics and as it is in the Bible, not through historical chronological accuracy and words to be taken literally, but as wisdom related to the cultural coding prevalent at the time of their creation, a cultural memory beyond time, which must be reinterpreted by each successive generation to preserve its deeper spiritual meaning.

Transmission through writing and printing, coupled with the authority of organized, institutionalized religion, which also grew in part out of these technologies, caused the great oral traditions to be "frozen." The Bible became a book to be ultimately held in one's hand, embodying the Hebrew tradition over thousands of years and subsequent Christian origins. The text throughout teems with apparent inconsistencies, contradictions, and unlikely miraculous events that have also been subject to errors inherent in copying and translation across three or more languages. In spite of such a record, there are those who believe that the text of the King James Bible of 1611 is the inerrant Word of God.[29] Bishop John Spong will have none of this.

Central to Spong's approach is a recognition of the use of a form of *midrash* by the Jewish authors of the Gospels, a Jewish tradition whereby "everything to be venerated in the present must somehow be connected in a new context. It is the affirmation of a timeless truth found in the faith journey of a people so that this truth can be experienced afresh in every generation."[30]

The midrashic form gives the impression of biographical, eyewitness accounts in a chronological order, whereas, in fact, many passages are drawn and adapted from the Jewish scriptures, which help to describe and illumine people and events that bear witness to timeless truth. Spong also provides evidence that suggests that the order of the gospels is designed to provide readings which harmonize with the Jewish calendar and liturgical year, since the earliest Christians were Jewish.

After the first century, Christianity spread to Hellenized Jews and Gentiles. An understanding of the midrashic form was lost, giving way to a literal linearity which has dominated Western culture. This is a remarkable example of how the provenance of earlier sources, their context, and the significance of order within the content can suggest a wholly different reading while preserving past and present truths seen in a different way—truths which cannot rely on literal certainty. Archival materials, especially images, teem with this kind of ambiguity. Folklore, likewise, attributes to its heroes actions performed by another because these illustrate the nature and character of the hero. There is a danger that our extensive accumulations of interviews with First Nations people may suffer the same fate as the Gospels referred to above and be treated literally, frozen in time on tape. It is essential that this material be made constantly available to the communities to which the tapes relate so that a living continuity of understanding can be maintained.

On the issue of certainty, Bishop Spong may have a message for archivists when he writes:

> In our contemporary world we have dedicated enormous energy to developing the technology that will enable us to freeze moments of history in their objective purity. Instant replay is a secular form of a liturgy. Like all liturgies, its purpose is to freeze objectivity so that we will not lose contact with it. Television, film, tape recorders, photographs—all become the tools of our obsession as we seek to stop the constant flux beneath our feet, to capture, relate to, and use objective reality to create a new security. It is a passionate human quest that will never succeed.[31]

As archivists, we too must abandon literal certainty at times in our search for meaning in records, in particular those which are nontextual. Even legal texts, drafted with the concept of certainty in mind, yield to interpretations, as every lawyer knows. Can we live with uncertainty in a digital and virtual culture exhibiting some of the qualities of neo-orality, where truth is located in myth?

The great truths, preserved in literary amber, are still there. Some are self-evident; theologians and other scholars are gradually revealing others through form criticism and the findings of related disciplines. Nevertheless, for all its great spiritual value, the Bible has, at times, been misused in good faith down the years and, in consequence, has become one of the most socially destructive books of all time. This is a tragedy of global proportions and a preeminent example of the need to understand the meaning and context of the record in a literate society, especially when literacy is coupled with a new technology. It is not without reason that we speak of computer "literacy."

Along with the sacred texts of other religions, the Bible is divine evidence for believers which can be made a great deal more relevant to our daily work and lives as archivists if the creational context is kept in mind and all life is seen as emergent and interconnected. The great mystics such as Meister Eckhart and Hildegard of Bingen believed this, in contrast to the polarity of the human being in conflict with the rest of nature. Fritjof Capra observes that "the concepts of science show strong similarities to the concepts of the mystics. . . . The philosophy of mystical traditions, the perennial philosophy, is the most consistent philosophical background to modern science."[32]

Matthew Fox in his book, *The Reinvention of Work*, makes the case for a return to a lost spirituality which is not related to one religion. Work, for him, is "the expression of the Spirit at work in the world through us . . . at the level of service to the community,"[33] the "Great Work," as he calls it. The long-established way of seeing the world no longer functions, and it is the desacralization of work at the heart of our alienation which is central to our problem. As E. F. Schumacher once said, "We in the West are clever aliens on this planet. We are now far too clever to survive without wisdom."

That word "wisdom" has been appearing more frequently in archivists' writings. The search for a lost spirituality has also resulted in a widespread interest in meditation whereby the perception of work as a secular and sometimes unpleasant necessity can be transformed by direct access to the love of God and the sharing of that love with others. All work has an element of drudgery, not least our profession, which is sometimes made unbearable for want of meaning in the midst of unrest and change throughout our repositories. Too often we work for outside rewards alone, or from an outside threat which is the death of work.[34]

Richard Klumpenhouwer, partly in the spirit of play yet revealing valuable insights as this approach often does, has recalled that

> Education and religion have, historically, intertwined one another, and . . . a kind of religious culture still pervades the University. . . . I began to see my MAS education as a kind of quasi-religious initiation into an archival culture and, at the same time, a process of revealing and defining archival culture as a personal identity.[35]

Klumpenhouwer then goes on to emphasize that the course left no firm foundations or "genetic imprint" as with more established professions, apart from certain principles. In short, through tensions and "creative

theorising" as "more ritual than catechism,"[36] the graduates found themselves as archivists through arguing over the right questions, which is
what a journey of discovery is about. He ends by saying:

> I have had the opportunity to climb the mountain of archival exploration, to
> talk about, feel and participate in archives as a powerful expression of hu-
> manity, and to be and become part of a larger mission, a community, a pro-
> fessional culture that believes in archives. In the end, it is a faith based on
> identity with something bigger than yourself. And if that is not religion, I do
> not know what is.[37]

The gift of creativity and imagination, such as Klumpenhouwer reveals
in his article, can help us break out of a sterile career culture based on a
life of things and busy-ness. Archivists by the nature of their work are surrounded by hundreds and thousands of "things" in the shape of documentary artifacts quite apart from all the bureaucratic busy-ness which
hinders our simplicity. There is much here that the mind desperately
needs to "let go" regularly if we are to understand and experience the nature of a reality beyond the external and the concrete. Fox has termed this
the "Inner Work" which many experienced meditators are sharing as a
"way" and not a "product."

Religion can "bind us back" to our common origins as revealed in the
new scientific creation story, and a creation myth as in the book of Genesis,
away from a paradigm which pits us against the environment and against
other humans as we chase after an infinitely expanding frontier where technology will "do it for us." We are deeply troubled by the digital impact. A
kind of creative relief may be found through more attention to the "Inner
Work" as a way, which is not so much a linear route as a process, a transcendent relationship which has everything to do with clarity and simplicity in a silence which quiets the teeming thoughts generated in the mind by
the ego. This is not easy. For instance, many who work in large cities now
seek this silence at lunch time either for peace or for strength.

Meditation is analogous to space, which creates power through the ab-
sence of continuity. One thinks immediately of the space between wheel
and axle, between words on a page, of the white space which dramatizes
graphic design, or the perfectly timed pause in a speech. The discipline of
meditation has ancient roots and is common to most religions, or no religion at all. According to Dom John Main, "In meditation we discover both
who we are and why we are; we are not running away from ourselves we
are finding ourselves; we are not rejecting ourselves, we are affirming
ourselves. We seek not just to think about God but to be with God."[38]

By contrast, Michael Heim, in his "philosophical study of word processing," discusses meditation as one "compensatory discipline" among
others: "to counter a ubiquitous technostress it is useful, then, to draw on

pretechnological cultures as their teachings become available."[39] This, surely, is just meditation as therapy—although it is none the worse for that. Consequently, Heim believes that

> any references whatsoever to inner psychic life runs counter to the pragmatic automation of writing and to the construal of language as information code to be manipulated. Inner life easily becomes a mere obstacle in the world of total management. But in the best analysis full human presence of mind is crucial for any endeavour.[40]

This is clearly one approach to meditation; but it seems to me rather arid and negative, a brief respite from the technological imperative.

Being grounded in a reality beyond the fragmented, contingent hustle of our lives may well radicalize us out of previously accepted social norms, and perhaps the norms of our profession. As archivists we may find ourselves at odds with, for instance, standards of acquisition and appraisal which fail to make an appropriate contribution to environmental studies, which is probably the most urgent priority today. It will take a great deal of imagination and insight to link Fox's "Great Work" to the necessary documentary sources in both the public and private sectors; but every imaginable kind of evidence shows that human beings are now responsible for the survival of the greater part of the natural world and that we are failing in this task.[41] "Environment" is a poor term in this connection as suggesting the natural world around us, whereas we are part of the problem. Perhaps the term "cultural ecology," with its implied contradictions, would be more appropriate.

The manner in which a radical approach to our profession can be inhibited by pressures of one form or another is clearly examined in a paper which was read by Howard Zinn, Professor of Government at Boston University, at the 1970 Society of American Archivists Conference in Washington. Radical in the style of the Vietnam War era, and himself a veteran of that conflict, he created a storm of controversy within the Society. The editor of the *American Archivist* at that time refused to publish the paper, which, of course, made it required reading for those of us who were known as the "activist archivists"!

Zinn's main point is that

> Professionalism is a powerful form of social control. By professionalism, I mean that almost total immersion in one's craft, being so absorbed in the day-to-day exercise of those skills, as to have little time, energy or will to consider what part those skills play in the total social scheme.[42]

He defines social control in this context as "maintaining things as they are, preserving traditional arrangements, preventing any sharp change in how the society distributes wealth and power," and leaving little time for reflection on what the social machine is designed for as we apply our specialized skills to one small corner of it. Archivists tend to perpetuate the status quo in the name of neutrality. For Zinn, rebellion was not the politicizing of a neutral craft, but the humanizing of an inevitably political craft,[43] as revealed in our acquisition and appraisal policies.

It may be argued that this whole paper is irrelevant, that we can have an ontological understanding of the spirit beyond the letter without spiritual belief; but there are, perhaps, some who may relate to the point of view developed in this paper and find it helpful. One way or another we must try to recognize the illusory nature of archives as repositories of truth waiting only to be uncovered. Heather MacNeil asserts that what distinguishes archives is the fact that they are the most impartial expression of socioeconomic values, although not the most truthful or objective.[44] Words point towards the truth; they are not in themselves the truth.

Perhaps as archivists we should learn to cultivate more impartiality in the way in which we allocate space and resources to neglected sources of records which we should appraise for what we need to know to ensure our survival, both globally and locally. MacNeil raises this question by asking "what balance needs to be struck between the preservation of individual and collective memory?"[45] This is not Zinn's false impartiality of avoidance, but a call for radical thinking and subsequent action by our Association as a group. A conference is needed in the near future combining the theme of environmental records with this kind of balance federally, provincially, and locally, within the context of a global problem which the ICA should also take up. Thus armed, we may be the better equipped to deal with the tension involved in "thinking globally and acting locally."

To return to the subject of archives and illusions, we must above all avoid falling into the trap of literalism, which has haunted the Bible, especially where a medium of record is new and unfamiliar. We are now learning how to interpret the meaning of photographs,[46] film, and maps as a function of appraisal and public service. The fact that the digital record gathers in all previous media (as printing once did) and dumps them onto a screen, will require the ability to read these records as a totality, and not individually. We have to avoid an archival fundamentalism which refuses to recognize that new forms of communication, both technically and semiotically, change the meaning of the content. Not only that, but our assumptions about our own practices may need reassessing followed by the abandonment of "dead certainties."[47]

Brien Brothman's often playful deconstructions, in the manner of Derrida, may irritate some, but "Derrida himself has invoked the term 'solicit,' derived from the Latin term denoting a shaking or disturbing of omnipresent structures to describe his deconstructive reading practice" as a way of undermining complacency.[48] If again we take deconstruction too literally and heavily, we begin to see it as destruction, which it most certainly is not. By analogy, it lets in a kind of meditative light and space where, as we have seen, new insights may occur.

Brothman's discussion about archives, myths, history, and mythistory[49] suggests that we perhaps claim too much for archives, as MacNeil warns, and that ultimately the majority of human beings will continue to identify with the great myths good and bad, among them Luke Skywalker, heir to the "hero with a thousand faces"[50] in *Star Wars* on the one hand, and Darth Vader caught up in the myth of progress on the other. Well-written history, no matter how scholarly and accurate, nearly always awaits the revisionist, which is quite proper, but both versions are, sadly, very forgettable and scarcely ever reach the general public, save in popular generalities which are the raw material of myths. Ultimate reality, as has already been suggested, lies beyond our grasp without a loving relationship with God.[51]

The celebration of our history will continue in one form or another as one valid expression of our heritage; but perhaps in the end Bearman is right when he emphasizes that, as we refashion our society, archivists should concentrate on the records of the immediate past to serve the present.

We are presently at a crossroads: either immensely powerful interests now driving an obsolete and discredited modernism will render the planet uninhabitable, or we will recognize the organic context of our lives and recover a sense of community that is in harmony with the "story of the universe." Public and corporate records will be absolutely vital as a means of increasing credible benchmarks towards ecological recovery and an ongoing accountability. The records of those who have striven to effect these changes will reveal not only successes and failures, but also the processes and modes of their activism for the guidance and understanding of their successors. Communities will cease to be more or less passive consumers of individualism and begin to share the warmth, passion, wise strength, and forms of spiritual growth already evident in hundreds of microgatherings of people determined to effect profound change. The records of this renaissance, with antecedents in and continuities with a remote past now being revealed,[52] will become immensely precious and central to historical research in national, regional, and community archives, using media of record that will help to reduce the problems of space and retrieval.

If community archives are going to proliferate as the local repositories of the future, we have to consider what is a community and what are its boundaries.[53] To begin with, they are likely to emerge as the result of special circumstances; but as the pattern becomes more generally accepted, then clusters of such archives will appear, each with its sense of place and space. If we look at the boundaries of the mandates of national, provincial, and municipal archives, they are quite clear: boundaries of power and authority determined by treaties and legislation. On the map, most of them are straight lines, which bear little relationship to the land they divide; they are the result of political decisions. Now consider the way in which the territory of native peoples has been determined over time with reference to mountains, rivers, watersheds, wildlife, forest, soil, coastline, the weather, and other natural resources which provide food, clothing, and shelter. All this gives them an abiding sense of place, in contrast to our tradition of movement, mastery, exploitation, and excessive consumption, with all the familiar threats to life that this implies.

We too can develop this same sense of place through the concept of bioregionalism, in which all forms of heritage resource can be appropriately accommodated. Kirkpatrick Sale, a leading exponent of bioregionalism, writes "Every place has a history, a record of how both the human and natural possibilities of the region have been explored and this must be studied with new eyes."[54] These eyes will determine local resources that have been abandoned, and will discover new ones derived from the land and the people who live there, as we seek to refashion our mindset and lifestyle in terms of sustainability, using local resources to their utmost.

First we must think in terms of our bioregion, its extent and its boundaries, and this will require not only those maps produced by government and industry, but citizens exploring and making an inventory of the resources of their district, city, or whatever, and mapping them as a means of empowerment and persuasion in the drive to make our place more habitable—"reinhabiting space," as it is called.[55] All this information, including oral history, folklore, and the archives of families, businesses, and institutions, will find a natural home in the community archives where all can feel and experience a dynamic heritage experience in which they can be personally involved, and which will be passed down to their descendants. There will, of course, be mobility, though less perhaps than at present; families will bring their own heritage with them, if not through their records, at least through their memory, and this will become part of the local heritage. I am thinking in particular here of immigrants to Canada.

There will, of course, be districts made up of many communities and then larger ecoregions embracing districts, until the entire land mass is covered by this natural configuration—but that is a long way off. The exciting thing is that communities can start now to prefigure this future, to stake out their boundaries and compile their inventories, since they have at present no statutory authority and no conflict with existing political institutions until their findings translate into political action.[56]

REFLECTION, 2000

The Association of Canadian Archivists' annual conference at Whitehorse in 1996 began with a plenary session titled "The Elders Speak." I had the privilege of sharing the task with Pearl Keenan, a native elder and Chancellor of Yukon College, who expressed her deep spiritual awareness through accounts of her younger life in northern conditions, sharply contrasting with today's technological and scientific world of stress and material comforts which distance us from the natural world, wherein lie our common roots. Following her I was very conscious of my somewhat academic presentation so dependent on the mind and intellect characteristic of European scholastic traditions, and lacking a fusion of this approach with a powerful sense of place and belonging.

The subsequent themes of the conference were to emphasize the technological aspect of our work and provide an opportunity for a focus we are inclined to avoid. As "elders," the two of us in our own ways stressed the need to transcend the purely secular but necessary imperative of technology if we are to become fully aware of our potential strength and role in society.

Quite recently I have been wrestling with the ponderous language of postmodernism, perhaps unavoidable with so much of the hitherto indescribable to describe. Stylistically there is something akin to those intensely theological papers issuing out of Oxbridge which delighted so many middle-class Victorians and set their minds to work. Epistemologically the objectives are, of course, poles apart. I was drawn to its rigorous examination of the nature of communication within our cultures, which I believe will help us to rise above so many assumptions which are the heritage of modernism and to release us into a dangerous, risky freedom which is the aim and essence of both radical religion and postmodern exploration. We are coming to realize that all forms of expression and communication are "signs" and not simply "statements" to be taken at their face value. We are probably directed as much by "signs," as by logical thought, which can defy explanation. This is also a spiritual phenomenon which may help us as we leave behind the illusions of "reality" which mark the "modern" age spanning 300 years.

Keith Jenkins is convinced (and I share his conviction) that "we live today within the general socioeconomic and political condition of postmodernity" which is not an ideology we can choose. "It is our historical fate to be living now."[57] Reconstruction of the works of historians has caused Jenkins to suggest that "the whole modernist . . . ensemble now appears as a self-referential, problematical expression of interests, an ideological-interpretive discourse without any nonhistoricised access to the past as such."[58]

This kind of criticism can be helpful and constructive in some respects, but there is a danger of postmodernism reducing everything it touches to meaningless, unrelated particles flying off into space, reminiscent of much digital communication. Archivists can also benefit from this approach, as Brien Brothman suggests in his review of Derrida's Archive Fever: A Freudian Impression:

"Those who are interested in rethinking the concept of archives as a public space, as a regulative source of authority, as a strategic concept, and as a mediative technological principle, however, may find the treacherous work of reading (let along summarising) Derrida's work worthwhile."[59]

Historians may have to admit that, in their zeal, they have claimed too much in their efforts to achieve a clear vision of the past. We archivists may have to recognize that an impeccable moral defence of the records will be beyond our grasp, if only because our control leaves a distorting imprint for which we are responsible. Postmodernists can teach us humility; but will they in turn realize that all those of us who project a past in one form or another must communicate successfully with our publics as honestly as we can? The public in turn must come to understand that everything we do provides only an approximation of the truth.

For me, absolute truth and reality only exist through faith within the bonds and insight between human beings in a relationship with their Creator. The rest is an asymptotic journey towards our full potential as we deconstruct ourselves in the context of the natural order.

NOTES

1. II Corinthians 3:6.
2. Discussed more fully in Hugh Taylor, "Information Ecology and the Archives of the 1980s," *Archivaria* 18 (Summer 1984): 25–37.
3. Ronald F. E. Weissman, "Archives and the New Information Architecture of the Late 1990s," *American Archivist* 57 (Winter 1994): 20.
4. Luciana Duranti, "Commentary," Ibid., p. 36.
5. Weissman, "Archives," p. 21.
6. Ibid., p. 29.
7. Duranti, "Commentary," p. 38.
8. Terry Eastwood, "Towards a Social Theory of Appraisal," in Barbara L. Craig, ed., *The Archival Imagination: Essays in Honour of Hugh A. Taylor* (Ottawa, 1992), p. 83.
9. Ibid., p. 88.
10. Ramon Gutiérrez, "Decolonising the Body: Kinship and the Nation," *American Archivist* 57 (Winter 1994): 91.
11. It is so typical of a fragmented approach common to all professions that we tend to polarize points of view. All this is done in good faith defending the "right." But, in the matter of appraisal, are we striving for synthesis or supremacy? Logical and empirical decisions that have been documented arise out of practical experience. This fact helps us recognize that we are dealing with artifacts which were created for a specific purpose and cast in a diplomatic form to serve that purpose and render it useful for the present and the future. Both polarities around the broader issue of classic philosophical rationalism *versus* postmodern analysis recognize the value of use, but not necessarily in the same terms. Wisdom grounded in an understanding of social change which incorporates accountability at the lo-

cal level should be recognized as an element in macroscopic realities. As in the natural world, can we settle for a "balanced turbulence"? Perhaps this is an issue requiring a holistic solution beyond opposing points of view which are so much a part of our literate culture of individualism.

12. Ursula Franklin, *The Real World of Technology* (Toronto, 1990). See also Hugh Taylor, "Chip Monks at the Gate: The Impact of Technology on Archives, Libraries, and the User," *Archivaria* 33 (Winter 1991–92): 173–80.

13. Peter Lyman, "Invention the Mother of Necessity: Archival Research in 2020," *American Archivist* 57 (Winter 1994): 125.

14. The debate took form, for the most part, in a series of articles in *Archivaria* culminating in Hugh Taylor, "Through the Minefield," *Archivaria* 21 (Winter 1985–86): 180–85.

15. Tom Nesmith, "Archives from the Bottom Up: Social History and Archival Scholarship," *Archivaria* 14 (Summer 1982): 26.

16. David Bearman, *Archival Methods:* Archives and Museum Informatics Technical Report No. 13 (Pittsburgh, 1989): 55.

17. Margaret Hedstrom, ed., *Electronic Records Management Program Strategies,* Archives and Museum Informatics Technical Report No. 18 (Pittsburgh: 1993): 98.

18. Terry Cook, "Mind Over Matter: Towards a New Theory of Archival Appraisal," in Barbara L. Craig, ed., *The Archival Imagination: Essays in Honour of Hugh A. Taylor* (Ottawa, 1991), pp. 38–70. The title may be seen as somewhat misleading. Cook is offering an alternative to the Cartesian philosophy of mind over matter.

19. Brien Brothman, "Orders of Value: Probing the Theoretical Terms of Archival Practice," *Archivaria* 32 (Summer 1991): 78–100.

20. Richard Brown, "Macro-Appraisal Theory and the Context of the Public Records Creator," *Archivaria* 40 (Fall 1995): 138.

21. Candace Loewen, "From Human Neglect to Planetary Survival: New Approaches to the Appraisal of Environmental Records," *Archivaria* 33 (Winter 1991–1992): 91.

22. Joan M. Schwartz, "'We make our tools and our tools make us': Lessons from Photographs for the Practice, Politics, and Poetics of Diplomatics," *Archivaria* 40 (Fall 1995): 40 74.

23. Brian Swimme and Thomas Berry, *The Universe Story: From the Primordial Flaming Earth to the Ecozoic Era* (San Francisco, 1992). This is recommended reading to grasp in lay terms the context and development of our planet whereby the universe from the "big bang" onwards tells its own "story" of evolution through time within a cosmic setting. Berry is a priest and geologist who calls himself a geologian and created the term "ecozoic." Swimme is an astrophysicist and cosmologist.

24. Arthur Kroker, *Technology and the Canadian Mind: Innis/McLuhan/Grant* (Montreal, 1984), p. 8.

25. Ibid., p. 12.

26. Brian Swimme, *The Universe Is a Green Dragon: A Cosmic Creation Story* (Sante Fe, 1984), p. 100.

27. Terry Eastwood, "How Goes it with Appraisal?" *Archivaria* 36 (Autumn, 1993): 112.

28. Ibid., p. 113.

29. For an introduction to this problem, see John Selby Spong, *Rescuing the Bible from Fundamentalism: A Bishop Rethinks the Meaning of Scripture* (San Francisco, 1991). This is a very controversial book among Anglicans, but contains a popular summary of the difficulties encountered in the Bible in terms of accepting it as literally the words of God, and Spong's solutions based on the meaning behind the words and other evidence from the midrashic tradition. See also his *Liberating the Gospels: Reading the Bible with Jewish Eyes* (San Francisco, 1996).

30. J. S. Spong, *Resurrection: Myth or Reality?: A Bishop's Search for the Origins of Christianity* (San Francisco, 1994), p. 8.

31. Ibid., p. 98.

32. Matthew Fox, *The Coming of the Cosmic Christ* (San Francisco, 1988), p. 36. Source not cited.

33. Matthew Fox, *The Reinvention of Work: A New Vision of Livelihood for Our Time* (San Francisco, 1994), p. 5.

34. Ibid., p. 77.

35. Richard Klumpenhouwer, "The MAS and After: Transubstantiating Theory and Practice into an Archival Culture," *Archivaria* 39 (Spring 1995): 89.

36. Ibid., p. 91.

37. Ibid., p. 95.

38. John Main, O.S.B., *Word into Silence* (New York, 1980), p. 4. One facet of meditation is apotheia in the stoic sense of freedom from domination and control by the voice of the ego, thereby reducing it to silence. This is far removed from the intellectual detachment of the Western mind and the modern meaning of "apathy."

39. Michael Heim, *Electric Language: A Philosophical Study of Word Processing* (New Haven, 1987), p. 236.

40. Ibid., p. 239.

41. Candace Loewen, "From Human Neglect to Planetary Survival: New Approaches to the Appraisal of Environmental Records." This article examines our plight: the fragmentary, piecemeal appraisal; the contributions of philosophers, feminists, and historians to the problem; an appraisal of the Atomic Energy Control Board; and holistic survival values. So far as I know, this excellent article is the first of its kind. See also, Hugh Taylor, "The Totemic Universe: Appraising the Documentary Future," in Christopher Hives, ed., *Archival Appraisal: Theory and Practice* (Vancouver, 1990), pp. 15–30 and Hugh Taylor, "Recycling the Future: The Archivist in the Age of Ecology," *Archivaria* 35 (Spring 1993): 203–13.

42. Howard Zinn, "Secrecy, Archives and the Public Interest," *Boston University Journal* 19 (Fall 1971): 38.

43. Ibid., p. 41.

44. Heather MacNeil, "Archival Theory and Practice: Between Two Paradigms," *Archivaria* 37 (Spring 1994): 13.

45. Ibid., p. 14.

46. Joan M. Schwartz, "'We make our tools and our tools make us.'" This is an admirable, ground-breaking addition to the work of Luciana Duranti.

47. Brien Brothman, "The Limits of Limits: Derridean Deconstruction and the Archival Institution," *Archivaria* 36 (Autumn 1993): 208. Brothman quotes this phrase in relation to archives as sign, "in Simon Schama's wonderfully ambiguous sense—a site of dead certainties."

48. Ibid.

49. Ibid.

50. This is also the title of a work by Joseph Campbell, who was consulted by George Lucas in the making of the *Star Wars* trilogy. Luke Skywalker was the mythic hero.

51. This I believe as a meditator in the tradition of the fourth-century John Cassian, the teacher and inspirer of St. Benedict, which the late Dom John Main has spread around the world through his workshops and tape-recorded talks. In order to make these reflections on spirituality in our profession as inclusive as possible, I have avoided discussing Christian beliefs and have referred to the Bible only as an example of the inherent dangers of literalism in dealing with a record of this kind.

52. For example, the Celtic world, with its remarkable fusion of pagan, and later Christian, spirituality with ecology, stands in contrast to the dichotomies bequeathed to us by Greece and Rome. For an excellent overview in a series of symposium papers, see Robert O'Driscoll, ed., *The Celtic Consciousness* (New York, 1981).

53. The remaining paragraphs in this article are taken from my unpublished commentary on the session, "Reconsidering Acquisition: The Total Archives Concept," ACA Conference, Ottawa, 1994.

54. Kirkpatrick Sale, *Dwellers in the Land: A Bioregional Vision* (Gabriola Island, B.C., 1991), p. 45.

55. Doug Aberly, ed., *Boundaries of Home: Mapping for Local Empowerment*, The New Catalyst Bioregional Series No. 6 (Gabriola Island, B.C., 1993). This was enthusiastically reviewed by Denis Wood in *Cartographica* 30 (Winter 1993), for which Ed Dahl was Review Editor.

56. To end on a personal note, this will be absolutely my last "stand alone" article to be published, and I would like to thank all my professional colleagues for their interest and support spanning forty-eight years. You have all been very patient! Once again, my warmest thanks to Jane Turner, Archivist of the University of Victoria, for her input digitally and critically, and to Terry Cook for very helpful criticism and suggestions.

57. Keith Jenkins, *The Postmodern History Reader* (London, 1997), p. 3.

58. Ibid., p. 6.

59. Brien Brothman. Review of Jacques Derrida, *Archive Fever: A Freudian Impression* in *Archivaria* 43 (Spring 1997): 192.

Afterword

On Reflection and Imagination

These afterthoughts, as well as the "Reflection, 2000" following each preceding chapter, are couched in a free-and-easy conversational style, in contrast to the essays. When my enthusiastic editors asked me for something fresh to garnish the main course already published elsewhere, I found this very reasonable request daunting. I have lost contact with archival developments on a daily basis as as result of retirement in 1982, so that I can no longer compare the progression from then and now with any authority. Once published, I never reread what I have written. I prefer to leave my contributions to the critical mercy of my colleagues without further comment. They can then make of them what they will, with one exception—I prefer not to explain or revisit.

I cannot always remember the occasion or theme which called for the paper. All 1 can now manage is an anecdotal and discursive approach with some rather wild comments, which defines to some extent where I was coming from at the time. The essays are themselves reflections on our development as a profession. Browsing, for example, through *Archivaria* and the *American Archivist* alone reveals that the standard of discourse and debate has greatly improved in recent years. Much of it is way over my head, which is as it should be. Each generation now faces up to and deals with constant change on a scale we never envisaged fifty years ago.

In 1965, my family and I emigrated from Northumberland, England, to Alberta, Canada, with thirteen pieces of baggage. I myself was additionally loaded with the mental baggage of an archivist which was to serve or impede me in the years which followed. Coming from England I was full to the brim of "know how" about 800 years of manuscripts within the County. Local government records after 1880 remained in the departments of creation. My priorities lay with the accumulated documents of landed families, churches, and other institutions. Consequently, my baggage about modern public records was light and knowledge of Canadian history even lighter; I never got beyond the university "101"-level course.

From the start of my encounter with an early church warden's minute book, my chief commitment was centred on records as silent communication, with history running second. This must sound rather stark, but I had learned enough about the historical method to grasp the essentials of Alberta's origins and development. As in Northumberland, where I had started up the County Archives, government departments were reluctant to transfer their records to anyone so obscure as an archivist (a what?). I managed to accession "old stuff" which relieved pressure on crowded shelves; trust and confidence had their origin in these small beginnings and modest services.

When I later moved to Ottawa and the (then) Public Archives of Canada as a branch manager, I realized quite early on that I could not fully grasp in archival terms the reality of so vast a territorial entity as Canada (a little more history would have helped!). I was much more comfortable in the Provincial Archives of Alberta (where I arrived), New Brunswick (which I also started), and Nova Scotia (where I ended my "formal" career). Canada for me remained an enormous "documentary expression" as far as federal public records were concerned, but I was supported by an immensely experienced staff.

For me, archives were grounded in locality as one aspect of the memory of a community, a powerful element of heritage with a rich contextual web of connections spun within public and private records alike. My concentration while at the PAC, as part of the demands of management, was to explore the mysterious power which the media of record exerted on archivists and users alike (we too were users)[1] and to enable the staff to join in this exploration, using all the professional skills at their command and merging this with the historical context. To what extent is this available to the public, given the limitation of finding aids?

A head curator of the Canadian War Museum once remarked that the artifacts did not belong to the Museum; they belonged to the citizens of Canada. Archives, likewise, but they are also silent witnesses to these citizens buried within a vast weight of documents from which, until recently, only the elites have had their voices heard. We must remain not only the guardians of countless memories, but also the champions of democratic access whenever possible, in spite of bureaucratic restrictions and shortage of funds. How much within our boxes and files are really accessible to the public for want of retrieval information about them?

It seemed to me that these relatively new approaches required leadership and enthusiasm, imagination and research, which would be in tune with changing times and a changing culture. The "young Turks" who banded together to form the Association of Canadian Archivists and publish *Archivaria* had just these qualities which those long on experience did not necessarily have. As one of the senior managers at the PAC, I was always conscious of our quite understandable generational limitations which equipped us with bows and arrows in the face of an emerging "high tech."

As a result of postmodern deconstruction, many assumptions about the exclusive nature of our profession as guardians of a form of "truth" are being called into question, which is what an effective discourse is about. We are now sufficiently sure of ourselves to recognize and accept changes which will include a measure of convergence with our colleagues in libraries, museums, art galleries, and beyond in our search for the citizens' collective memory and for what records should be retained. Quite recently I lighted upon a publication which has given me pause with regard to research and archival theory such as it is.[2] Stephen Toulmin, while discussing research within the social sciences, contrasts the "ivory tower, High Science" endeavours with what is called "action research," which in many academic quarters had been dismissed as lacking the necessary intellectual rigour. Under the chapter "Elitism and Democracy among the Sciences" contributed by him, Toulmin notes that "mainstream social sciences themselves rarely meet the strictest demands of empiricism."[3] At the same time he recognizes that action research bears little relation to general theory and "does not seek to escape from the particularities of its historical and cultural situations—let alone raise itself to abstract, timeless cosmological heights: its style is historical and anthropological."[4] There is now a widespread suspicion of the "High Science" model and the assumption that "the only authentic knowledge is universal, general and timeless . . . which came to be called *episteme* (theoretical grasp)."[5] This was an element in Plato's model to which, according to Toulmin, Aristotle added *techne* (know-how) and *phronesis* (the ability to spot the action called for in any situation). In a section on "action research as a clinical art," Toulmin defines clinical medicine not as applied physiology; rather "its substance is the body of experiential maxims that are passed from one generation of doctors to another by apprenticeship, not theoretical argument."[6]

I make no apology for quoting at length from Toulmin because he does not deny the value of purely theoretical endeavour, but seeks recognition of a genuine research activity which can challenge timeless theories: "In short, action research shares two features with clinical medicine. First, it focuses on concrete cases in particular times and places. Secondly, it tries to improve the current mode of operation in these situations."[7] We should never forget that we are surrounded by action research carried out by NGOs, among others, which has also been termed "citizen research," often at a very high standard, which also seeks to challenge the academic "High Science" that is used as a powerful argument by the corporate world since it carries a great deal of weight. These evidences of democratic action to improve situations rather than simply achieving theoretical discovery, coherence, or consistency should also find a place in our archives along with the "High Science."

All this gives a background and wider context within the social sciences to Barbara Craig's thoughts which perfectly articulate action research for archivists as part of archival education.[8] We can now be quite proud of the research we are doing and increasingly will do in the new millennium. The change is quite spectacular when we look back to the 1950s and '60s in North America when we were still treated as simply an auxiliary support for historical research. Then, we published "how-to" articles (Aristotle's *techne*) spanning our idiosyncratic processes. Half a century later, I have been greatly impressed recently by two articles, one discussing curriculum changes in preappointment graduate studies to meet changing needs, the other exploring areas of enquiry into the necessary knowledge that archivists will require in the next century.[9] Both have a thoughtful depth which indicates how two Canadian archival educators are facing up to the multifaceted challenges that will face us. There is no more I can say short of a detailed review except to admire the high standard reached by Terry Eastwood and Tom Nesmith who, in their different ways, complement each other. Clearly we will no longer be auxiliary to anyone, but rather partners with many as we work with other disciplines to preserve social memory amid virtual uncertainty.

Richard Cox brings up a less complex subject, but one which I have been wondering about for some time, namely the value of textbooks.[10] I myself had published a particularly bad one, so I feel a bit of an authority![11] In a preappointment degree programme, they are useful as a point of rapid takeoff into the considerable published material now available, which may well challenge the textbook, and so much the better if a good case is made. I remember the first series of booklets, the "Basic Manual Series"on various subjects (some better than others) published by the Society of American Archivists on the recommendation of the Committee of the 1970s, which were quite successful, given the limits on other sources at that time. Their principal value was in conjunction with workshops which were the most common form of archival instruction. Some are probably still used by volunteers in the small community repositories, and more up-to-date volumes have also appeared. Yet at the heart of good archival education lies discourse and discussion, far removed from the rigidity of the textbook, which encourages resourcefulness and flexibility through the development of communication which is what the records themselves are all about.

* * * * *

I have been asked to say why I think my approach is so important, and this I find difficult, as I believe the reader is the best judge. It may help if I make clear at the outset that I do not have that mix of Plato and Aristotle, *episteme* and *phronesis*, characteristic of Terry Cook, Luciana Duranti, Terry Eastwood, Tom Nesmith, Brien Brothman, and Richard Brown, to name but a few Canadians, with their generous wealth of footnotes supporting theoretical structures and action research. To be honest, I suppose I do more thinking than reading in a search for connections which link the work of others to archives and thereby reveal unexplored relationships through "probes" in the McLuhan tradition—which may touch on a useful revelation or spin wildly off track. My citations appear to range widely, far beyond the boundaries of archivy, but they are not carefully selected from groups of Dewey decimals or Library of Congress alphanumerical schemas. Rather they are the product of the "new book" shelves which I devour for their stimulating freshness.

As a practising archivist I have always developed my repository with a broad brush, leaving my colleagues and successors to fill in the details, which is just as important and demanding, and it has worked quite well. Dare I say that I'm an Impressionist rather than a Pre-Raphaelite! Likewise we cannot possibly read "all there is" on anything, but we can build bridges of communication between hitherto insulated and isolated endeavours which can result in a whole which is far greater than the parts. My bridges are constructed in a manner beyond reason alone and require imagination to span the gap. If deconstruction reveals fallacies, then the bridge will collapse. So be it, but on the other hand deconstruction may result in a span built from the ruins of a castle of logical positivism no longer serving its original purpose. If we fail to use our imagination in what we do, then we will lose our sense of the full magnitude and possibilities of our professional task of becoming involved in the large picture which may be context. Failure to use our minds in this way could lead to ceaseless drudgery and burnout.[12]

As an example of what I mean by seeking possible solutions in unlikely sources, Janine Benyus has reminded us that for centuries we have devised technological advances using human resources arising from necessity and have totally ignored immensely suggestive models in the natural world.[13] Benyus has a degree in forestry from Rutgers where she studied each aspect separately, in the best scientific reductionist manner: "We practised a human centred approach to management assuming that nature's ways of management had nothing to teach us."[14] Her book contains examples of those scientists who, by means of highly sophisticated experiments and models, seek to mimic natural processes which if successful over time will revolutionize the way we relate to nature. One example is Wes Jackson and the Land Institute in Kansas seeking a sustainable agriculture based on a "herbaceous, seed yielding perennial" after the manner of the virgin prairie and in contrast to agribusiness and the destructive chemical mono-culture of today.[15] Many other examples follow in great technical detail, one of which is "How will we store what we learn,"[16] which introduces Michael Conrad and computing based on carbon, not silicon. Our brains are made of carbon and "compute in massive parallel; computers use lin-ear processing."[17] Silicon attempts to mimic the brain by using "connec-tionism," and "neural net" will not match carbon. This kind of research has serious but positive implications for archives in the future, but it is also a facet of environmentalism which will, as I have said so often, become a part of our lives if we are to survive on this planet. Here surely is a field for the archival imagination as carbon communication approaches com-mercial reality, whenever that might be.

So much for storing what we learn with carbon, in what could be a mid-dle distant future, but to what extent has the created past become a part of our culture? This is a vast subject which spans heritage and in particu-lar history and memory as far as we are concerned. We must in some way remember what is significant to us that survives the present moment as it becomes past time, but also recognize this process as a linear concept which is now challenged. Our memory can be fed by a history which may be reliable in a general way, but is essentially the ever-changing product of historians seeking in good faith an accurate rendition, which inevitably will be challenged and overturned by colleagues, including postmodern deconstruction. What then are citizens to believe? How much history taught in school remains in the memory? Is this really the source of our early, retained knowledge of the past, unless we are deeply interested later in an amateur or professional capacity. I doubt it. More likely the early source resides in "pop" culture, illustrated magazines in story form, historical novels, and "period" features on film, television, and video, which at their best can convey a powerful sense of time, place, and peo-ple stored in our minds as we join the myths which order our lives. This is not all bad and may lead on to historical awareness in a broad sense, es-pecially if archaeology, historic sites, art galleries, libraries,[18] museums,[19] and archives[20] are taken seriously. The created past also consists of the natural environment that surrounds us which we have valued, in the main, for recreational tourism. The rest is at the mercy of the consumer, and this accurately reflects one facet of our present culture which rarely thinks in terms of our integrated human and natural past in the present, unless we are aboriginal people.

All this and more can be classed as heritage, but to what extent can we connect this with our own families and communities in an unbroken understanding of what the word really means? Too often it now stands for all that we want to remember with little recognition of the violence, waste, and destruction which we also inherit. We are all stakeholders. We all create records of our lives which link us to this heritage of which we are a part as thousands of "family albums" bear witness. We are very present and future oriented, but is a family fonds out of the question, which reflects the life and times of its members?[21] Space, of course, is a problem, as is constant moving. This surely is "bottom up" heritage which goes beyond just names on a family tree, helpful as that is. Perhaps digital family memories will have possibilities in the future.

For us archivists, there can be no conclusions, no finality, no *obiter dicta*. We are builders of bridges, not castles, as we cross from the assurance of "now" to the uncertainty of "new." We are coming to realize that all we can do is stand by the principles of "now" until we cross yet another bridge where new principles will greet us, which may be closely related to the old ones, or radically different as another generation breaks away from tutelage and returns with the knowledge and wisdom of the young who will build yet more bridges. There is, I believe, a spiritual element in all this which resides perhaps in the imagination, with faith as a neighbour, through which we come to recognize the humans we are meant to be, our reality in the fullest sense, which will guide us from the now to the new.

I found myself looking up "imagination" in the *Oxford English Dictionary*, and you may wish to ponder a moment on some of the meanings which are significantly different, as you can well imagine with such a diaphanous word. There is the "fleeting forms of things," which suggests day dreams which evade our capture, and that in turn is related to "an impression of what is likely," which is firmly down-to-earth. Then again there is "memory as reproductive imagination" which can be collapsed into the bittersweet abstract noun, "nostalgia," which as concept should not be derogated. It is also the memory which recalls heritage to life in the mind and the spirit. Finally, I will leave you with "the faculty of the mind by which are formed maps or concepts not present to the senses." Does this fit our case? I rather think so, but leave you to your own conclusions.

NOTES

1. Hugh A. Taylor, *Archival Services and the Concept of the User: A RAMP Study* (Paris: International Council on Archives, 1984).
2. Stephen Toulmin and Bjorn Gustavsen, eds., *Beyond Theory: Changing Organisations Through Participation* (Amsterdam and Philadelphia, 1996).
3. Ibid., p. 203.

4. Ibid., p. 205.

5. Ibid., p. 206.

6. Ibid., p. 210.

7. Ibid., p. 211.

8. Barbara Craig, "Serving the Truth: The Importance of Fostering Archives Research in Education Programmes, Including a Modest Proposal for Partnerships with the Workplace," *Archivaria* 42 (Fall 1996): 105–17. For an example of action research on clinical records, see Hamish Maxwell-Stewart and Alistair Tough, "Cutting the Gordian Knot: Or How to Preserve Non-Current Clinical Records Without Being Buried in Paper," *Archivaria* 41 (Spring 1996): 61–77.

9. Terry Eastwood, "Reforming the Archival Curriculum to Meet Contemporary Needs," *Archivaria* 42 (Fall 1996): 80–88; Tom Nesmith, "'Professional Education in the Most Expansive Sense: What Will the Archivist Need to Know in the Twenty-First Century?" *Archivaria* 42 (Fall 1996): 90–95.

10. Richard J. Cox, "The Real Problem of Archives Textbooks," *Archivaria* 40 (Fall 1995): 5–7.

11. Hugh A. Taylor, *The Arrangement and Description of Archival Materials*, International Council on Archives, Handbook Series 2 (Munich, 1980).

12. Hugh A. Taylor, "From Dust to Ashes: Burnout in the Archives," *The Midwestern Archivist* 12.2 (1987): 73–82.

13. Janine M. Benyus, *Biomimicry: Innovation Inspired by Nature* (New York, 1997).

14. Ibid., p. 3.

15. "How will we feed ourselves?: farming to fit the land: growing food like a prairie," in *Ibid.*, pp. 11–58. I met Wes Jackson sometime in 1983 and was much impressed by his remark that "agriculture was the first industry." I refer to him in my "Information Ecology and the Archives of the 1980s," *Archivaria* 18 (Summer 1984): 25–37.

16. Benyus, *Biomimicry*, "How will we store what we learn?" pp. 185–237.

17. Ibid., p. 196.

18. Hugh A. Taylor, "The Collective Memory: Archives and Libraries as Heritage," *Archivaria* 15 (Winter 1982–1983): 118–30.

19. Hugh A. Taylor, "Heritage Revisited: Documents as Artifacts in the Context of Museums and Material Culture," *Archivaria* 40 (Fall 1995): 8–20.

20. For a joint approach by a librarian and an archivist, see Cynthia J. Durance and Hugh A. Taylor, "Wisdom, Knowledge, Information and Data," in *Alexandria* 4.1 (1992): 37–61. For an earlier example of the use of archival material in schools, see Hugh A. Taylor, "Clio in the Raw: Archival Materials in the Teaching of History," in *American Archivist* 35 (July/October 1972): 317–30.

21. Hugh A. Taylor, "Family History: Some New Directions and Their Implications for the Archivist," in *Archivaria* 11 (Winter 1980–81): 228–31; Hugh A. Taylor, "Archives in the Home," *Federation News* [Federation of Nova Scotia Heritage] 9.1 (Winter 1985): 11–12.

About Hugh A. Taylor

Hugh Taylor was born in 1920, served in communications in the Second World War, and was educated at Oxford and Liverpool. In his English archival career, he was Archivist, Leeds Public Libraries (1951–54); Archivist, Liverpool Public Libraries (1954–58); and founding County Archivist, Northumberland (1958–65), as well as Archivist to the University Library, University of Newcastle-upon-Tyne (1963–65). Coming to Canada as the founding Provincial Archivist of Alberta (1965–67), he was later the founding Provincial Archivist of New Brunswick (1967–71); Director of the Historical Branch, Public (now National) Archives of Canada (1971–77); and Provincial Archivist of Nova Scotia (1978–82). A consulting archivist since 1982, he has specialized in teaching archival studies and continued writing a wide range of articles and books about archives and their connection to social, cultural, and philosophical issues. He has been awarded his country's highest civilian honour, the Order of Canada, and a *festschrift* was published for him in 1992: *The Archival Imagination: Essays in Honour of Hugh A. Taylor.* A past president of the Society of American Archivists, he also received an Honorary Life Membership of the Association of Canadian Archivists. Additional biographical information may be found in the autobiographical chapter, "A Life in Archives: Retrospect and Prospect," and in the editors' introductory essays.

About the Editors

Terry Cook is Visiting Professor in the postgraduate archival studies programme at the University of Manitoba. He has also taught at the School of Information, University of Michigan. Before 1998, he was a senior manager at the National Archives of Canada, where he directed the appraisal and records disposal programme for government records in all media. He has been published on every continent on a wide range of archival subjects; has conducted numerous institutes, workshops, and seminars on appraisal, electronic records, and archival ethics across Canada and internationally, especially Australia and South Africa; and has served as General Editor of *Archivaria* as well as Editor of two scholarly series/journals of the Canadian Historical Association. He is the author of *The Archival Appraisal of Records Containing Personal Information: A RAMP Study With Guidelines* (1991) and editor of *Electronic Records Practice: Lessons from the National Archives of Canada* (1993).

Gordon Dodds is the Archivist of Manitoba. Since 1972, he has worked at the Archives of Ontario, the National Archives of Canada, and the Provincial Archives of Manitoba where he was manager of the Government Records Office and an Associate Provincial Archivist. In 1975–76 he was the inaugural president of the Association of Canadian Archivists, subsequently chair of its education committee, and later General Editor of *Archivaria* (1978–81). He has taught courses in history and archives, including most recently in the archival studies programme at the University of Manitoba, and published both in England and Canada. In addition to several articles on archival issues, he is coauthor of four books: *Tyneside Classical: The Newcastle of Grainger, Dobson and Clayton*; *A Picture History of Ontario*; *Canada: A History in Photographs*; and *The World of William Notman*.